W9-AMX-269

Faulkner's Women

DAVID WILLIAMS

Faulkner's Women

THE MYTH AND THE MUSE

MCGILL-QUEEN'S UNIVERSITY PRESS

MONTREAL AND LONDON 1977

DALE H. GRAMLEY LIBRARY
SALEM COLLEGE
WINSTON-SALEM, N. C.

PS
3511
.A86
Z9857

This book has been published with the help of a
grant from the Humanities Research Council of Canada,
using funds provided by the Canada Council. Permissions

© McGill-Queen's University Press 1977
ISBN 0 7735 0257 2
Legal Deposit second Quarter 1977
Bibliotheque nationale du Québec

Printed in Canada by
The Bryant Press Ltd.

ACKNOWLEDGEMENTS

The author and publisher are grateful to the following for permission to reprint excerpts from the works of William Faulkner:

Random House, Inc., for *Sartoris*, copyright, 1929, renewed, 1956 by William Faulkner; *The Sound and the Fury*, copyright, 1929, by William Faulkner; copyright renewed, 1956, by William Faulkner; copyright, 1946, by Random House, Inc.; *As I Lay Dying*, copyright, 1930, and renewed 1957, by William Faulkner; *Sanctuary*, copyright, 1931, and renewed, 1958, by William Faulkner; *Light in August*, copyright © 1968 by Random House, Inc.; copyright 1932 by William Faulkner; copyright renewed 1959 by William Faulkner; *The Unvanquished*, copyright 1934, 1935, 1936, 1938 by William Faulkner; copyright renewed 1961, 1962 by William Faulkner; copyright renewed 1964, 1965 by Estelle Faulkner and Jill Faulkner Summers; *The Hamlet*, copyright 1931, and renewed 1958, by William Faulkner; copyright, 1932, and renewed 1959, by the Curtis Publishing Company; copyright, 1940, by Random House, Inc.; copyright, 1936, by Charles Scribner's Sons, and renewed 1964, by Estelle Faulkner and Jill Faulkner Summers; *The Town*, © copyright, 1957, by William Faulkner; © copyright, 1957, by the Curtis Publishing Company; *The Mansion*, © copyright, 1955, 1959, by William Faulkner; *The Reivers*, © copyright, 1962, by William Faulkner.

The Author's Literary Estate and Chatto & Windus, Ltd. for *Mosquitoes, Sartoris, The Unvanquished, The Hamlet, The Town, The Mansion,* and *The Reivers.*

The Author's Literary Estate and Curtis Brown, Ltd. for
*Soldiers' Pay, The Sound and the Fury, As I Lay Dying,
Sanctuary,* and *Light in August.*
Liveright Publishing Corporation, a division of W. W. Norton
& Company, Inc. for *Soldiers' Pay,* copyright 1926 by Horace
Liveright, Inc., and renewed 1954 by William Faulkner;
Mosquitoes, copyright 1927 by Horace Liveright, Inc., and
renewed 1955 by William Faulkner.
Permission is gratefully acknowledged from The Viking
Press, Inc., for excerpts from the following:
The Faulkner-Cowley File by Malcolm Cowley. Copyright
© 1966 by The Estate of William Faulkner. Copyright ©
1966 by Malcolm Cowley.
Writers at Work, ed. Malcolm Cowley. Copyright © 1957,
1958 by The *Paris Review,* Inc.
Studies in Classic American Literature by D. H. Lawrence.
Copyright 1923, 1951 by Frieda Lawrence. Copyright ©
1961 by The Estate of the late Mrs. Frieda Lawrence.
The Portable Nietzsche, ed. and trans. Walter Kaufmann.
Copyright 1954, © 1968 by The Viking Press, Inc.
Permission to quote from the following works is also acknow-
ledged:
The Collected Works of C. G. Jung, ed. by G. Adler, M. Fordham,
W. McGuire, and H. Read, trans. by R. F. C. Hull, Bollingen
Series, Vol. 9i, *The Archetypes and the Collective Unconscious.*
Copyright © 1959 and 1969 by Bollingen Foundation.
Copyright © 1959 by Routledge & Kegan Paul, Ltd. Re-
printed by permission of Princeton University Press and
Routledge & Kegan Paul, Ltd.
Faulkner: The Major Years by Melvin Backman. Copyright
© 1966 by Indiana University Press.
Ishmael: A Study of the Symbolic Mode in Primitivism by
James Baird. © 1956, The Johns Hopkins University Press.
Faulkner's Olympian Laugh: Myth in The Novels by Walter
Brylowski. By permission of The Wayne State University
Press. Copyright ©, 1968 by Wayne State University Press.
The American Novel and Its Tradition by Richard Chase.
Copyright © 1957 by Richard Chase. Reprinted by per-
mission of Doubleday & Co., Inc.
"Preface to *The Sound and the Fury,*" by Maurice Coindreau,
trans. George M. Reeves. Copyright 1966 Mississippi State
University. Reprinted by permission of *Mississippi Quarterly.*
Love and Death in the American Novel by Leslie A. Fiedler.
Copyright © 1966, 1960 by Leslie A. Fiedler. Reprinted with
permission of Stein and Day/*Publishers.*
Faulkner in the University, ed. Frederick L. Gwynn and
Joseph L. Blotner. Copyright 1959 by University of Virginia
Press. Reprinted by permission of The University Press of
Virginia.
Man and His Symbols by Carl G. Jung *et al.* © 1964 by
Aldus Books Limited, London.

Faulkner's Revision of "Sanctuary" by Gerald Langford. ©
1972 by Gerald Langford. Reprinted by permission of
University of Texas Press.
The Odyssey of Homer, trans. Richmond Lattimore. Copyright © 1965, 1967 by Richmond Lattimore. Reprinted by
permission of Harper & Row, Publishers, Inc.
Laocoön by G. E. Lessing, trans. Ellen Frothingham. Copyright © 1957 by The Noonday Press, a division of Farrar,
Straus & Giroux, Inc.
The Achievement of William Faulkner by Michael Millgate.
Copyright © 1966 Michael Millgate. Reprinted by permission
of Constable & Company, Ltd.
The Great Mother by Erich Neumann, trans. Ralph Manheim. Bollingen Series XLVII. Copyright 1955, © 1963 by
Bollingen Foundation. Reprinted by permission of Princeton
University Press.
The Idea of the Holy by Rudolf Otto, trans. John W. Harvey,
2nd edition. Copyright 1950 by Oxford University Press.
Dionysus: Myth and Cult by W. F. Otto, trans. Robert B.
Palmer. Copyright © 1965 by Indiana University Press.

To Darlene

CONTENTS

PREFACE

Walter F. Otto's *Dionysus: Myth and Cult*, at once a study of Dionysiac religion and of the creative act, lays claim to the precedence of godhead in all monumental creations of the human spirit. "How could man," Otto asks, "who had been touched by the Divine remain inert and motionless when all genuine revelation awakens the power of creativity?" (p. 43). He likewise maintains that "the creative phenomenon must be its own witness. And its testimony has only one meaning: that the human mind cannot become creative by itself, even under the most favorable circumstances, but that it needs to be touched and inspired by a wonderful Otherness; that the efficacy of this Otherness forms the most important part of the total creative process, no matter how gifted men are thought to be. This is what the creative ones have told us in all ages when they appealed to an inspiration which emanated from a higher being" (pp. 25–26). Otto finally says of all creative acts of worship that "something great must have occurred, a revelation of such miraculous force that the community of men made a living monument for it out of themselves, surrendering themselves completely to the holy ecstasy of being, in themselves, an answer to, and an expression of, the transcendent" (p. 38). These acts "could exist only thanks to a great emotion, a feeling of passionate exaltation. And such exaltation can have been aroused only by a mythic vision which had taken possession of the human spirit" (p. 36).

Woman as such is evidently not the subject of this essay; woman as the living monument of the presence of deity, or as an expression of some great and inspiring power in the creative act, is nearer to what is meant by "the myth and the muse." Although Jungian terminology—particularly that of "rediscovering the gods as psychic factors"—is used in theoretical portions of what follows to describe the nature and being of the Great Goddess, her manifestation is not to be regarded (any more than it is by Jung) as less than a living reality.

Terms and their concepts can give too easily the impression of explaining away the content of great emotions. The creative phenomenon in Faulkner is the most telling witness of the influence of an awesome and wonderful "otherness"; the novels themselves (or at least some of them) are testimony to the artist's inspiriting encounter with godhead. It is, as Otto suggests, not a new idea in the study of poetry, if the appeals to the Muse of Homer, Hesiod, and Milton be accepted in the spirit in which they are uttered. The poet of an age of mechanistic thinking would hardly be taken seriously, however, should he formally address his Muse. Quite as likely he, as the product of a rational culture, could not say what exactly it is which has informed the feelings he must set down. It is then the task of a certain kind of criticism, oriented toward the sacred in a secular age, to bring to light the symbols and the narrative prepotency of the Muse wherever she is felt, though not acknowledged, in her awe-inspiring reality and activity.

Certain Faulknerian women are encountered in this

study in the course of having become, in themselves, an answer to, and an expression of, the sacred Being, configuring for their human community the miraculous force of deity. The efficacy they re-present stands, as it has before, at the beginnings of culture, at the foundations of whatever emotions, practices, and institutions support the basic existence of a people. This manifestation in fictional communities has absolute effects. But such a presence has also a decisive effect upon art. Literature itself becomes one of the great languages with which mankind speaks to godhood, speaking to it for no other reason than that it must. Man, as Otto affirms, owes the highest of which he is capable to the feeling of the deity's imminence. Faulkner, the man and artist, is then seen as having given voice to a mythic vision—itself inaugurating and directing the outcome of his art—by virtue of the great emotion attached to women in whom the Holy is incarnate. Paradoxically, however, the artist, in the act of exalted expression, thereby frees himself from the vision which has taken possession of him, at the same time that he delivers everyone who is deeply affected by his work. The creation of mythic art is thus simultaneously an act of communion and of individuation.

This last statement is proposed as much as a principle of selection as of substance. While I feel a definite responsibility, as a specialist, to all of Faulkner's work, I admit at once that it is motivated neither uniformly nor completely by the myth of woman. *The Sound and the Fury* (1929), *As I Lay Dying* (1930), *Sanctuary* (1931), and *Light in August* (1932) are, I think, the only four works by Faulkner which are describable as full and uniform (in representation, not in personae-response) incarnations of the goddess. I am grateful to Richard Chase for having already pronounced these four to be "among the best novels of the twentieth century" (*The American Novel and its Tradition*, p. 205), lest the usual reservations about

Sanctuary make my argument seem tendentious. More than half of this study is devoted exclusively to these four works, and they are accepted throughout as the fulfilment (or norm) of the subject. Most of the judgements of my theoretical introduction refer only to them. The second chapter, dealing with *Soldiers' Pay* (1926), *Mosquitoes* (1927), and *Sartoris* (1929), though not in that order, is designed to reveal Faulkner's intellectual grasp of the myth, to trace his failing attempts to use it, and to suggest the probable reason for his sudden emergence of genius in *The Sound and the Fury* and what follows.

The last chapters, succeeding full-dress analysis of the myth, its content, and its varying form in the four novels, deal with the artist's freeing of himself from old compulsions in *The Hamlet* (1940), *The Unvanquished* (1938), *The Town* (1957), *The Mansion* (1959), and *The Reivers* (1962), although the latter work marks a return, if in altered form, to "the heart's desire." The former two works chronicle the actual defeat by man of daemonic powers, if by differing means and for different purposes, and the latter three define and variously demonstrate what is meant by "individuation"—the process of the artist's personal liberation from divinity which parallels that of individual women from mythic women. This course, artistically speaking, is not always a happy one. It is already being pursued in *Pylon* (1935) and *The Wild Palms* (1939), but I do not consider them, preferring, on the one hand, to let inferior work lie, and on the other, to avoid redundancy. The Snopes trilogy, itself profoundly uneven, together with "An Odor of Verbena" say what is essential about the progress of demythification.

Absalom, Absalom! (1936) and *Go Down, Moses* (1942), each in their own way mythic and equally great works of art, do not figure in the mythology of woman. Thomas Sutpen, whose Faustian ambition leads inevitably to self-destruction, looms above the

female world of Ellen and Rosa Coldfield, Judith and
Clytie Sutpen, or Eulalia Bon, leaving his male heirs
subject in his defeat only to the jungle itself and the
loins of African kings. Isaac McCaslin, who encounters
a native American deity in the forest, is defeated by
the inescapable Fall into history, by the laying waste
of the wilderness which has mothered him, and by
his refusal to accept divinity's presence on anything
less than literal, historical terms. He becomes a carpenter, heir to his own destruction and victim of a
powerless identity as Christ. Finally, *A Fable* (1954),
the estimation of which is yet publicly in doubt, must
receive but a passing judgement upon its attempt to
reactualize the Christ myth in a modern world—the
failure of Christ and Protestant Christianity to provide
sanctions for existence being the obverse meaning of
the goddess's incarnation in the earlier works.

I owe much in this study to many, but to the following I am specifically grateful. Professors A. W.
Plumstead and David Porter read a version of this
manuscript and gave me valuable criticism. Professors
Morton Berkowitz, John Blanpied, Philip J. Gallagher,
John Paskus, Rev. Albert F. Reddy, S.J., Killam
Fellow Evelyn J. Hinz, and Mr. Christopher Diamond
provided by their conversation a forum for inter-
disciplinary studies.

The Canada Council granted me leisure to write;
twice the University of Manitoba Research Grants
Committee contributed assistance toward the produc-
tion of a final typescript. To both I am deeply in-
debted.

With much pleasure I can say that Professor John
Teunissen, who introduced me many years ago to
Faulkner's novels, has yet an incalculable part in this
work. Needless to say, the errors or infelicities which
persist herein are still my own. To Professor Teunissen
and to another colleague, Evelyn J. Hinz, I can be
more particularly grateful for premises adopted from
their essay, "The Attack on the Pietà: An Archetypal

Analysis," *The Journal of Aesthetics and Art Criticism* (Fall 1974).

Finally, my wife Darlene has helped pragmatically and personally, more than I can say.

DAVID WILLIAMS

PART ONE

INTRODUCTION

Man as the secondary artist is man who is
servile to art; man as the primary artist is man
who commands art to incarnate what had not
before attained form. He alone is the artist
who dares to make new symbols to describe
the relationship of man to his God.
James Baird, *Ishmael.*

Cultural Failure and the
Modulation of Idiom

A Critical Orientation to
Faulkner's Women

T he beginnings of Faulkner criticism remark a *Weltanschauung*
which several decades of critics have been busy to deny. Early
readers thought they had discovered in Faulkner a pessimistic
naturalism: his obsession with horror and violence, his liking for
idiots, neurotics, and nymphomaniacs, and his brooding over a moribund past seemed even to found a "cult of cruelty."[1]

To a certain extent such a view is justified, even in retrospect.
A significant character group in the novels does regard the world
in almost naturalistic terms as if it were blind, purblind, indifferent
—if not actually hostile—to man's personal fate. Benjy and Quentin
Compson are agonized by the inexorable processes of growth and
change; Darl Bundren is cast by his own family behind the bars of
a mental institution; Lee Goodwin is executed in a gasoline blaze
for a crime he did not commit; Horace Benbow, the champion of
law and reason, is thwarted by a mandate having no connection
with justice; Joe Christmas is run to earth through thirty years by
some malevolent, though hidden Player and is castrated at last in a
preacher's kitchen.

These narratives notwithstanding, the Nobel Prize Address of
1950 and much criticism from that date have dispelled the notion
that for Faulkner the universe is out of joint. His contrapuntal
technique, whereby destructive modes of behaviour are precisely

counterpointed to creative states, has been widely heralded. The world (or some remote cosmic Player) is no longer seen to be at fault so much as are the characters who inhabit that world. Mounting evidence points one way or another to Faulkner's men as the source of prevalent moral bankruptcy and to his women as primal heirs of life and moment. This shift in emphasis from cosmic failure to some sort of fault in personality or gender stops short, however, of probable conclusions. Current estimation stints an understanding of woman's significance in Faulkner's art largely because the function of male victims in a cult of cruelty is evaded with a Neville Chamberlainean kind of optimism. Admittedly, Faulkner's address is to blame for such willed optimism, but the evidence of his work reveals a far different kind of belief, a hope born of arduous trial. Rather than reviewing at this point the critical response to fateful sexual polarities in the novels, it is best to let the male victims themselves expose the roots of any cult of cruelty.

One of the most poignant examples in Faulkner of this masculine dilemma occurs in *The Sound and the Fury* in the character of Quentin Compson whose sensitivity, perception, and idealism make him so sympathetic a voice, and yet whose quest for a "clean" damnation beyond the flux of life, and whose mounting nausea at the scent of honeysuckle, the illicit sexuality of his sister, and the engendering "filth" of womankind leave his flesh so terribly vulnerable to his own anti-vital fanaticism. Quentin's suicide, in fact, sums up not only his own hatred of the flesh but also his father's conditioning nihilism and his brothers' shared resistance to life in Caddy. Benjy's bellowing despair at the memory of his sister and his attempt to arrest her in her childhood mark his unwitting effort to deny her power to give life, while Jason's cynicism, his greed, and his hatred of the "bitchery" of both sister and niece betray in a similar, if more consciously destructive, way his loathing of life.

Analogously, Simon McEachern, Doc Hines, and Gail Hightower of *Light in August* share variously with Joe Christmas a preference for martyrdom over life, a commitment to the ruthlessly logical justice of men, and a revulsion from bitchery, from menstruation and sap-flowing trees. Horace Benbow, who elaborates in *Sanctuary* this apparent condition of rational nausea, believes that existence were better ended: "Perhaps it is upon the instant that we realize, admit, that there is a logical pattern to evil, that we die, he thought.

. . . Better for her if she were dead tonight, Horace thought, walking on. For me too . . . thinking how that were the only solution. Removed, cauterized, out of the old and tragic flank of the world."

Darl Bundren—whose mother dies, is removed, and yet remains vitally related to other members of the family in symbols of the fish, horse, wagon, and tree—accepts no symbol for existence, but proclaims instead his unrelenting nihilism: "How do our lives ravel out into the no-wind, no-sound, the weary gestures recapitulant: echoes of old compulsions with no-hand on no-strings: in sunset we fall into furious attitudes, the dead gestures of dolls. Cash broke his leg and now the sawdust is running out. He is bleeding to death is Cash." Although Darl yearns for some sort of primal belief, he can discover nothing beyond a logical relation to his symbolic mother. Yet the subsequent convolutions and tortured doubt of his syllogisms have but a temporary staying power against his cynical despair and eventual madness: "Since sleep is is-not and rain and wind are *was*, it is not. Yet the wagon *is*, because when the wagon is was, Addie Bundren will not be. And Jewel *is*, so Addie Bundren must be. And then I must be, or I could not empty myself for sleep in a strange room. And so if I am not emptied yet, I am *is*." Darl's Cartesian sanity does not survive his family's insane symbolic undertaking, and yet it is painfully apparent in conclusion that his rationalizing is the real madness, his family's "mad" configuring of images the life-giving power.

The refusal, then, in each foregoing instance of the natural, and a related persistence in the merely rational leads to repeated fulfilment of Horace Benbow's nauseated desire to be cauterized, the act of which is stunningly cruel. In every case, however, the option (woman, nature, life, the non-rational) which is refused not only "endures" but, narratively, at least, "prevails." The health and vitality which are available in some sort of prevailing symbolic alternative indicates that Faulkner's view of human destiny is more urgent and of greater consequence than these memorable platitudes of the Nobel Prize Address suggest. The presence of some life-promoting factor in the midst of an operative cult of cruelty or nigh cosmic pessimism requires not less than the fullest possible study. But for the moment, the corollary proposition—that Faulkner's despairing men are symptomatic of a pervasive sort of failure—must be wholly engaging.

The recurrence among some of Faulkner's male victims of a Christ-figure has been recognized in criticism with varying degrees of irony.[2] This irony is typically realized in the discrepancy between Christ-like destinies, at least of martyrdom, and un-Christ-like dispositions—whether the unlikely temperament be that of the idiot Benjy Compson or of the murderer Joe Christmas. Usually these figures are interpreted humanistically as emblems of a pitiable human condition. Here, they enjoy at most a compassionate function, being sanctioned to recall the Gospel story without presuming either to be gospels in themselves or to be possessed of the actual properties of the unique religious occurrence. Since they are identified with Christ, no one bothers very much about their moral natures, recalling, perhaps, the Son of Man's exhortation, "He that is without sin among you, let him first cast a stone." The unrecognized probability, however, that these personations are heretically configured alters the purpose and the meaning of a great majority of instances of Faulkner's "humanism."[3]

Most of Faulkner's Christ-figures are at fault, not only in the moral and psychic sense previously mentioned, but in the further sense of being powerless—even through immolation—to offer life, of whatever sort or however lasting. Lee Goodwin of *Sanctuary*, for example, who is lynched as the scapegoat of a supposedly pharisaical society is not innocent if one recalls Christ's dictum of the equivalence between thoughts and deeds. Goodwin (like the idiot Tommy who is explicitly identified with Christ in the galley version[4]) lusts after Temple, even though it is Popeye who alone, and in parody, accomplishes the lustful deed. If Goodwin's "merited" crucifixion offers little hope for man, the fruits of his life hold less. He leaves behind him a son who has been cradled in a farmhouse, "flushed and sweating, its curled hands above its head in the attitude of one crucified." The son is not only emblematic of the sexual guilt bequeathed by the father—Goodwin has killed a man over a black woman in the Philippines—but of the disease and moribundity of the central Christian symbol. For the health of the cultural-religious icon, set against the vengeful image of Temple Drake, cannot be otherwise than involved in the health of the artistic Christ-child.

Faulkner's awareness of this debility in his inherited religious symbols is sustained conclusively, if less obviously, in *As I Lay Dying* by the two agents who most nearly succeed in halting the progress of Addie Bundren's funeral cortège. The log in the river, which stands "for an instant upright upon that surging and heaving desolation like Christ," dislodges the casket from the foundering wagon, but it cannot dislodge the family fancy that Addie even now impels them. Likewise Darl, who is violently sacrificed for trying to burn his mother's coffin with the Gillespies' barn, is unable to resist that force which refuses to stop in the New Hope cemetery. These two agents suggest concurrently the powerless identity of their principle and the authority of some other principle which overrides them. While such a changed prepotency forms the basis of the present study, it is necessary to consider further the import of this dispelling of the once authoritative Christian symbol.

The artist's awareness of inefficacy in his religious tradition, particularly as it is specifically demonstrated in the impoverishment of Christian symbolism, is defined by James Baird, in his remarkable study of the "symbolic mode in primitivism," as "cultural failure."[5] The idea, stated briefly for the moment in words meant to apply to the practice of Herman Melville's "existential primitivism," is that "society may cease to possess a common agreement upon the meanings and the purposes of existence; it may experience moral death; it may ultimately accept nihilism as its destiny" (p. 4). Cultural failure, in this sense, *"means the loss of a regnant and commanding authority in religious symbolism, since religion is here understood as the ultimately effective symbolic authority in the total culture of a race"* (p. 16, Baird's italics). Both the nihilism of Faulkner's men and the vitiation of his received symbols tend to offer, at least in this artistic phase of culture, less than an inspiriting kind of vision.

The extent of the presumed bankruptcy of Christian civilization in Faulkner's work will be considered more precisely in succeeding chapters, but its general character conforms nearly to the account provided in Baird's survey of acknowledgements during the past one hundred years from representative philosophers and theologians of the failure of a *"reason-doomed* culture" (p. 23, Baird's italics). Minds as diverse as Oswald Spengler and Albert Schweitzer, Ernest Renan and Paul Tillich, or Carl Jung and Jean-Paul Sartre have pointed to a "spirit of negation of life" arising from "a universal incapacity to grasp significance from the facts of *being*" (p. 21, Baird's italics).

Where this negation of life is viewed, as it is in the existentialist philosophy of Sartre, as a logical expression of the contingency of existence, nausea is invariably its graphic symptom. "The very quality of the viscous matter that promotes growth throughout nature evokes disgust; for Sartre it becomes entirely obscene" (p. 21). Life and fertility in all its forms are loathsome, regardless of what symbolization of existence is made, because they perpetuate existence for which there is no reason. This philosophy, which Baird describes as "the sickness of over-reason," manages to avoid moral death (unlike the majority of Faulkner's men) only by offering an existential assertion of the will-to-be in the blind face of recognized "absurdity." It admits, however, of no purpose outside the conscious will of man and of no transcription for existence beyond the barren rendering of such consciousness.

Where an insufficiency in the reading of existence is understood, on the other hand, as the inevitable outcome of Protestant iconoclasm, two radically different solutions to the problem of meaning are presented. Each, following the observations of Nietzsche and Paul Bourget, presumes a common deficiency in the practical history of Protestantism. It is best described as an intolerable refinement of the "I-You" relation (the I representing an elaboration of personality and consequent overvaluation of the self, the You standing for a personalized and desymbolized God), to an extent where the You-symbol has "lost the authority to absorb and to render inconsequential the individual's consciousness of himself" (p. 24). The only sufficiency then envisioned in the mid-twentieth century Protestant theology of Tillich is an ultimate extension of the personality, calling for "a new courage to be and to believe in a meaning of existence without symbols" (p. 32), as if man were, like God, now beyond the pale of symbolism.

This kind of spiritual bleakness which is limited to the over-refinement of the relation between man and God is curiously delineated by Faulkner in the experience of Darl Bundren. The character of Darl's relation to that You which, if decidedly un-Christian, has the power to absorb the remaining family individuals into symbolic corporateness with itself, oddly enough reveals the uniquely Protestant mechanism of human personality contending alone, that is, minus the mediation of images, with its God. The upshot of Darl's self-conscious courage to be and to believe in a meaning of existence without iconolatry is the downfall of consciousness and the destruction of personality. His solitary insistence upon denying, even while depicting its value for others, the authority of symbolism epitomizes the dilemma of a purely rational culture. Those who ride with him on the wagon find their only viable alternative, like the artist, in private symbolizing activity, and they are alone these artists who, rediscovering the primal stuff of revelation, emerge from the wasteland of cultural failure. The meaning of existence, as Baird says, is thereupon heard in a "new tonality."

The literary artist choosing to write in a new key thus commits himself, in the act of making different icons to replace the lost symbols of Protestant Christianity, to an ever-unique experience of divinity. Such a "modulation of idiom," as Baird calls it, *"occurs only when art is confronted with an inheritance of exhausted symbols which can no longer describe the belief or feeling antecedent to the forms of art"* (p. xiv, Baird's italics). This hypothesis rests, of course, on the supposition that man has an inherent *"need for symbolization,"* the symbol-making function which, in [Suzanne] Langer's view, is one of man's primary activities, 'like eating, looking, or moving about' " (p. xiv, Baird's italics). Baird is not content to rest, however, in the proposition of an aesthetic need for symbolization. Because he holds that the feelings antecedent to artistic forms shall be communicated only by a power charged with consequence, the need for image-making must be seen to be essentially religious. The predominant feature, then, of any true modulation in the idiom of literature is "atavism" or "primitivism," since *"atavism arises from the artist's awareness of his impoverishment in Christian symbolism"* (p. 19, Baird's italics). Thereupon, *"The symbols of primitivism are formed in answer to the basic human need for sacrament, when previously authoritative forms of sacrament have become powerless"* (p. 55, Baird's italics). Alternatively, the artist, in his quest for forms by which, *"through corporateness the individual is made one with his fellows in communion with the deity"* (p. 56, Baird's italics), of necessity reverts to the primal source of feeling or belief, and out of this unchanging source, returns with different images and premonitions of the divine, with a power which is uncannily convincing and alive.

The artist of primitive feeling is consequently "the maker of life symbols reconstituting an archetypal reality" (p. 8). In several key respects, he is like the archaic shaman who, by his ecstatic experience, "attempts to restore the 'communicability' that existed *in illo tempore* between this world and heaven," in order to "attain to ultimate reality."[6] Such reality, within the scheme of archaic ontology, "is a function of the imitation of a celestial archetype," where profane time and space are revitalized by an "eternal return" to the sacred time of the beginnings, to "the Center," to the "Zone of Absolute reality."[7] Although archaic societies as a whole are characterized by this tremendous thirst for *being*, it is the shamans "who experience the sacred with greater intensity than the rest of the community . . . who, as it were, incarnate the sacred, because they live it abundantly, or rather, 'are lived' by the religious 'form' that has chosen them" (*Shamanism*, p. 32). The shamans, in relation to their communities, are then the psychopomps who "accompany their dead to the 'Realm of Shades,' and serve as mediators between them and their gods, celestial or infernal, greater or lesser. This small mystical elite not only directs the community's religious life but . . . guards its 'soul.' The shaman is the great specialist in the human soul; he alone 'sees' it, for he knows its 'form' and its destiny" (p. 8). So too the primitivistic artist, by his personal and ecstatic experience, serves as a psychopomp; his case is unique only in that, for him, the religious life of the rest of the community has been exhausted and the community now stands in danger of losing its soul. He alone seeks to avert that danger by entering singlehandedly into the presence of the sacred and by emerging with a "new" iconic language through which man might speak to godhead.

A contrary transposition of idiom must also be remarked, however, since it does not shape reality from archetypes of primitive feeling. It seeks, rather, to glorify a culture or cultures which are distant in time or space, assuming that exotic truths so met are culturally transferable. But the means of this method constrain it; it is able to proceed only by erudition, by collecting historic instances, the presentation of which must be a pale surrogate for the primal feelings which once inspired an alien language. Baird terms this "a contrived or 'assembled' and hence *academic* primitivism" (his italics), as opposed to an "authentic primitivism": "Hence we must see the distinctions between the artist of nostalgic reference, the symbolist of externalities which are apparent in the flow of profane time; and the artist of primitive feeling, the restorer of the sacred center" (p. 8). The invigoration of a cultural wasteland—it cannot be overstressed—shall never be accomplished through the use of exotic lore; any possible means of grace has to be indigenous and hence expressible only in its unique idiom.[8]

When Faulkner presents in the fourth section of *The Sound and the Fury* a Negro preacher holding service on Easter morning: "And the congregation seemed to watch with its own eyes while the voice consumed him, until he was nothing and they were nothing and there was not even a voice but instead their hearts were speaking to one another in chanting measures beyond the need for words," the essence of sacramental experience is revealed in an authentic native idiom. Dilsey, who is "crying rigidly and quietly in the annealment and the blood of the remembered Lamb," is seemingly made one with her fellows in communion with the Christian God. Nonetheless, the "blood of the remembered Lamb" is not that of the man, but the infant Jesus who is snatched by Herod's men from Mary's lap and is crucified, as it were, on the same day. At the same time, the Negro "mother" is portrayed in the midst of the congregation, weeping beside her idiot "son" who is "rapt in his sweet blue gaze." The new accent heard in this double account of the dying god is achieved in the shift of emphasis from the traditional Protestant image of the Heavenly Son, the Redeemer sent by the Father, to the conflated pagan figure of the Madonna-Pietà.

The remarkable thing is precisely this shift in emphasis, for the new elements in the image have always been present, if latent, in its cultural apperception. Obviously it is the key, not the notes, which has been changed, even though the woman, by her relation to the "son", images in human form and temporal space the ancient mother-goddess. For the spent religious icon—thoroughly illustrated in the infant, moronic, gelded Christ, in the disruption of the Easter dates, and in the inclement weather of the "resurrection" morning—has not been discarded in the quiet tonal change which makes of woman a life symbol in the midst of a story of despair and death.

DALE H. GRAMLEY LIBRARY
SALEM COLLEGE
WINSTON-SALEM, N. C.

It was earlier suggested that the mother in *As I Lay Dying* symbolizes some overriding principle or archetypal reality, notwithstanding (even because of) the grotesque aura coming out of that story. Cash, Jewel, and the rest who, like the shaman, undertake a perilous journey and who emerge from it successfully symbolizing their relation to the deity (in this case the "mother"), underscore Darl's rational inability to accept shamanistic vision and so to guard his own soul. *Sanctuary* nevertheless points up the error in assuming that motherhood is in Faulkner both the major instance and the final explanation of a modulation of idiom or even of shamanistic vision. Ruby Lamar, the common-law wife to the lynched Lee Goodwin and mother of the sick "Christ-child," affords little more than images of a lost feminine efficacy, while Temple Drake incarnates the symbolic presence of a vengeful, yet life-giving reality (see chapter 5). Evidently the novel tone heard in this repeated symbolism of the feminine is more complete and more complex a rendering of the meaning of existence than the first phase of it—the Christian adaptation of the weeping mother—would suggest. For the concept of a change in idiomatic key presupposes that "symbols exist invariably within larger symbols." Baird greatly enlarges the scope of inquiry when he adds that "the system to which the symbol belongs is an aggregate of symbolic parts," originating in an "unconscious community" (p. x). Any iconology could not be complete so long as it concerned only the conspicuous symbolic parts which the artist creates. It should include as well that community of feeling that gives to his abstracted forms their impulse and authority. The burden of this study is meant to comprise an interpretation of such symbolic parts, as well as a description of the unconscious community to which the symbols of woman in Faulkner belong.

Sally R. Page, in a recent and first full study of *Faulkner's Women*, subtitled *Characterization and Meaning*,[9] essays to order a range of characterizations according to principal themes in the work. Faulkner's meaning is said to depend upon woman's symbolic participation in an image system broadly defined as "nature." Part

One, "Woman: The Image of Romantic Ideality," sets out the leading version of this premise: woman's alliance with nature makes her represent for man ideals of beauty and transcendence, although these ideals fail because spring fades, beauty doesn't last, and the real, un-innocent nature of woman mocks the ideality which her beauty seems to represent. A second concept, "Woman: The Image of Moral Order," develops the significance of her greater closeness than man to nature. Submission to the natural reproductive process, to the bearing and sustenance of life, and to the ethic of self-sacrificial serving symbolizes her moral decision to act for the good of others without regard for herself. This submission, seen in Caddy, Dilsey, and Ruby Lamar, is often counterpointed by the refusal to submit to or by even the perversion of the natural sexual process (as with Mrs. Compson, Temple Drake), leading to the eruption of forces which deny and defeat life. These polarities in the nature of woman provide essential ethical choices for man and for human society.

A subsequent theme, "Woman: The Image of Death," details woman's misuse of her natural purpose—the bearing of children— by which process she might achieve "serenity and virtue." She becomes equated with death (dying literally, or living, metaphorically, a death-in-life) whenever she is prevented from or finds herself incapable of entering into the reproductive process. If, like Addie Bundren or Charlotte Rittenmeyer, she does bear children but at the same time "attempts to use sexuality as a means of escaping the reality of life's limitations rather than as a means of reproducing life, she aligns herself with the forces which destroy life, and, ironically, in her search for life's vitality she embraces decay and death" (p. 134). A fourth and final idea, "Woman: The Image of Life," elaborates in terms of *Light in August* and the Snopes trilogy the continuing dialectic in Faulkner's work of "the life-nourishing female principle versus the life-destructive male principle" (p. 153). Lena Grove and Eula Varner represent a human need for obedience to the ongoing process of life, while the men or masculinized women of each novel portray the human drive for self-assertion and personal freedom. Generally, then, women are regarded as being more capable of accepting evil and/or the limitations of life, while men strive in a kind of desperate innocence to assert the reality of an ideal, unlimited world. At this point, however, woman is no longer seen simply as an ethical choice for man but as a part of a dialectic "which is forever unresolved in Faulkner's fiction" (p. 173).

The difficulty presented by this view of Nature as iconography lies in the meaning assigned to it: non-innocent womankind, being merely natural, cannot be said to represent an ethical choice for men. Nature itself is double, involving seasons of life and death and hence destroying even as it creates. Thus the natural process—and any woman imaging it—must stand outside of concepts, save for the pre-Homeric idea of *Moira* (destiny),[10] of moral order. Even recourse to the mythic Fates, however, would not support a case for an ethical system of Nature. For Nature, let alone Zeus himself, is subject to their order; the Fates' and Nature's only common feature is a feminine identity. Evidently this female principle of destiny is more than nature or woman, but not vice-versa. The order then represented by the Fates, at least as a psychic phenomenon, is supra-natural. If ethical choices happen to be imaged in certain human women, they proceed not from Nature but from a farther dimension. Thus when a woman like Temple Drake is envisioned in Faulkner as the image of death but is represented within the symbol system of nature, she must connote an ultimate and more profound natural purpose than the ethic of submission to child-bearing whereby is offered, says Mrs. Page, "the means by which man achieves his immortality—the survival of the human race" (p. 186).

The fuller perception of an ongoing dialectic in Faulkner's fiction between effeminate nature and masculine ideality is a notable finding in regard to the symbology of woman, but the former's inadequacy as a system is further discovered in man's imputed relation to it. If woman can relinquish herself to the reproductive processes of nature, man cannot. Even though "the feminine force of life demands" (p. 164) that man "submit himself to domestication and reproduction" (p. 163), Mrs. Page admits that "in real life man is simply incapable of submitting himself to woman and to nature as the idiot [Ike Snopes of *The Hamlet*] can submit himself to the cow. Man is not natural; he is human and fallen" (pp. 164–65). Nature (or woman) as such cannot save him. A fixed gulf intervenes between him and this plan of supposed efficacy.

The apparent *cul de sac* of such a symbol system duplicates the impasse created by an exotic modulation of idiom: the impoverished community has no native part in the alien communion. Axiomatically, the "life-destructive male principle," if it is to find a vital point of contact with the "life-nourishing female principle," must discover that within itself. But the possibility of man's psychic community in "muliebrity" cannot be accounted for within an order so inexactly defined as nature. Nor can the obvious fact that images of the female take their existence from the male imagination be understood solely in terms of nature. They are a remarkable instance of man's capacity to bear life; they are also a compelling argument for interpreting his iconography as being in some greater sense "feminine." For in the creation of symbolic women, the artist himself seems to have evinced a healthful and productive inner reconciliation with "the feminine force of life." This sort of primitivism which assumes its being within a widening sphere of symbols speaks not so much of a projected (or external) reference, but of an inward authority which shapes "reality" from that farther dimension. Man's relation to these larger symbols of womankind is finally no relation to nature as such, but to inclusive (if as yet undefined) archetypes of primitive feeling.

Delores E. Brien, anticipating the subject of the present study in "William Faulkner and the Myth of Woman,"[11] contends that to a host of Faulkner's men, "woman [sic] are not human beings like themselves, but avatars of ambiguous, supernatural forces" (p. 133). In some measure these women take on archetypal proportions, being "seldom individualized human beings, but shadowy, enigmatic creatures, incarnations of the 'Eternal Feminine' " (pp. 132–33). The "eternal" notwithstanding, it is evident that fictionally individualized women are here preferred as being of greater value than incarnations of an insubstantial (and possibly ominous) "Feminine"—this in all likelihood because of an a priori assumption that myth performs an important social, rather than religious, function.

The root fear in a social prospect of myth is its potential misuse. Brien believes that the myth of the feminine depersonalizes woman, empties her of human value, and so perpetuates a male-imposed role upon her. She implies that it stereotypes one sex in the mind of both sexes, preventing the mutual encounter of human beings on an individual basis. Faulkner, to be sure, is not accused of prohibiting women from the equal status of personal existence; it is the men of his reflected culture who are so arraigned: "Significantly, the women in Faulkner's novels are usually perceived through the eyes of the male characters, who have taken upon themselves the role of priest, prophet, and victim of a mythic cult they have compulsively created" (p. 132). Paradoxically, however, this mythic cult so created by men in answer to "whatever it is that deeply disturbs the male psyche" (p. 132) does not make of women "things to be used" (p. 140) to a male advantage. Instead, the cult is said to be the reason for man's destruction and the cause of disease, not of dominion, within his social system. Ironically, then, the myth must possess some sort of psychic and religious validity; were it to consist merely in such social and utilitarian office, it would prove to be more manipulable in the hands of its creators.

Once the true creator of this feminine myth (whatever its valence) is recognized as an archetype or a kind of woman within, then the province of the myth might be best understood as the crucial attempt of a desacramentalized artist to "rediscover the gods as psychic factors."[12] The archetype can now be accounted for in Jungian terms as a psychic factor which exists as a structural potentiality in the collective unconscious; it is at once the producer of patterns of behaviour (these of special interest to the psychoanalyst) and patterns of vision[13] (the finished form of which is alone the prerogative of art). Archetypes themselves, however, are not the patterns of vision nor the image contents *per se* of psychic experience. They are rather " 'factors,' which comes from *facere*, 'to make' " (Jung, p. 23). Primitive man, says Jung, was quite right to call these factors gods; they are the a priori element in psychic experience, "eternal presences" by whose vision man is often overcome; they bring into our timebound consciousness an unknown psychic life belonging to a remote past; they are that which "lives of itself, that makes us live" (p. 27); they are equally productive of ecstasy, devotion, allegiance, exaltation, but also of danger and terror. They are, in brief, a great creative power, a primal "Otherness" which gives life to artistic symbols whenever, in Baird's words, "the I-You relationship of the Protestant condition eludes the authority of traditional dogma perpetuated in Christian symbols and reverts to archetypal patterns which were always there in the unconscious, but earlier 'controlled' or 'obscured' by traditional symbols" (p. 52). In this atavistic state, more than one archetypal pattern is available to the artist who seeks by symbolic means to reactualize an ultimate reality. The choice of which archetype shall now be ascendant is governed almost entirely by a psychic law of compensation: whatever has been most excluded from consciousness (both individual and collective) must again find its place therein.[14] The anti-vital consciousness of so many of Faulkner's men and the countering presence of feminine life symbols in his art tend to indicate that from first to last the vision he most frequently reverts to is the archetype of woman in man (to be defined as the *anima*).

Since the feminine-in-man shall be the subject here of a good deal of aesthetic study, some brief account of the modus operandi in art of a psychic factor is by this time imperative. First, it should be stressed that if archetypes are makers of symbols, they become such only as pre-existing elements of unconscious feeling. Although they are a collective element—in this sense primordial common "factors" —they serve as "bases of feeling antecedent to the shaping of a symbol," or as those " 'drives' in the sentience of the primitivist which elicit individuated forms and authorize the purpose of genuine artistic construction" (Baird, p. 55). The symbols which appear in art are not, in other words, the collective product of the archetypal unconscious, but are begotten by a psychic factor upon the singular perception and sensibility of the artist. That sensibility is tempered not only by the unique history and native disposition of the artistic personality, but also by a cultural, though simultaneously imaginative, recollection of traditional forms of sacrament. Adopting, then, this final principle from Baird, *"the creator of genuine art forms his symbol by the act of fusing an aggregate of symbolic materials"* (p. 65, Baird's italics).

To select from Faulkner the first example to come to mind, the image of the pregnant Lena Grove progressing progressionless through a town transformed by her coming is not derived merely from dream content but equally from Faulkner's sensed experience of the South, from acquired knowledge of women around him, from perhaps a glimpse of a young pregnant woman or the hint

taken from a story of maternal faith, from his conscious attitudes
and feelings. For proof, nonetheless, that a significant measure of
his fused symbolic materials is gained from his "lost" Protestant
icons, it need only be discerned how the story of the crucifixion, as
Hightower calls it, of Joe Christmas is an integral part of the lyric
beauty of the feminine processional. Faulkner, too, seemed altogether aware of this integrative character of symbolic materials
in his art. When questioned at Virginia, for example, about the
possible symbolic meaning he had given to the dates of *The Sound
and the Fury*, he responded, "I'm sure it was quite instinctive that
I picked out Easter, that I wasn't writing any symbolism of the
Passion Week at all. I just—that was a tool that was good for the
particular corner I was going to turn in my chicken-house and so
I used it" (*University*, p. 68). Asked more closely about the frequent
occurrence of crucifixion images in the novels, he gave an inti-
mation of the artist's certain recollection of traditional, if re-
imagined, forms of sacrament in his work: "Remember, the writer
must write out of his background. He must write out of what he
knows and the Christian legend is part of a Christian's background,
especailly [sic] the background of a country boy, a Southern country
boy. My life was passed, my childhood, in a very small Mississippi
town, and that was a part of my background. I grew up with that.
I assimilated that, took that in without even knowing it. It's just
there. It has nothing to do with how much of it I might believe
or disbelieve—it's just there" (p. 86). This presence of Christianity
is decisive; it is an essential element in the art of symbolic fusion.

The problem, then, of sovereignty of expression in religious primitivism, turning on the question of whether archetype or artist
has final authority over form, is resolved by Baird only in terms of
the capacity in art for synthesis. The artist is said to fuse an autotype, "*a facsimile of singular experience* . . . with some archetypal
emblem from atavistic reversion [which] thus determines the primary elements of a symbol" (p. 18, Baird's italics). Baird extends
himself a little further than necessary, however, in demanding
that the autotype be a facsimile of sensed experience from a physical
journey to the Orient, toward "a country of the mind" (p. 66),
albeit a geographical Orient which might "provide the greatest
store of symbolistic material and the superior possibility of infinite
and sustained variation" (p. 29). For having claimed that "archaic

man, whether vestigial or dominant, is preserved" (p. 7) in modern man, Baird does not need the uniqueness of the journey to account for the unique expression of the archetype. The singularity of artistic personality, interpreted at least partially through the state of decay of a received culture and expressing itself out of an intuitive sense of the "archaic," is sufficient to explain what is particular or genuinely individual in symbol making. Personality, in this sense, is its own stamp upon what is necessarily transpersonal.

The presumed necessity of a supra-personal factor in authentic image creation is best discovered in the question of how images acquire their authority of being. Jung has said that archetypes "are, at the same time, both images and emotions. One can speak of an archetype only when these two aspects are simultaneous. When there is merely the image, then there is simply a word picture of little consequence. But by being charged with emotion, the image gains numinosity (or psychic energy); it becomes dynamic, and consequences of some kind must flow from it."[15] Limiting discussion for the moment to a lack of dynamic consequence, images which are void of feeling exist pretty much as rational abstractions. They are signs, or assembled artifacts, representing little more than that conscious thought which, if they have been learned, is extracted from them, or if made, went into the construction of them. Authentic symbols, on the other hand, "are pieces of life itself—images that are integrally connected to the living individual by the bridge of the emotions" (Jung, *Symbols*, p. 96).

The stick-woman insignia on the door of a women's washroom is, for instance, not more than a word picture. It may, as a sign, convey implicit cultural premises such as the right to privacy, differentiation by sex, or the correctness of bourgeois habiliment, but it is not stored with awesome and sublime reserves of feeling. As such, the stick woman is no more than an implement of conscious (or at most, subconscious) thought. The icon of the Pietà, however, may be a profoundly moving formulation of woman's non-rational association with death, depending on the individual's response to it. The "consequences" it might possess will depend entirely upon the attitude of consciousness expressed in any given response. Axiomatically, then, "Those who do not realize the special feeling tone of the archetype end with nothing more than a jumble of mythological concepts, which càn be strung together to show that everything means anything—or nothing at all. All the corpses in the world are chemically identical, but living individuals are not. Archetypes come to life only when one patiently tries to discover why and in what fashion they are meaningful to a living individual" (*Symbols*, p. 96).

The authentic symbol is hereinafter defined as a natural and spontaneous product arising from a life-giving archetype, and so possessing vital significance and great emotions for its human architect. Like all truly spontaneous products which are, as Jung says, "so fashioned that they must forfeit every sort of meaning, unless the symbolical one is accorded them,"[16] this archetypal image must promote and create life wherever it is admitted in its archaic force. The artist's compulsion to give it form is one consequence of its authoritative being; through it he feels the dynamic of existence. Faulkner's observation on the artistic act of creation, made to Jean Stein of *The Paris Review*, speaks amusingly but graphically of the impelling life and perhaps the transcendent worth of the dream in art's coming to form: "The writer's only responsibility is to his art. He will be completely ruthless if he is a good one. He has a dream. It anguishes him so much he must get rid of it. He has no peace until then. Everything goes by the board: honor, pride, decency, security, happiness, all, to get the book written. If a writer has to rob his mother, he will not hesitate; the 'Ode on a Grecian Urn' is worth any number of old ladies."[17] On the other hand, the responses of narrative personae to the dream are a different matter, to be dealt with in context. To the artist, however, as well as to the sympathetic reader, the only way the dream image might lose its dynamism would be to become exhausted by the understanding; the only way it might lose its meaning would be to receive a more compelling formulation in a new and different icon. Apparently, then, the authentic symbol is the communicator, irrespective of its individuated form, of an astounding reality—a totality filled with true existence.

Richard P. Adams, in *Faulkner: Myth and Motion*, suggests one mode by which the symbol might be empowered to communicate this aliveness. He avers that the contrapuntal opposition in *The Sound and the Fury* consists in "a fertile female principle of life [set] over against a male principle which is sterile and therefore essentially static, or dead" (p. 232), at the same time that he requires this counterpoint to be viewed in the context of an attractive, though sometimes difficult, aesthetic doctrine. The motion or flow of life, represented for the most part by women, must in art be arrested by whatever means "for esthetic and moral contemplation" (p. 15), but its very obstruction, if accomplished by male characters resistant to life, is intended "to dramatize the unquenchable vigor of life by showing it in the act of overwhelming and crushing static obstacles in its path" (p. 5); while, if achieved by the technical devices of the artist, it is designed to "contradict . . . the flow of time and [to provide] an artificially static moment into which [he] can compress great quantities of life" (p. 11).

The first of these putative aims seems discerning and exact. The great majority of Faulkner's men are indeed "desperate because a living world keeps forcing them into action in spite of their desire for security, peace, and stasis," while his women, although "so much in harmony with the motion that they, by themselves, could hardly show it at all" (p. 13), by contrast yet image the dynamic movement of life. Less apparent is the description of the means by which Faulkner aims at holding great quantities of life in a "vibrant moment of static awareness" (p. 248). If "Caddy, in her close association with trees, flowers, and water," is said to be "a fertility symbol like the hyacinth girl in *The Waste Land*" (p. 232), she is not necessarily a life symbol. The inadequacy of nature, even of the Grail-fertility-ritual type[18] referred to by Adams, as a system figuratively extending life to man needs no further discussion. Should the artist be dependent like the critic, however, upon traditional sources for his iconography, then either that cultural tradition must possess a felt authority in the symbolism of existence, or the artist must assign to his created form a meaning which "is informed more by erudition and the abstractions of learning than by emotion" (Baird, p. 73).

The critic says that "Caddy resembles not only the Arician Diana but the Egyptian Isis, whose lover, Osiris, was also her brother" (p. 233), and that it is chiefly by this symbolic counterpoint that she comes to represent all "the power of motion." The gulf between cultures and collectivities of belief cannot be so easily crossed; it must not be forgotten that Faulkner as artist is neither Arician nor Egyptian, or that *The Golden Bough* and *From Ritual to Romance* as myth furnish no more than instances of primitivism. The primary artist, it must be asserted, does not create, like the critic would have it, from inert ideas but from the reaches of great emotion. The implications for secondary art are damaging. Eliot's hyacinth girl in *The Waste Land* takes whatever significance she possesses second-hand from Frazer; she does not spring from the life source out of which, presumably, the original myth of Arician Diana arose. But that is only to say what the primal creator could not mistake—that the truly creative act is nothing like the critical attempt at its re-creation.

If Caddy's obvious fertility in *The Sound and the Fury* is accounted for by way of Eliot by way of Frazer by way of an alien source (or even by one of these), then Faulkner's fertility symbol is only a sign—a lifeless idea—and his potential primitivism is merely academic. Should Caddy's abundance of life, on the other hand, be realized in an image of primitive feeling, then Dilsey, who is omitted from the foregoing discussion of "motion"—presumably because she is too old to be fertile or because she is identified with death—would regain her portion in Faulkner's emblem of existence; and that peculiar ability (or mode) of the symbol to impart life would be readmitted to critical consciousness.

Conversely, Walter Brylowski, in *Faulkner's Olympian Laugh: Myth in the Novels*,[19] defines a more broadly symbolic mode by which the artist is enabled to re-establish a mythic reality. Noting that "several critics have remarked the dissatisfaction Faulkner expresses in his early novels with 'talk, talk, talk,' " he asserts that it is Faulkner's "felt need to discover a mode of communication which carries an aura of meaning beyond the bounds of what might be recognized as a scientifically rational mode of knowledge that leads him to employ the perceptions of irrational characters, characters whose 'truth' is a configuration of the mythic mode of thought" (p. 15). This concept of a "mythic mode of thought," derived from Ernst Cassirer's attempt to achieve a philosophic definition of myth as symbolic form, appears to have undervalued Cassirer's premise in *Mythical Thought* of a culturally incipient process of cognition, whereby "man can apprehend and know his own being only insofar as he can make it visible in the image of his gods,"[20] and to have emphasized instead the formative operation effected by intuition in mythical consciousness, as opposed to that effected by " 'pure thought' . . . in theoretical-scientific or rational-empiric" (Brylowski, p. 13) consciousness. By this account, the laws which govern the formation of mythic thought, having an intuitive base, are distinctly different from the laws by which scientific-empiric thought is formulated; consequently, differing versions of reality take shape. Mythic thought is seemingly defined as a spiritual configuration of reality unattended by an attitude of inquiry and doubt toward the "object" with its claim to objectivity and necessity (Cassirer, p. 74); mythic thought, in other words, instead of seeking to understand an object by articulating it with a complex of causes and effects, is simply overpowered by the object's immediacy. Badly stated in the only available terms, its activity is characterized by an epistemology which admits of no spatial differentiation between subject and object and of no temporal distinction between past and future. It operates through the configuration of a non-objective reality and through the destruction of empiric time.

Brylowski's hypothesis seems to be essentially right about the disposition of Faulkner's world view. The rational-empiric mode of thought is said to be narratively connected with the disclosure of a demonic world; the mythic mode of thought provides a necessary dual focus for the resolution of the problem of evil: an admission, on the one hand, of the "folly, misery, and corruption" in existence, and an affirmation, on the other, of its ultimate transcendence. Nonetheless, mythic thought can be narratively operative only in the mind of a created character, not within the mind of the artist who is already one step removed by his art from the essential unity of subject-object. Art, by this standard, is not myth; there are in art only characters who think mythically. In much of Faulkner's work, characters who perceive the world empirically are counterpointed by characters who think in the mythic mode; pessimistic naturalism is thus offset by a transcendence perceived in symbolic form.

The mythic mode may outline a proper outcome—one which is true to a general tendency—in Faulkner's fiction, but it is less reliable in analysing processes by which that end is reached. In *The Sound and the Fury*, for example, the mythic mode of thought is limited to Quentin. He is spiritually committed to the destruction of empiric time, yet his attempt is unsuccessful; the clock-world of ordinary logic pains him to the point of self-destruction. He identifies his shadow, as in mythical thought, with the object casting it (his body), but he assays to trample the bones of that shadow into the pavement. He tries to incorporate the fact of Caddy's pregnancy into his undifferentiated, unchanging reality by the substitution of himself for Dalton Ames as lover, but he is forced at last to kill himself to keep the persistent facts of empirical reality from impinging on his fantasy. If Quentin rejects the rational-empiric mode in favour of the mythic mode of thought, his suicide marks the failure of that mode to be a viable reality. It can offer him neither sacrament nor sanction for existence because it is at base no more than thought; as a noted linguist once said, "No one prays to a concept." So Quentin's death, in terms of this perspective, is far from evidence of a mythic optimism. It is even more life-denying than Jason's cynical configuration of the world by the laws of the rational-empiric mode. The character's mythical thought alone cannot then be sufficient to realize the artist's symbolic aim. Evidently, the symbolic mode of the artist must extend beyond those "intuitive" laws of thought revealed in his persona's intra-symbolic response.

Quentin's resistance to time, occurring within the containing symbolic parts of *The Sound and the Fury*, opens up to discussion one territory deliberately overlooked by Baird in his account of iconographic primitivism. It concerns the temporal process of narrative form, especially with an eye to its participation in the symbolic mode. Baird admits forthrightly to having "proceeded upon the assumption that . . . literature . . . may be regarded as poetry in the sense of *poesis* [poetic form]," and further acknowledges that his "purpose is to isolate and to examine the symbols of each [work] which belong to the system of primitivism" (p. xx). But Lessing's *Laocoön*, in its own right a classic of aesthetic criticism, defines the limits of painting and poetry (the plastic arts and the epic) in such a way that any isolation of symbols from narrative art is effectively ruled out. Lessing says, "The rule is this, that succession in time is the province of the poet, co-existence in space that of the artist."[21] Thus, while pictorial art might achieve its desired end of beauty through representing the harmonious whole of adjacent parts, it will lack the ability of narrative art to imitate change and even contrariety in the same subject. The pictorial artist must so arrange his subject in space as to give an apparently static image the dynamic character of a great action, even as that image retains the quiet and restraint which is essential to unchanging form. The poet, on the other hand, "alone possesses the art of so combining negative with positive traits as to unite the two appearances in one" (p. 60). The great sculpture, then, is not an incident drawn from a story, but the epitome of it; the great narrative should be not only a gallery of pictures but, potentially, an imaging of paradoxical figures.

The icon in literary art, while it is a product of word succession, is curiously projected through the eye of the imagination into spatial form. Lena Grove, for example, "advance[s] in identical and anonymous and deliberate wagons as though through a succession of creakwheeled and limpeared avatars, like something moving forever and without progress across an urn." Although she possesses all the dynamism (or psychic charge) of the Baird-Jung symbol, she is perceived in the moment of perpetual stasis, the beauty and power of this image ever potential, but essentially suspended as the "thing in itself." There is as well the image of Temple Drake who is conflated with "the dead tranquil queens in stained marble" and with "the sky lying prone and vanquished in the embrace of the season of rain and death," which, if regarded in that moment as the essence, is the arrested power of all life. Temple, unlike Lena, has the added disadvantage of appearing to be negative, not positive, if held in a suspended image. That she is not negative, however, becomes apparent only by examining within the narrative the complex of responses to her symbolic being. The temporal movement of the story, then, is the sole means of releasing the symbol's dynamism even as it is the sole revealer of the icon's doubleness.

At this point an analogy from Lessing's discussion, even a provisionally applicable one, might serve to illuminate the function of narrative within this symbolic process. "The gods," Lessing argues, "and other spiritual beings represented by the artist are not precisely the same as those introduced by the poet" (p. 58). Since Aphrodite is to the artist the epitome of love, she must be endowed with every beauty and charm which might represent the "frozen," though undiminished power of such love. The pictorial artist may choose, much like the bard Demodokos, to represent her lying with Ares in the toils of Hephaistos's snare. If so, he must similarly depict her in her unabated loveliness. "But when [Aphrodite], intent on revenging herself on her contemners, the men of Lemnos, wild, in colossal shape, with cheeks inflamed and dishevelled hair, seizes the torch, and, wrapping a black robe about her, flies downward on the storm-cloud,—that is no moment for the painter, because he has no means of making us recognize her. The poet alone has the privilege of availing himself of it. He can unite it so closely with some other moment when the goddess is the true [Aphrodite], that we do not in the fury forget the goddess of love" (p. 59). While it is obvious that the authentic symbols of primitivism require no such allegorical tagging—in fact, could not permit it—it is equally apparent that their dynamic suspension, like the representations of pictorial art, leaves them essentially uniform, admitting of but one impression. In other words, the symbol as an entity has but one aspect—the life-enhancing, existential expression of its source. But Jungian theory, let alone the recollection of a Faulkner novel, offers evidence that "every archetype is 'two-faced,' ambivalent, and has a 'good' and a 'bad' side according to the attitude the conscious mind adopts toward it."²² The limits which apply in Lessing's discussion of poetry and painting apply equally to Baird's iconic mode of primitivism; to ignore them would, in a critical sense, be to court the same aesthetic failure which is attendant upon any creative violation of such limits. Some other tool is consequently needed to define the narrative presence and process of an archetypal factor.

The term "mythos" is here adopted to refer to the structural organizing principle of symbolic form by which the face of an archetype is revealed in the precise attitude—two-fold now by virtue of personae and artist—of consciousness toward it. The essential uniformity of the image, it should be stressed, is still perceptible in the artist's indirect (because projected in narrative arrangement) response to it, since the very disposition of narrative action about the symbol's presence constitutes a private coming to terms with it, resulting in artistic creation. But the immediate responses of narrative characters to the symbol's power need not be uniform, resulting quite possibly in the emergence of either face, or indeed, the Janus-face of the archetype. Mythos, then, is meant to retain the adumbrative definition Aristotle gave to it of plot or narrative as theme. but it takes on a wider meaning in the context of the symbolic mode. A part of this meaning has to do with the structural ordering of unlimited power in humanized form, the other part with the structural resolution of time (the medium of the narrative and its characters) and timelessness (the eternal presence of the archetype).

Northrop Frye has suggested two variants of mythos:[23] archetypal narrative, which in his anatomic terms is the imitation of a recurrent action or ritual; and anagogic narrative, the imitation of the total conceivable action of an omnipotent god or human society, both of which have a limited correspondence to these designated structural factors. To take the more problematical definition first, Frye means by anagogic simply that which is all-encompassing, both in action and manifestation, although he finds (with Durkheim, whose social theories propose that society deifies itself) the action of an omnipotent god interchangeable with that of an "omnipotent" society. Contrarily, anagogy is meant more narrowly here, retaining the etymological meaning of spiritual uplift, as the expression of divine activity within the action of a narrative. Where the archetypal feminine, for example, is present in a literary work, its power is absolute. Society, on the other hand, is polarized by its presence; each character is forced to choose for or against the expression of its power. The literary artist cannot violate with impunity, however, accepted canons of credibility within his culture. The particular tension of mythos in a rationalistic culture must then consist in its accommodation of supra-personal power to personal form. *Sanctuary* provides an interesting case in point because the structural revisions of the galleys help to invest a brashly human coquette, Temple Drake with a supra-human authority which she did not formerly possess (see chapter 5). That authority, of course, is ultimately derived from the archetype which is present in the psychic experience of both characters and author (presumably the reader also), but manifest as well in the outer world. The real difference here with Frye, then, has to do with his contention that in the anagogic phase, narrative is a self-contained universe dependent only upon unlimited individual thought. His assertion that plot and theme no longer depend, in this phase, upon the imitative word (high or low mimesis), but upon the Logos, the shaping word of reason and the creative act (p. 120), happily places symbolic art beyond the constraints of realism. The idea, nonetheless, that this paternal

Logos or reason is the maker of omnipotent symbols ill accords in general with their being emotions as much as they are images, or, more particularly, with their being identified at any time as feminine.

The ritual aspect of mythos which Frye terms archetypal narrative is more easily translated as a recurring response to the eternal presence of the archetype. It is the momentary and unique experience of something which is both transhistorical, appearing throughout human time, and supra-personal, more than the ephemeral consciousness of the individual. The myth of the feminine, for example, is the story of the Great Mother repeated again and again in life and art from the paleolithic period to the modern era. "Mythos" then implies a particular narrative within a containing tradition. More importantly, however, it refers to the particular artist's encounter with one of several transpersonal factors which shall be thoroughly defined as the archetypal feminine. The historical individual somehow brings the non-historical and the supra-personal down (or up) into his world. He forges a narrative structure which contains a vital two-dimensional reference in time. This resolution of time and timelessness is itself a vital objective of mythos.

T. S. Eliot's "mythical method" should here be identified in its concern with periodicity, as evinced in his dictum concerning *Ulysses*, that "[in] using the myth, in manipulating a continuous parallel between contemporaneity and antiquity, Mr. Joyce is pursuing a method which others must pursue after him."[24] This leads to a different sort of temporal resolution in the aesthetic proposition of intruding myths of antiquity into the contemporary situation in order to contradict the flow of time and to produce an artificially static moment into which all time, or history, or experience, or life can be compressed. The Christ pattern, the Persephone pattern, and the Grail-fertility pattern as they are used in the story of the Compsons, act, by this account, to obstruct ordinary time and to impede the motion of life so that the artist can give his story temporal and cultural dimensions it would not otherwise possess.

The Sound and the Fury's three interior monologues appear to support the arrest, by intrusion, of ordinary time and to gainsay any prospect for timelessness within the chaotic time of the story. The temporal dislocation in narrative structure (7 April 1928 to 2 June

1910 to 6 April 1928 to 8 April 1928) parallels the radical disordering of time in Benjy's and Quentin's minds. Where this confusion serves as the desperate attempt of consciousness to reactualize the past, it parallels the attempt of the mythical method to suffuse the moment with all history. Neither attempt succeeds, however; the despair attendant, in the first instance, upon the mind's inability to hang onto time leads, in the second instance, to the Joycean fear of history as nightmare. The impulse of the mythical method to impose by artificial means order and meaning upon the present terminates in the terror of Stephen Dedalus and of Benjy or Quentin Compson. This terror seems essential, nevertheless, to Faulkner's strategy. For if the Compson brothers are predisposed to the synchronous limitations of the method, the artist is not. In the novel's fourth section, Dilsey says "I've seed de first en de last." Because her speech is located at the conclusion of the Easter service in the Negro church, it is often assumed that her "first" and "last" are the Alpha and Omega, the apocalyptic god of Christian tradition. What is less often noticed is that the sermon and Dilsey's symbolic part in it are not Christian but pagan. She is identified with the icon of a pagan Pietà; Caddy, in the first section, has already been figured as a primitive madonna; the Christ of both symbols thus serves only to evoke the attributes of the Holy Mother (see chapter 3). What Dilsey envisions in "de first en de last" is the ceaseless beginning and end of human life; what she sees as she looks into the very depths of being is that the feminine contains them both; she is somehow outside of time, comprising it. Mythos, as it then refers to the story of Caddy and Dilsey, projects a symbolic immanence of eternity in the historical world of the novel, even as it orders the responses of limited human creatures·to the unlimited power expressed in symbols of woman.

At last, it is possible to say plainly that Faulkner has written—at least in some of his works—testaments in worship of the Great Goddess. Sensible of the failure of his Protestant culture to provide symbolic mediation (or some abiding mythic awareness of the other world of the Thou), he has used his inherited religious materials as tools for striking a new key in the feeling-tone of existence. This need of the artist in his Protestant aloneness to redescribe the relationship of man to his deity does not, however, insure the creation of successful works of art. The making of new symbols of existence is primarily religious, not artistic, in intent; it is an attempt to provide renewed contact with the source and value of existence, to image the range and course of human destiny. The obverse effect that creative worship might have upon the story will occur in the realm of form. The artist who is possessed by an arche-type and feels impelled to render it incarnate will not only be the maker of dynamic life symbols, but will be as well the composer, in narrative terms, of a compulsive counterpoint. But such posses-sion can be regarded as authentic, in that art will be invigorated only when the feeling component of symbol and the structuring component of mythos have entered into elemental combination, or, alternatively, when the awesome and inspiriting presence of god-head has met in vital confrontation with mankind, and whatever then opposes life or denies it is judged in terrible fury, whatever embraces or accepts it is confirmed in lyric animation. Obviously, no literary achievement with aims of this magnitude can be expected to be forthcoming overnight. Faulkner's early novels afford evidence of his repeated, if miscarrying, attempt to achieve a sacramental mode of primitivism.

2

The Portrait of the Feminine in Faulkner's Early Novels

Primitivistic Materials
Antecedent to Form

It is with reference to woman, wrote Cleanth Brooks, "that those who claim that Faulkner is a primitivist could, if they cared to attempt it, come closest to making out a case. But I think that they had better not try to make the case unless they are prepared to claim Aristotle and St. Thomas and Milton as primitivists too."[1] The difficulty appears to be with what is meant by "primitivist"; Brooks means by it one who holds to the "noble savage" concept of man as being essentially good in a natural state and as becoming progressively perverted in a state of civilization. Faulkner, of course, does not believe in natural goodness any more than does the classical philosopher, the Christian theologian, or the classical-Christian poet; each takes the view that man is inherently limited or sinful. Faulknerian woman, however, is said to be closer than man "to nature, and in the persons of Eula and Lena she comes close to being nature itself—and nature is scarcely innocent" (p. 23). If the nearest, then, that we can come to primitivism in Faulkner is by means of woman, and if the pursuit of that argument is hindered only by a moral-philosophical definition of the end, then the hypothesis of an un-innocent, sentient kind of primitiveness should make the case for Faulkner's women not only possible but necessary.

From the time of his apprenticeship, Faulkner was aware of the importance of woman to a primitive world view. In *Mosquitoes* (1927), the novelist Fairchild and the "Semitic man" stand before Gordon's sculpture of a "virginal breastless torso of a girl" which is "motionless and passionately eternal";[2] the presence of the stone image prompts Fairchild to say: " 'Creation, reproduction from within. . . . Is the dominating impulse in the world feminine, after all, as aboriginal peoples believe? . . . There is a kind of spider or something. The female is the larger, and when the male goes to her he goes to death: she devours him during the act of conception. And that's man: a kind of voraciousness that makes an artist stand beside himself with a notebook in his hand always, putting down all the charming things that ever happen to him, killing them for the sake of some problematical something he might or he might not ever use' " (p. 320, Faulkner's ellipses). Fairchild's rhetorical question shows Faulkner's knowledge of primitive mythology, of the belief that the dominant impulse in the world is ambivalently feminine; more than that, it presumes that the existence of life, whether biological or artistic, is governed in its waxing and in its waning by a feminine power.

Mosquitoes, its awareness of mythology notwithstanding, is not mythic; it is a novel of ideas, not of symbolic primitivism, at times an interminable satire (rarely crisp, most often heavy-handed) of a kind of insectivorous bohemian sub-culture of Jazz Age New Orleans. Its central debate turns on the issue of the nature of woman and her bearing upon male life and art. Most of the men on board the conversation-ship *Nausikaa* (named for King Alcinous's daughter to whom Odysseus owed, in some measure, his life) are deeply troubled by woman; she is variously represented as being more vital but less spiritual than themselves, as being more naturally creative than the artist, as being the unattainable object or the betrayal of man's impossible desire.

Fairchild, the novelist, is most concerned with differentiating the functions of the sexes; he objects to the charge that women are stupid, claiming that "their mental equipment is too sublimely sufficient to do what little directing their bodies require" (p. 240). Feminine life, he claims (and he seems to anticipate characters such as Caddy Compson, Lena Grove, and Eula Varner) is a self-contained organic process transcending intelligence; man, on the other hand, is able to contain life only through artificial means.

Consequently he defines art as "getting into life, getting into it and wrapping it around you, becoming a part of it. Women can do it without art—old biology takes care of that. But men, men. . . . A woman conceives: does she care afterward whose seed it was? Not she. And bears, and all the rest of her life—her young troubling years that is—is filled" (p. 320, Faulkner's ellipsis). Fairchild feels driven, however, to assert the superiority of male creation: "But in art, a man can create without any assistance at all: what he does is his. A perversion, I grant you, but a perversion that builds Chartres and invents Lear is a pretty good thing." He ends with the reflection already quoted, that all creation is feminine, that all organic-artistic conception is a devouring of life, and that the world-dominant feminine impulse maintains a negative ascendancy (as it does to a certain extent, for Faulkner, in Temple Drake, as well as in Addie Bundren and Caroline Compson).

Julius, the Semitic man, is more cynical and more directly misogynous than Fairchild in response to woman's non-intelligent organic creativity. He argues, implicitly, that only men have souls: "If [women] are not born with them, it's a poor creature indeed who can't get one from some man by the time she's eleven years old" (p. 241). Man's spiritual and intellectual creations represent, for him, the dominant human achievement; when Fairchild qualifies his definition of art to say that women have created some good things, Julius retorts, "They bear geniuses" (p. 248). The satiric portraits of Eva Wiseman and Miss Jameson give almost cruel vindication to his idea that women are subordinate to the purposes of art. Mrs. Wiseman, for presuming to write poetry, is characterized as a lesbian who yearns for "the divine inevitability of [Jenny's] soft body" (p. 178); Miss Jameson uses painting as an ineffective means of seducing artistic men. The one becomes perverted (pseudo-masculine) through her artistic ambition; the other prostitutes art to her spirit-weakened biological purpose.

Mr. Talliaferro, who is neither an artist nor a man, holds a different view of women; they are the unattainable object of his desire. Like his literary ancestor Prufrock, he is tormented by a nubile sexuality often bordering on oblivious provocation; he is torn between physical desire and his psychic fear of it, between surrender to the moment and endless indecision. At one point, Fairchild offers him advice about womankind which is later heard from Faulknerian characters as different as Byron Bunch and Addie Bundren: "They ain't interested in what you're going to say: they are interested in what you're going to do" (p. 112). Talliaferro, however, is too afraid of what they are going to do ever to act boldly; the novel ends with his calling Fairchild on the telephone to say what course of action he thinks he will follow. The narrator (with the implication that it is Gordon thinking) sums up this male perplexity of mind—figured most fully in Talliaferro, but represented to various degrees in the other men as well—with a despairing observation about both pure consciousness and the novel of ideas: "Talk, talk, talk: the utter and heartbreaking stupidity of words. It seemed endless, as though it might go on forever. Ideas, thoughts, became mere sounds to be bandied about until they were dead" (p. 186). The idea that the male estate—mind, spirit, intellect—is a dead thing of itself prefigures the predicament of the majority of Faulknerian men; Quentin Compson and Darl Bundren will represent the tragic, Gavin Stevens the pathetically comic possibilities of that dilemma.

Gordon is the only man and artist in *Mosquitoes* who seems to have made a separate peace with the feminine impulse. He rarely speaks; at our last sight of him, once the interminable talk of the voyage is ended, he is entering a New Orleans bordello where Fairchild and Julius see him "in a narrow passageway lift a woman from the shadow and raise her against the mad stars, smothering her squeal against his tall kiss" (pp. 338–39). The novel also opens in Gordon's studio where stands his sculpture of "the virginal breastless torso of a girl, headless, armless, legless, in marble temporarily caught and hushed yet passionate still for escape, passionate and simple and eternal in the equivocal derisive darkness of the world" (p. 11). Patricia, one of the nubile females of the book, is strangely moved by it; through it, she is attracted to its creator. Although the figure does not dominate the course of the novel, it serves in conclusion to elicit Fairchild's observation about the dominance of the feminine impulse. Within this frame, Gordon says two things about the image: it "is my feminine ideal: a virgin with no legs to leave me, no arms to hold me, no head to talk to me" (p. 26), and "She is dark, darker than fire. She is more terrible and beautiful than fire. . . . Marble, purity. . . . Pure because they have yet to discover some way to make it unpure. They would if they could, God damn them!" (p. 329). The first is the semi-facetious portrait of a "still unravished bride of quietness"; the second is a desperate assertion of the changeless feminine, one which exists only in the world of male ideality and is untouched by feminine realities of sex, growth, and change. The violence of Gordon's despair prefigures the violence Quentin will commit upon himself to preserve his sister Caddy in that eternal state of purity.

The role of art, in Gordon's view, is finally little different from the narrator's view that "Dante invented Beatrice, creating himself a maid that life had not had time to create, and laid upon her frail and unbowed shoulders the whole burden of man's history of his impossible heart's desire" (p. 339). The fact, at this point, that the "heart's desire" is impossible suggests only that the ideal is unreal; Gordon and the narrator believe that the artist fashions what never was nor will be so that he will not have to acknowledge what is. The fact that Faulkner later spoke of Caddy as "the heart's darling" (*University*, p. 6) suggests he learned as an artist that he could create not an ideal but something with a life of its own, something which always was and will be; fortunately, the tension between the real and the ideal can now exist in the discrepancy between narrators and the narrative outcome.

Although *Mosquitoes* anticipates the tendencies and dispositions of a number of Faulkner's mature novels, it does not function in the archetypal mode. The dominance of a feminine impulse in the world might be an accurate mythological statement but it is not mythographically expressed. The women artists of the narrative dominate nothing; they are only derided. And the two young girls, Jenny Steinbauer and Patricia Robyn, whose sexual force makes them the centre of attraction for every man in the book never accomplish their biological ends; they become neither pregnant like Lena Grove (around whom a world revolves) nor violated like Temple Drake (in whom a male world is annihilated). Their sexual power remains merely potential, and they are invested with no supra-personal numen.

Likewise, the few symbols of the book relating to the "feminine impulse" (such as Gordon's statue) do not evoke a sense of the unknown or the inexplicable—the sculpture is, for Gordon, the expression of a logical ideal—nor do they contain a dynamic autonomy. Patricia comes the closest, in her response to the statue, to suggesting its affective potential, but her statement, "It's like me" (p. 24), and her desire to place her "hands on the marble, hard, hard" (p. 30) suggest a latent narcissism, nothing in the image. The other sentient factors embodied in it are only such ideas as "passionately eternal" with which the author drapes it. Several scattered images do anticipate authentic symbols from the mature work: Patricia walking about the studio "straight as a poplar" (p. 27) and having about her the "clean young odor . . . of young trees" (p. 21) anticipates Benjy in his haunting refrain "She smelled like trees." The difference, in the latter instance, is that Caddy's association with trees is part of a much larger symbol complex which in turn is suggestive of something larger than a personality behind it. Still there is an awareness in *Mosquitoes* of the primordial and hallowed forces felt to be resident in trees. When David West, the ship's steward, and Patricia slip away into the aboriginal chaos of the swamp, they face "always those bearded eternal trees like gods regarding without alarm this puny desecration of a silence of air and earth and water ancient where hoary old Time himself was a pink and dreadful miracle in his mother's arms" (p. 174). The cypresses of this formless and abysmal swamp seem to antedate creation, themselves the timeless fountainheads of the fabric of the temporal. Their aspect is patriarchal (bearded), but they share a matriarchal identity with the mother older than time. They do not share that identity with Patricia, however, either in action or in significance. They stand unrelated to human life or to the shape of the narrative; they do not have the power to project David and Patricia into their non-historical time, they have no impact upon events, and they do not hold image and incident throughout the novel subservient to their inner meaning. This, finally, must be the index of a novel of primitivistic ideas over against a novel of symbolic primitivism.

Soldiers' Pay (1926) is not only Faulkner's first published novel; it is also an indication of his earliest predisposition in narrative toward the power of woman in the world. Donald Mahon, the young aviator who has been critically wounded in the Great War, is shipped home from France to Charlestown, Georgia; along the way, he blindly attracts the sympathy of a young war widow, Mrs. Margaret Powers. She seems, in assuming his care, to be atoning for an act of spiritual infidelity to her husband of three days; her letter informing Richard Powers of her decision to annul their hasty, war-hysterical marriage had not reached him before he was killed in action. She feels he has died believing in her, and the war-disfigured aviator becomes for her a welcome surrogate. Donald, who has almost no awareness of who he is or where he is going, is, in fact, returning to his fiancée, Cecily Saunders. Throughout the course of the story, these two women will be the most active agents in Donald Mahon's lingering death-in-life.

Much of the plot of *Soldiers' Pay* turns on the question of whether Cecily will keep her engagement to marry the wounded man, or whether she will give herself to one of the youths about town. She is flighty and immature, something of a flapper in the sense that Temple Drake of *Sanctuary* seems to be: using her sexuality irresponsibly to arouse desire, then fleeing the act (or its result) with a ruthless, desperate self-concern, seeking fiercely to forestall her public disgrace. She is tearfully willing to marry Donald at one moment, hysterically unwilling to look at him the next. At last, she tells Donald's father, the rector, that she is not a good woman any more, and she elopes with George Farr who has seen "her body, like a little silver water sweetly dividing."[3] Margaret, who has in the meantime become the source of strength in the widowed rector's home and who has quietly sought to bring about the marriage of Cecily and Donald, marries him herself. Shortly thereafter, Donald flares in a moment of bright lucidity (during which he remembers being gunned down out of the sky), then dies.

Margaret and Gilligan, the enlisted man who has also come to Georgia out of devotion to Mahon, agree—as Joe puts it—that they have "tried to help nature make a good job out of a poor one without having no luck at it" (p. 309). Emmy, the servant girl who is linked to nature by allusions and by the girlhood night she spent with Donald in the grass, does not agree. As Margaret gently attempts to persuade her to come to the funeral, Emmy cries silently "I would have cured him! If they had just let me marry him instead of her!" (p. 301). She speaks, nevertheless, more in desperation than in belief; she lives in a world of memory where "she went to him, and wet grass and dew under her and over her his head with the whole sky for a crown, and the moon running on them like water that wasn't wet and that you couldn't feel" (p. 277);

hers is a world (like the sculptor Gordon's) of impossible desire. One further aspect of woman should be juxtaposed to this concept of the life-giving nature of the female. Margaret inexplicably associates herself with death as Gilligan asks her to marry him: "Bless your heart, darling. If I married you you'd be dead in a year, Joe. All the men that marry me die, you know" (p. 312). She seems to have identified herself with the dominant feminine impulse of *Mosquitoes*, with the female spider who devours the male in the act of conception; at the very least, she gives her woman's nature a mysterious and unfathomable relation to the power of death.

Upon more hard-headed reflection, however, the failure of Faulkner's mythos in *Soldiers' Pay* is quite evident. Donald Mahon is destroyed by a war which has little connection with a "feminine impulse." After Donald is injured, it is true, he becomes the helpless recipient of feminine attention; but his condition is neither produced nor palliated by woman (much like Jake Barnes's condition in Hemingway's *The Sun Also Rises*). Granted the thematic turning of the novel, the war-wounded hero is a false start in the story; yet even then, its thematic elaboration is neither grounded in necessity nor possibility: Margaret has no real or intrinsic connection with Donald's death (he ought not to have lived this long anyway except for some undetailed and unexplained military surgery), Cecily has done nothing by her infidelity to shock him to death (he does not remember her), and Emmy does not have the burgeoning power of the spring season to restore life (despite her allusive connection with earth and water, grass and trees). All these potentialities of woman exist as a sort of unfocused feeling, an incipient mythos, in the author's mind, but they fail to be vitally integrated with the action which the story relates. Theme, in other words, fails to merge with plot.

There is evidence, nevertheless, that the young artist possessed some understanding of what his theme entailed; in the opening lines of the final chapter of *Soldiers' Pay*, his emerging *Weltanschauung* is given rather lugubrious emphasis: "Sex and death: the front door and the back door of the world. How indissolubly are they associated in us! In youth they lift us out of the flesh, in old age they reduce us again to the flesh; one to fatten us, the other to flay us, for the worm. When are sexual compulsions more readily answered than in war or famine or flood or fire?" (p. 300). Sex, as one has begun to suspect from *Mosquitoes*, is central to the myth of the feminine; in copulation, in pregnancy, most mysteriously in death, it constitutes the underlying force of woman. The problem in *Soldiers' Pay*, illustrated by the above passage, is that the artist does not yet know how to give this potency dynamic and compelling expression.

Cecily Saunders is the focus, more than Emmy, of female sexuality in the novel. The greater number of the images attempting to convey this force are tree-associated; Januarius Jones—classicist, Faun, and fool—sees Cecily as a "Hamadryad, a slim jewelled one" (p. 71); with his eyes he abuses "her body created for all men to dream after. A poplar, vain and pliant . . ." (p. 225); in her slim figure he glimpses something "like a flower stalk or a young tree relaxed against the table: there was something so fragile, so impermanent since robustness and strength were unnecessary, yet strong withal as a poplar is strong through very absence of strength, about her" (pp. 74–75). The redundancy of images in Jones's mind does not, however, make Cecily play the wood nymph to his satyr. The narrator links poplars over and over to young girls; they assume several important qualities in this context, most often being vain and pliant, pristine and epicene, but always caught in arrested motion. The initial portrait of Rector Mahon's garden establishes this Grecian Urn significance of budding sexuality contained forever in perpetual virginity: "Beyond the oaks, against a wall of poplars in a restless formal row were columns of a Greek temple, yet the poplars themselves in slim, vague green were poised and vain as girls in a frieze" (p. 55). Sergeant Madden crossed France, "seeing the intermittent silver smugness of rain spaced forever with poplars like an eternal frieze giving way upon vistas fallow and fecund" (p. 175). Something eternal or "non-historical" is glimpsed in the tree-nymph image, and that timelessness is somehow linked to both virginity and fecundity, but the artist is not yet sure what its inner significance is, or how it relates to the whole; it is an image, like the "blue hyacinths . . . dreaming of Lesbos" (p. 55), extrinsically alluding to Ovid.

The same allusive method marks the use of the myth of Atalanta in the novel. Jones, who stares at Cecily with the same redundancy in which he thinks of her, "could imagine her long subtle legs,

like Atalanta's reft of running" (p. 72). Nevertheless it is Emmy
whom he pursues with his goat-like agility and pertinacity; Margaret suggests quite archly that he is preparing to write a poem
about Atalanta (p. 292). By the end of the scene, it is the poplar
in the yard which has become "a leafed and passionate Atalanta,
poising her golden apple" (p. 296). In the myth, of course, Atalanta
was both virginal like Artemis and was punished by Aphrodite for
her obstinacy in remaining a virgin. So inclusion of the poplar in
alluding to Atalanta is not merely the undisciplined exuberance of
a young artist; the myth reinforces the sexual ambivalency of the
tree-nymph image. That ambivalence, however, has little bearing
on the meaning of Cecily's story (the social question of whom she
will marry); it stands as a *tour de force* of the artist's insight into the
sexual nature of woman. The image complex of tree, woman, and
Atalanta is shaped by allusion from the "outside," and it fails to
achieve an internal unity with the story; it does not, as the true symbol must, govern both the energy and the outcome of the narrative.

One final image must be treated in the terms already set out; it
is an important image because it will reappear in Faulkner in a
different manner, by a different process. Jones, who is seeking by
fair means or foul to seduce Cecily, sits with her "in the vaguely
gleamed twilight of the room, Jones a fat Mirandola in a chaste
Platonic nympholepsy, a religio-sentimental orgy in grey tweed,
shaping an insincere, fleeting articulation of damp clay to an old
imperishable desire, building himself a papier-mâché Virgin" (p.
226). Two important features of the allusive method are highlighted in the final phrase: first, one notices that the symbol of the
Virgin has no intrinsic life, it is only "papier-mâché." Second, the
artist builds himself a symbol; that is, the image is neither spontaneous (the only manner in which something otherwise unknowable could be revealed) nor necessary, but only desired. It is fabric-
ated entirely out of consciousness. Jones's image-process comments
on the style of the work as a whole—luxuriously allusive in the
manner of *fin de siécle* poetry, yet garishly over-conscious of its art.

It hardly seems that Faulkner set out in *Soldiers' Pay* (as he
did, say, in *Sanctuary* or in *Light in August*) to portray man's
mysterious dependency upon feminine powers; nevertheless it
seems that he discovered—perhaps took hold of—something about
the human condition in the writing of his first book. Nonetheless

he lacked a total vision yet of the scope of that condition, and he lacked the technical means to give it symbolic formulation.

Sartoris (1929), which preceded publication of *The Sound and the Fury* by only some nine months, establishes for the first time Faulkner's microcosmic county; it introduces us to a number of his people, and it prefigures some of his major themes—a crumbling aristocracy, for example, obsessed in a romantic sense with its own past. It is still very much, however, a vestigial work of the Old Plantation South, filled with the ghosts of an outmoded history. Old Bayard Sartoris, though he runs the Jefferson Bank, is still "Massuh, yassuh" to Simon Strother who tells his son Caspey, "You go'n git dat mare, and save dat nigger freedom talk fer town-folks: dey mought stomach it. Whut us niggers want ter be free fer, anyhow? Ain't we got ez many white folks now ez we kin suppo't?"[4] The joke, of course, depends upon a double form of benevolent paternalism: the comic-literal version which recoils upon its caricatured maker, and the amused but more lofty version of the novelist himself.

If *Sartoris* depicts a vestigial society, it also portrays vestigial characters like Miss Jenny Du Pre, widowed by the Civil War but not reconciled after half a century to the defeat of the South. Miss Jenny is very much the grand old Lady of the South, possessed of a crisp mind, a sharp tongue, and a wisdom bred of an indomitable strength; she also participates, however, in a feminine nature which is markedly different from the male estate. In fact, all the women of *Sartoris*, despite their uneven blend of antebellum, Reconstruction, post-Great War, and non-historical characterizations, are consistently set off against the wild, reckless, despairing world of Sartorises as being themselves more peaceful, prudent, and abiding.

Jenny Du Pre came all the way from Carolina to Mississippi in '69, travelled alone to her brother's house wearing "that expression of indomitable and utter weariness which all Southern women had learned to wear, bringing with her the clothing in which she stood and a wicker hamper filled with colored glass" (p. 9). Fifty years later when her great grandnephew Bayard and the Negro servant Caspey have returned home from another war, she says of Caspey, "Give him one day to get over the war. But if it made a fool out of him like it did out of Bayard, he'd better put that thing on again and go back to it. I'll declare, men can't seem to stand anything"

(p. 53). The Sartorises are, nevertheless, a peculiar case, a special breed of men; they can stand anything save the lack of glamour and of fatal glory. One of Miss Jenny's favourite stories is of the young Carolina Bayard who rode in a mad, reckless dash through Yankee pickets to capture General Pope's anchovies; he and a companion died in the attempt, but over the years "what had been a hare-brained prank of two heedless and reckless boys wild with their own youth had become," in Miss Jenny's mind, "a gallant and finely tragical point to which the history of the race had been raised from out the old miasmic swamps of spiritual sloth by two angels valiantly fallen and strayed, altering the course of human events and purging the souls of men" (p. 9). The modern young Bayard recently returned from France proves, however, the folly of belief or hope in male action; Miss Jenny comes to believe that the old Sartoris penchant for headlong self-destruction has on every occasion been "just another rocket to glare for a moment in the sky, then die away" (p. 358). She sees that the moody, willful, petulant violence of young Bayard is antithetical to life and its real significance. After Bayard kills himself in the crash of an experimental aircraft, she goes to the cemetery to survey the Sartoris gravestones; she contemplates "their dust moldering quietly beneath the pagan symbols of their vainglory and the carven gestures of it in enduring stone; and she remembered something Narcissa had said once, about a world without men, and wondered if therein lay peaceful avenues and dwellings thatched with quiet; and she didn't know" (p. 376).

Narcissa Benbow, who reappears somewhat changed in *Sanctuary*, is quite certain, however, that men are disruptive of life, "thinking that there would be peace for her only in a world where there were no men at all" (p. 245). She reinforces some of the Faulknerian ideas about the opposition between feminine and masculine; she says to her brother Horace, "I never knew a woman that read Shakespeare at all. . . . He talks too much" (p. 177). She is nevertheless upset, not on behalf of her sex but for the sake of her brother, at the prospect of Horace becoming involved with a married woman:

> "But that woman," Narcissa wailed suddenly, like a little girl, burying her face in her hands. "She's so dirty!"

Miss Jenny dug a man's handkerchief from the pocket of her skirt and gave it to the other. "What do you mean?" she asked. "Don't she wash often enough?"

"Not that way. I m-mean she's—she's—" Narcissa turned suddenly and laid her head on the piano.

"Oh," Miss Jenny said. "All women are, if that's what you mean." (pp. 201–2)

Miss Jenny's quiet acceptance of female sexuality as being natural—beyond morality—leads not only to Narcissa's acceptance of her own role but to the negation of her desire for a world without men. The day that Bayard dies, she bears a son. So the Sartorises continue in spite of themselves; woman proves to be the mediator between life and death, as inevitable as either of them.

Sartoris recapitulates a number of ideas about woman and her bearing upon male life to which Faulkner has already been attempting to give form. This third novel represents a vast improvement over *Mosquitoes*, and a fair development beyond *Soldiers' Pay*. Something in the fabric of the male character, for example, now makes Bayard innately "wounded" and disposed to death; woman stands above this moribund world, capable (unlike Margaret Powers) of renewing its life. Two conditions, however, contribute to the failure of *Sartoris* to provide a structural resolution for its theme. The first is that woman is partially separate from the male world, seeking to be detached from it. This disjunction seems to be unintentionally successful, for Bayard never is totally dependent upon the feminine, as Donald Mahon is, in life or in death; his desperate drive toward destruction is empty of any relation to Narcissa or to Miss Jenny. In other words, there is present no redeeming factor for him, even should he elect it. The second lack in a potential mythos is a corollary of the first; neither woman is invested with a suprapersonal authority. Miss Jenny holds a position of matriarchal power in the Sartoris household; she boxes the ears of servants and she beats the men in reasoned argument; but she has no connection with forces which are ultimately non-rational. Nor is Narcissa characterized, despite her power to bear life, by a dynamic of unknown origin. She is represented finally by her human hopes and limitations; she attempts to alter the Sartoris nature of her son by changing his name. To which Miss Jenny reasonably replies, "Do you think . . . that because his name is Benbow, he'll be any less a Sartoris and a scoundrel and a fool?" (p. 380),

There is another kind of woman in *Sartoris*, however, who anticipates the world dominance that the feminine impulse will maintain in the later work. She is Belle Mitchell, the "dirty" woman to whom Horace is attracted; adumbratively, her sexuality connotes her power: "Belle had freed her mouth, and for a moment, her body still against his, she held his face in her two hands and stared at him with intent, questioning eyes. 'Have you plenty of money, Horace?' And 'Yes,' he had answered immediately, 'of course I have.' And then Belle again, enveloping him like a rich and fatal drug, like a motionless and cloying sea in which he watched himself drown" (p. 257). By the time of *Sanctuary*, she will have become, in action and in symbol, "la *belle* dame sans merci," one of the female agents of Horace's utter collapse. She will, however, have become that agent from the inside, herself as intrinsically mythic as is Keats's nightmare lady or Graves's White Goddess Bel.

One authentic symbol nonetheless comes to life near the end of *Sartoris*. It grows, surprisingly, out of a setting which is closer than anything to Rousseauistic primitivism. Young Bayard, who cannot quite live up to the old Sartoris code of reckless gallantry, flees from his responsibility in the death of his grandfather to the home of his relative Virginius MacCallum and his rough brood of sons. There, within the precinct of the log house, the farm, and the surrounding woods, Bayard encounters a world of simple human verities, truthfulness and courage and respect and love, and of elemental male practices, such as hunting with dogs at night and drinking corn liquor with logs blazing on the fire. This world of primitive innocence is beyond the dereliction of the modern world; it defines itself by its remoteness from civilization. As Stuart MacCallum says, " 'Sposin they all broke up in town . . . and moved out here and took up land; you'd hear pappy cussin' town then. You couldn't git along without town to keep folks bottled up in, pappy, and you know it' " (p. 336). It is also apparent, however, that Bayard, despite his presence in the hunters' household, is bottled up in the town world; he can't go back to an aberrant remnant from the past, any more than his civilization can return to the time before the Great War or the Civil War. In the night, as he lies on the dry corn shucks beside Buddy, he tries to enter his cousin's heavy and untroubled sleep by breathing with him: "As though he were one thing breathing with restrained, laboring pants, within himself breathing with Buddy's breathing; using up all the air so that the lesser thing must pant for it. Meanwhile the greater thing breathed deeply and steadily and unawares, asleep, remote; ay, perhaps dead. Perhaps he was dead" (p. 321). Bayard's groping surmise measures Faulkner's unequivocal insistence upon the truth: the literal world of the primitive is dead. The narrative proves it conclusively; Bayard cannot take refuge with the MacCallums; their world has no bearing upon his own.

Another sort of primitive world, however, is crucially related to the man and his fate; this primitiveness is centred in woman. After Bayard rides away from the farm, he seeks shelter, on a clear and crisp Christmas Eve, in the home of a Negro sharecropper. The nameless family puts him up in the barn loft for the night. As young Sartoris wraps himself in the rank Negro quilt, the narrator underscores the situation: "Before he slept he uncovered his arm and looked at the luminous dial on his wrist. One o'clock. It was already Christmas" (p. 343). It appears quite certain that, as will be found in the stories of Benjy Compson and Joe Christmas, Faulkner is not seriously re-presenting the Christ myth in the tale of Bayard Sartoris. More likely, he is parodying the myth or at least its failure in a modern world, for he who sleeps in this stable on this new Christmas Eve is no saviour of the world; he cannot even hold to his own moral code. There is, however, a deeply positive side in the telling of the story. It draws its strength from the portrait of the nameless mother and her children. As the dirty pickaninnies stare at Bayard out of watchful eyes, squatting by the wall on Christmas morning, their mother chides them: " 'Show de white folks yo' Sandy Claus,' she prompted. . . . 'Show 'im,' she repeated. 'You want folks to think Sandy Claus don't know whar you lives at?' " (p. 345). There is only a toy tin automobile, a wooden string of beads, a pocket mirror, and a stick of filthy candy to show to the man who slept in the stable. The man adds nothing to their pitifully simple gifts; but there is little he could offer to equal the quiet love and fierce pride which the Negro woman feels for her brood.

As well, on this Christmas morning, Faulkner juxtaposes the bright cold outdoors to the atmosphere of warmth indoors, the smells of the food the woman is cooking. Before dinner, Bayard uncorks his whisky jug and the three of them, Negro husband and wife and the white man, drink together for a moment; " 'Chris'mus,' the woman murmured shyly. 'Thanky, suh' " (p. 347). The final impression we have of the home and of the family is the overview, the scene exposed in relief as it were on the Christmas card as we move away from it: "He looked once back at the cabin, at the woman standing in the door and a pale, windless drift of smoke above its chimney" (p. 347).

Faulkner was undoubtedly aware of the religious nature of his symbol of the woman dominating both the doorway of the dwelling and the fire inside on the hearth. It would be implausible to argue that he gives us a portrait only of the externals of the facts, however deeply felt, of primitive life, because the context in which he places this vignette, the time period of Christmas Eve and Christmas Day, gives it a symbolic, very clearly religious, life. The only question remaining concerns the nature of the symbol's relation to Bayard Sartoris. Faulkner seems to imply that the Christ in the stable is not (and perhaps never has been) the important element in the Christmas story. The true primitive feeling in that story is for the mother and child (children); each defines the other. (In the latter sense, Faulkner is of one spirit with the paganism that has proved ineradicable in the long history of Christian art—as an obsession with Madonna and Child, and finally in Christian theology—with the Assumption of the Virgin Mary.) As the son in the manger, Bayard is encompassed within the feminine sphere; he is subject to the dominant impulse of the feminine in the world. Bayard's death follows hard upon the symbol of his dependency, but his destruction is not symbolically linked to the Mother; he dies by his own design in a world where the feminine has no part. The icon of the Madonna does not then lead, as it must if the myth is to be fulfilled, to the icon of the Pietà. *Sartoris* fails to provide a structural resolution for the theme which it adumbrates, while at the same time its discovery of a symbolic mode of primitivism heralds the coming use of Faulkner's great poetic theme.

The sudden and otherwise inexplicable genius of *The Sound and the Fury*, Faulkner's next published narrative, seems to spring from the same origins that he had uncovered in the conclusion of *Sartoris*. The artist enters into a fully archetypal mode.

PART TWO

INCARNATION

He seeks to create an archetypal and
essentially sacral art in a secularized age
whose canon of highest values contains no
deity, and the true purpose of his art is the
incarnation of this deity in the world of today.
Erich Neumann, *The Archetypal World of
Henry Moore.*

❧ Prologue ❧

James Baird's theory of authentic primitivism recognizes in literature one of its most ancient abilities: the capacity to function as myth. Myth is by definition sacred story; it is charged with affective power which can put us (corporately) back in touch with the value of existence. Baird calls this sentient dimension the sacramental property of myth. Symbols are always the means of such sacrament, being (as it were) vast reserves of unconscious feeling. Certain of these symbols become in time the prerogative of religious orthodoxies; they are the commanding force in sacramental experience. But when they grow dogmatic, they are gradually impoverished. They lose their emotive force; they lose their power to give life. In the midst of this sort of cultural failure, it is the artist who, feeling his privation, reverts to an archaic world in search of different symbols. He returns to the authority of primitive feeling and the emotive life. He is thus the primal artist who commands art to incarnate what has long been dispossessed of form. To paraphrase Baird further, he alone is the artist who dares to call up archaic symbols to describe the relationship of man to his gods.

The authentic primitivist is not, however, a refugee from his own time and place; if he were, he could not affect the reader from his culture. Instead, he is somewhat like the last prophet of culture, the one human being who puts us into contact with things of value beneath (or behind) our civilized consciousness. He can touch us with life-giving energy for the very reason that we continue to be moved by powers we do not understand. Archaic man, whether vestigial or dominant (and whether we recognize it or not), is preserved in each of us.

The hypothesis of an inherent primitivism is best expressed by Jung. In his well-known theory of the collective unconscious, he calls the affective powers archetypes. Whatever is irrational or sentient has its origin in them; they are the a priori element in psychic experience. They bring into our ephemeral consciousness an unknown psychic life which is immensely old because they "live in a world quite different from our own; in a world where the pulse of time beats ever so slowly; where the birth and death of individuals count little, and where ten thousand years ago is yesterday."[1] Jung says that primitive man was quite right to call these factors "gods" since they constitute an eternal psychic presence; they contain a history of the psyche beyond its individual manifestation. Even a changeless, deathless pattern-producing element cannot, however, account solely for the empirical fact that man is the object of factors. A structural presence *per se* is often no more than a past or future potentiality; its present symbol complexes are all too capable of becoming drained through excessive consciousness. Man then becomes the object of dormant factors; he is moved by different images. When discussing archetypes, it is necessary to speak of their activation, whatever the cause. The dynamic of the archetype, the way in which it relates to the individual, is all important (*Symbols*, p. 98).

Jung expresses both this category of infinite trans-

cendence (eternal presence) and the state of mind the
archetype engenders by the term "numinous." The
word is borrowed from a Christian theologian who has
essayed to analyse the non-rational element in
religious experience.[2] "Numinous" is meant to convey the original significance of "holy," not the
rational qualities of moral goodness or logical behaviour, but the uncanny sense of a *mysterium tre-
mendum* which evokes in the beholder feelings of
fascination, awefulness, overpoweringness emanating
from some "Wholly Other." In Jung's terminology,
the archetype becomes this alien presence which is
"not quite human, but is rather a breath of nature—a
spirit of the beautiful and generous as well as of the
cruel goddess" (*Symbols*, p. 52). The first observer,
the theologian, speaks of "creature-feeling" in the face
of the "Wholly Other"; the more empirical psychologist speaks of the archetype's dynamic relatedness to
the unique human being. Each in his own way tries to
account for the experience of the numinous.

The psychologist's observation about the trans-
human origin of numinous experience betrays a
larger proposition: the archetypes have given rise to a
sexual symbology. They are a "breath of nature";
more than that, they are "a spirit of the . . . goddess."
It might seem banal to speak of Mother Nature in an
age of television advertisements for Mother Nature's
margarine. Nevertheless, earth has from time immemorial been allied with human females in the
mysterious generation of life. Erich Neumann extends
this analogy beyond material occurrence into psychic
origins: "In both sexes the active ego consciousness is
characterized by a male symbolism, the unconscious
as a whole by a female symbolism" (*Great Mother*,
p. 28). The unconscious thus identifies itself as the
creator of living things; the "masculine" consciousness,
trying to stay in touch with the value of existence,
must remain accessible to the life-giving female
factors.

Jung terms this underlying expression of the feminine-in-man the anima. It is a multi-layered concept, meaning much more than the vague term "soul." First, man is genetically composed of both sexes, one of which predominates; so there is a biological femininity pertaining to man, and a biological masculinity pertaining to woman. The conjunction of the sexes is continued in the cultural sphere; man has experience of woman and vice versa. This experience helps to personalize the inner compensatory sexual element. The more vital experience of the opposite sex, however, occurs on a transpersonal plane: "Since the collective unconscious is *more* than personal, so the anima is not always merely the feminine aspect of the individual man. It has an archetypal aspect—'the eternal feminine'—which embodies an experience of woman far older than that of the individual" (*Integration*, p. 73). This archetype of the anima is said to be "incarnated anew in every male child";[3] it is a direct experience of the feminine, of the creating and relating factors in the unconscious. The animus is the corresponding archetype in woman; it is a direct experience of the masculine, of the cognitive, discriminating powers of consciousness. Although anima and animus are in character both personal and transpersonal, each would seem to be a very different archetype, the latter corresponding to "the paternal Logos," the former to "the maternal Eros" (*Psyche*, p. 13). The anima, however (and here at least Jung seems to be contradictory), is also said to be the mother of consciousness: "It is a 'factor' in the proper sense of the word. Man cannot make it; on the contrary, it is always the *a priori* element in moods, reactions, impulses and whatever else is spontaneous in psychic life. It is something that lives of itself, that makes us live; it is a life behind consciousness that cannot be completely integrated with it, but from which, on the contrary, consciousness arises" (*Archetypes*, p. 27). Here, "anima" seems to

contain the animus as well; it appears to be a personi-
fication of the whole unconscious.

Neumann is one follower of Jung who differentiates
the anima from the total unconscious. He locates the
anima in a position much nearer to ego-consciousness,
already part of the personality, though still transpersonal.[4] The larger factor giving rise to consciousness
he says, is the primordial unconscious; it is symbolized
by the Archetypal Feminine. The feminine in
Neumann's schema, however, is more than the life-
support of consciousness. It is the Great Round bearing
within it life and death, gestation and growth,
consciousness and the unconscious, and the whole
realm of human creativity. It contains each of the
physical, psychic, cultural, and spiritual planes of
existence: "If we survey the whole of the symbolic
sphere determined by the vessel character of the
Archetypal Feminine, we find that in its elementary
and transformative character the Feminine as 'creative
principle' encompasses the whole world. This is the
totality of nature in its original unity, from which all
life arises and unfolds, assuming, in its highest transformation, the form of the spirit" (*Great Mother*,
p. 62).

This elementary and transformative character is
vital to an understanding of the archetypal feminine.[5]
The elementary figure is essentially bound up in the
physical sphere with the bearing of life; its function
in the zone of the unconscious might be thought of in
the same way as bringing into being the spontaneous
images of the psyche, still as yet undifferentiated and
sinking back into the unconscious. The central symbol
for this elementary character of the feminine is the
vessel as the container of all life, the generative womb
of the Great Mother.[6] The mother of life has been
worshipped variously as Demeter (goddess of the
Eleusinian mysteries), Egyptian Isis, Babylonian Ishtar, Buddhist Kwanyin, and innumerable other goddesses of all nations and ages. Her specific maternal

functions are those of containing, bearing, protecting, and nourishing. But she can also fixate, ensnare, and hold fast. Gorgon of pre-Hellenic Greece, Kali of India, Hecate of Greece, as well as the terrible Ishtar, Artemis, and Isis are several of her negative personifications. In this dual aspect, she is the Great Round or the maternal Uroboros (the serpent devouring its tail), virtually complete in itself. The thing created—son, consciousness, spirit—is not yet of individual importance; it exists merely to define her as mother. For the duration of this elementary phase, "the Archetypal Feminine not only bears and directs life as a whole, and the ego in particular, but also takes everything that is born of it back into its womb of origination and death" (p. 30). So, depending on whether the ego-consciousness is totally dominated by, incipient in, or emergent from the matriarchal unconscious, the elementary character of the Great Mother will be experienced in either a positive or a negative aspect. The accent on the former will be as the mother of life (womb), on the latter as the mother of death (tomb).

On the other hand, the transformative character of the feminine, incipient even within the Great Round as the agent of nourishment toward change, is directed wholly to the goal of growth as development. Growth itself is the most numinous of all the transformation mysteries. In the human world, it has been experienced in the blood-transformation mysteries of woman, in the inexplicable development of the menstrual female, in the numinous growth of pregnancy, and in the mystery of nursing—the transformation of blood into milk. On the corresponding natural plane, primitive man has been perennially overwhelmed by the archetypal numen of vegetation. In his culture, he has identified objects such as pot, kettle, oven, and retort with the body-vessel of the feminine in its transformative phase. On the cosmic plane, the Great Mother's symbology has included the night as womb and tomb of the sun (day). A new accent is heard in this symbol-category; the feminine reveals a side of her character which is radically different from the elementary stage. Now the physical relatedness of mother and son is of vital importance; the thing created has gained a developmental significance.

At the same time, the earthly sphere of the transformative character is only too closely associated with the Great Round. For whatever grows in the physical world is also subject to decay; whatever lives must die because of change. "But this tragic aspect, this expression of the predominance of the Great Round over what is born of it and, psychologically speaking, of the unconscious over consciousness, is only one side, the dark earthly side, of the cosmic egg. In addition to its earthly half, the Great Round has also a heavenly half; it embodies not only a transformation downward to mortality and the earth, but a transformation upward toward immortality and the luminous heavens" (p. 54).

The domain of spiritual transformation is the uppermost achievement, in the cultural sphere, of the archetypal feminine. It encompasses the arts and all of human wisdom. On this plane, the pagan Muses and the Christian Sophia are incarnations of the Great Mother; it is she who offers transformation leading upward toward the spirit. Primitive peoples have universally regarded the female as the primal seeress; she was the divine prophetess Sibyl and she was the original oracle at Delphi, Apollo notwithstanding. The more civilized Greeks of Homer's age worshipped Athene as the goddess of wisdom; the Byzantine Church expressed her by the name Sophia, spirit of eternal wisdom. In the arts, she has continued, throughout the ages, to be the Muse of poetry, appearing as the triple Muse on Helicon, the nine-fold Muse under Thraco-Macedonian influence, the daughter-goddess of Zeus in Homer, as Beatrice in Dante's

Paradiso. She has continued to be Muse in spite of this evident "progressive" historical subordination to a father God. Originally, she was autochthonic, self-begotten, the Muse mother and inspiration of even Apollo (the classical-civilized god of poetry).[7] At this stage of matriarchal consciousness, the thing created (son-consciousness-spirit) was her culminating creation; poetry, though dependent, was of value in its own right. Later, when the Muse became inferior to the thunder-god, she lost her place, but not her power. At the height of the Judaeo-Christian era (and in the tradition of DuBartas and Sylvester), Milton appealed to her as the "Heav'nly Muse," Urania, though "The meaning, not the Name I call." Perhaps derogatively, he envisions her playing with her sister, Eternal Wisdom, in the presence of "th'Almighty Father." He does not, however, derogate her potency. In the ninth book of *Paradise Lost*, as he prepares for the critical moment when he shall soar—or fail to soar—above "th'Aonian Mount," he offers one prayerful qualification of his poetic ambition:

> If answerable style I can obtain
> Of my Celestial Patroness, who deigns
> Her nightly visitation unimplor'd,
> And dictates to me slumb'ring, or inspires
> Easy my unpremeditated Verse.

It is as fine a description of the Muse's operation as exists in poetry; she reveals herself as the inspiring anima of the poets.

As a positive function, the anima can be the greatest sort of dynamic force compelling to creation; but the individual must in his own person close the dynamic circuit, fixing his feelings "in some form—for example, in writing, painting, sculpture, musical composition, or dancing."[8] Negatively, the artist who is authentically possessed of the anima must come to terms with the archetype, he must assimilate its contents into consciousness, or be overwhelmed by it.

Consciousness, then, is finally the decisive factor; where the artist co-operates with his life-giving factors, he can be led to the very depths of being; he can also transport us with him. This kind of anima-driven art is, objectively speaking, part of the process of individuation, of coming to individual terms with unconscious contents.

From his subjective standpoint, the anima-possessed artist can have but one true purpose: to give his transpersonal factors incarnation. Three things are implied by this term: First, Neumann's location of the archetypal image is accepted as being neither in the mind nor outside it but on a plane beyond both (*Henry Moore*, p. 12). Its tremendous creative force, its capacity to take possession of man, much in the manner of epiphany which Walter Otto claims to be the beginning of cultus, is also admitted. Finally, Jung's admission that the primordial images of the unconscious "do not refer to anything 'that is or has been conscious, but to something *essentially unconscious*. In the last analysis therefore, *it is impossible to say what they refer to*' "[9] must close the gap between a science of psychology and religious experience. In short, the collective unconscious might be considered synonymous with numinous gods. Leslie Fiedler says just that: "A final way back into the world of the Archetypes, available even in our atomized culture, is an extension of the way instinctively sought by the Romantics, down through the personality of the poet, past his particular foibles and eccentricities, to his unconscious core, where he becomes one with us all in the presence of our ancient Gods, the protagonists of fables we think we no longer believe."[10]

The archetype of the anima might then be viewed as both the subject and object of a certain form of literary creation. It can be present both as incarnation and inspiration. Man, it is ultimately realized, is the bondsman of female powers in artistic creation even as in infant dependency. Herein consists his supreme

experience, in the transformative phase, of the archetypal feminine: by the power of the anima, "the male
rises to a sublimated, intoxicated, enthusiastic, and
spiritualized existence of vision, ecstasy, and creativity,
and to a state of 'out-of-himselfness' in which he is
the instrument of higher powers, whether 'good' or
'evil' " (*Great Mother*, p. 305). This approximates
the definition thus far developed of a literature of
myth, in which this state of "out-of-himselfness"
experienced by man is itself endowed with sacramental properties, which is to say that the individual
is made one with his fellows in communion with the
deity. In times past, primitive societies have employed
a broad cultural range of such feminine aids as the
magic philter, the love potion, the intoxicant, soma,
nectar, and poetic incantation to deliver man up as the
instrument of higher powers. In our modern world,
the arts (and especially a primitivistic, symbolic literature) single-handedly administer the same function as
the last cultural remnant of the life-giving factors.

When one speaks of literature, however, an important question remains to be considered: the
personality of the artist. If the archetype is charged
with affective, sacramental power, its symbols are also
channelled through a uniquely individual celebrant.
In the form transmitted to us, the archetype has to be
carried on the frequency of its transmitter. This
problem of causative duality has already been anticipated in the concept of individuation—of coming to
personal terms with transpersonal contents. Perhaps
the most vivid definition of this literary *modus
individuationi* is expressed in Fiedler's "Archetype
and Signature." He uses the latter to mean the sum
total of individuating factors in a work, such as
diction, patterns of imagery, the heard voice of the
author, the biographical experience, the tonal response of artist to archetype. In any literary return
to the world of numinous gods, archetype and signature must be considered as indissoluble entities.

William Faulkner once said the true artist was "demon-driven" (*University*, p. 19); Fiedler equates the act of evoking the archetype with "demonic power" (p. 467). In the ensuing chapters an attempt shall be made not only to name Faulkner's "demon" archetype, but to consider it as a piece of life itself—an image complex which is "integrally connected to the living individual by the bridge of the emotions" (Jung, *Symbols*, p. 96). It will be an attempt particularly to explore the manner in which the archetype of the feminine is incarnated in certain of his works. Alongside this sacramental property of the art, however, the signature of the artist must be traced. Although the biographical experience will be introduced wherever pertinent, the examination of signature shall be centred more upon patterns of imagery in the novels, upon diction (the heard voice of the author), and upon the tonal response—the bridging of emotions—of the artist to the archetype.

3

"The Heart's Darling" and the Brothers Compson

The Sound and the Fury

It was more than the gallantry of a Southern gentleman which prompted Faulkner to say at Virginia of Caddy Compson that "To me she was the beautiful one, she was my heart's darling. That's what I wrote the book about" (*University*, p. 6). Much earlier—about the time of *Light in August*'s completion—he had disclosed in a piece of unpublished autobiography that "in *The Sound and the Fury* I had already put perhaps the only thing in literature which would ever move me very much: Caddy climbing the pear tree to look in the window at her grandmother's funeral while Quentin [sic] and Jason and Benjy and the negroes looked up at the muddy seat of her drawers."[1] The author has in retrospect condensed the whole of his novel into one image; it is a symbol of great value; it is also an atavistic symbol cluster: it reverts to a personal childhood of family experience, and to a racial childhood of mythic experience (death discovered via a tree).

The content of the image is of less interest for the moment than its effect. Caddy's curiosity and her muddy drawers are said to be the emotive factors of the symbol. Perhaps in a more inclusive sense, Caddy herself is the dynamic of the image. To Maurice Coindreau, Faulkner admitted that "the same thing happened to me that happens to so many writers—I fell in love with one of my characters, Caddy. I loved her so much I couldn't decide to give her

Caddy & her absence

life just for the duration of a short story. She deserved more than that. So my novel was created, almost in spite of myself."[2] Two points of interest emerge from this profession of love: First, the author understands his relationship with an "inner" created character as a more than individual occurrence; other writers too fall in love with an "inner" feminine being, so that some trans-personal factor seems to be present. Second, the personal relatedness between author and character leads to creation; Faulkner says he wrote almost in spite of himself. His statement is tantamount to a confession of inspiration; his fascination with Caddy has compelled him to incarnate her, to let her give herself life in the consciousness of art.

Caddy's dynamism seems nonetheless to have influenced more than the author's choice of material. Millgate quotes Faulkner from another unpublished piece of autobiography—perhaps an introduction to a limited draft edition of the novel—to say that "Only *The Sound and the Fury* had given him 'that emotion definite and physical and yet nebulous to describe: that ecstasy, that eager and joyous faith and anticipation of surprise which the yet unmarred sheet beneath my hand held inviolate and unfailing, waiting for release' " (p. 26). Creation of this sort has much less to do with the purposive and formative act of masculine consciousness than with a passively receptive obedience to unconscious factors. Faulkner confesses to a sort of surprised openness, a reverence before the unknown material; he speaks of his ebullience in the grip of its affective power. One can safely say, from the biographical evidence cited, that what awaits release on his unmarred page is the anima itself, the woman within, the archetype of creative powers.

Later in the same autobiographical passage, Faulkner acknowledges his sudden creative liberation in the writing of *The Sound and the Fury*: "One day I seemed to shut a door between me and all publishers' addresses and book lists. I said to myself, Now I can write. Now I can make myself a vase like that which the old Roman kept at his bedside and wore the rim slowly away with kissing it. So I, who had never had a sister and was fated to lose my daughter in infancy, set out to make myself a beautiful and tragic little girl" (Millgate, p. 26). Perhaps in this declaration more than in any other, the cellar door has been left open to Freudian analysts who would interpret Caddy as wish-fulfilment. To some extent she is; but it must be remembered that Faulkner is speaking with hindsight: his infant daughter had not been conceived by the time *The Sound and the Fury* was published, and the purposiveness of his setting out is apparent to him only after the "surprising" words are down on paper. The best gloss on this desire of the artist to create "a beautiful and tragic little girl" ought to be taken from the novel itself. Quentin, who would deny his sister's vital sexuality, turns instead to his little sister death, echoed in the words running like a refrain in his mind, "And the good Saint Francis that said Little Sister Death, that never had a sister."[3] Faulkner, like Saint Francis, never had a sister, but he could create one where the saint could not; he could bring her to life where the brother could take her only into death. Quentin and Saint Francis testify unwittingly to a "male" sterility of consciousness—the desire of the spirit for absolute autonomy—while the artist confesses his reliance upon the uncanny life of the anima. Perhaps the belief that he would never again be published freed Faulkner to follow the dictates of his artistic compulsion; in any event, that compulsion was now a private affair of the heart, insofar as his heart responded to a being with intrinsic life.

Observing something of the dynamism of Caddy in private relation to the author, the content of the symbol-complex which surrounds her should be examined within the artifact itself. In a fuller account of the genesis of *The Sound and the Fury*, Faulkner denied that "impression" was the right word to describe the "little girl up in a tree":

It's more an image, a very moving image to me was of the children. 'Course, we didn't know at that time that one was an idiot, but they were three boys, one was a girl and the girl was the only one that was brave enough to climb that tree to look in the forbidden window to see what was going on. And that's what the book—and it took the rest of the four hundred pages to explain why she was brave enough to climb the tree to look in the window. It was an image, a picture to me, a very moving one, which was symbolized by the muddy bottom of her drawers as her brothers looked up into the apple [*sic*] tree that she had climbed to look in the window. And the symbolism of the muddy bottom of the drawers became the lost Caddy. (*University*, p. 31)

The first striking thing in this explanation is Faulkner's changing of the tree from pear to apple. Perhaps, after twenty-five years, the man had begun to see his story in terms of Christian folklore; Eve must taste of death through an apple tree. The artist, on the other hand, had not established in his work this overt equivalence between Caddy and Eve. The story of *The Sound and the Fury* is apparently not a retelling of the Fall through knowledge; not even Caddy's muddy drawers are linked to the problem of evil. Her sexual development and eventual surrender to Dalton Ames are a part of the natural order of the world; as Quentin's father says, "Women are never virgins. Purity is a negative state and therefore contrary to nature. It's nature is hurting you not Caddy" (p. 143). Caddy's bravery, her connection with a tree, and her physical dirtying take on some of the amoral significance of nature; what this means in the wider sense shall be considered in due course.

The second aspect of Faulkner's perception of the picture is that he is not its sole perceiver: there are several male observers within the symbol. They see Caddy in the tree; Faulkner sees them looking up at her. The nature of the image suggests something about the narrative technique of the story: Caddy is only an indirect presence in it; she exists as a projection of the minds of her three brothers. When asked why the girl was never given a voice of her own, Faulkner said, "Caddy was still to me too beautiful and too moving to reduce her to telling what was going on, that it would be more passionate to see her through somebody else's eyes, I thought" (*University*, p. 1). Like the pre-Olympians, Caddy has no face, no voice; since she is too beautiful and too moving to be reduced to the ordinary stature of human spokesman, she in turn becomes larger than life,[4] dwelling at the back of life as the significant agent of all response and change. At least within the mind of each brother, she assumes, willy-nilly, such a character. That the author should find this indirect apprehension of her more passionate only suggests more emphatically that she is a shadowy presence like the anima, never a voice in its own right, but an expression of some inner feminine being. The fact of the three male perceivers (presumably a fourth in the omniscient voice of the final section) serves but to underscore this contention.

In view of Faulkner's remarks, then, it seems that the conflicting voices of Benjy, Quentin, and Jason are intended to draw a fuller portrait of Caddy, before they reveal themselves in relation to her. She is the common factor in their stories, both as subject (seen from limited points of view) and as object (her relation to each has caused him to speak out). Her centrality throughout the novel also offers the best explanation for the arrangement of its sections, for the retreat in time from 7 April 1928 in the Benjy section to 2 June 1910 in Quentin's chapter, and the return again to 6 April 1928 in Jason's portion of the story. Each of the brothers is haunted by a different period in Caddy's life; the moment her existence is accepted as the underlying matter, the narrative falls into a straightforward chronology which accounts for Caddy's childhood, adolescence, and maturity[5].

Benjy is the narrator who re-creates the girlhood of his sister. His ubiquity in time (at least within the period of 1898–1928) makes it possible for him to render past events as present; this reactualization is made even more forceful by his being limited to sensory experience, thus expressing an occurrence with perfect immediacy. Because he is mentally three years old, he has a pronounced tendency to re-present his earliest experiences, for they are the most moving episodes in his life. Time, through a mental limitation, has thus stopped for Benjy in the childhood which is shared with Caddy. For Quentin, on the other hand, time has not stopped at all, though he would try to fix it at a certain moment in Caddy's adolescence, before time and change had brought her to sexual fruition. Failing to obstruct her physical transformation, the eldest brother kills himself, hoping to arrest his sister (in his own mind, at least) forever in her nonage. Jason, however, to whom time is money, would preserve Caddy in her maturity, for by fleecing her, he gains his wealth and his revenge. His story then concerns itself exclusively with the adult Caddy, both in the past, and in the present by means of proxy through her daughter Quentin.

This tentative explanation for the arrangement of the novel's four sections accounts in reality for the ordering of only three of the divisions. In the fourth telling of the story, there is a decided shift from Caddy to Dilsey as "the beautiful one." It is enough to recognize here that such resolution of the novel's structure demands proportionately higher emphasis on *The Sound and the Fury* as the story of Caddy, and that the thematic concern for differing obsessions with time might be concluded in the very process of transference.

Establishing Caddy's priority, however, cannot fully account for the passion and fascination with which her image has been invested. There must be some reason for her prominence, both in the minds of her brothers and in the mind of the artist. If one looks at the totality of her story, one gathers that its major theme is the warping of her great capacity for love.[6] Both her devotion to Benjy and her affection for Quentin are circumvented by the brothers' aversion to her growing up; their refusal of her transformation (the ability to bear new life in which they have no part) leads all the more urgently to her union with Dalton Ames and her eventual casting out from the family. Caddy's metamorphosis appears to be a resistless force; Benjy and Quentin might just as well try to stop the seasons from coming. If, however, their all-or-none personal requirements warp her wider capacity for love, they have in turn been warped by a mother who is incapable of love. The initial situation, then, is what must first be examined in *The Sound and the Fury*. Therein exists a microcosmic family which is deeply affected by antipodal sorts of females.

On facing pages very early in *The Sound and the Fury*, one is invited to compare both Caroline Compson and her daughter Caddy with the Negro woman at the conclusion of *Sartoris*: " 'What is it.' Caddy said. 'Did you think it would be Christmas when I came home from school. Is that what you thought. Christmas is the day after tomorrow. Santy Claus, Benjy. Santy Claus. Come on, let's run to the house and get warm.' " (p. 6). On the next page the neurotic Mrs. Compson is found saying, "Nobody knows how I dread Christmas. Nobody knows. I am not one of those women who can stand things. I wish for Jason's and the children's sakes I was stronger" (p. 7). It seems likely, from the sheer temporal proximity of the end of *Sartoris* to the beginning of *The Sound and the Fury*, that an intentional collation exists. The thematic importance of "Chris'mus" to the earlier story, together with the protective and caressing utterance of "Sandy Claus" (*S*, p. 345) and the significance of the fire on the hearth, link the primitive madonna of that Negro cabin to Caddy with her idiot brother. In the self-centred dread of

Mrs. Compson, however, one discovers a symbolic repudiation of the maternity represented in Christmas. Caroline Bascomb Compson is an anti-madonna.

The son Benjy, the idiot Christ (see chapter 1), is the real touchstone among the women of the Compson family. Because of his retardation, he is a perpetual child, innocent in the sense of "mindless," dependent on woman completely for the physical and psychic necessities of life. He corresponds to the eternal child in man. Caddy provides this child with the only love he knows. She cares for him, comforts him, holds him fast. When she carries him into Mrs. Compson's presence, the mother objects:

"He's too big for you to carry. You must stop trying. You'll injure your back. All of our women have prided themselves on their carriage. Do you want to look like a washerwoman."

"He's not too heavy." Caddy said. "I can carry him."

"Well, I don't want him carried, then." Mother said. "A five year old child. No, no. Not in my lap. Let him stand up."

"If you'll hold him, he'll stop." Caddy said. "Hush." she said. "You can go right back. Here. Here's your cushion. See." (p. 77)

The incident in Mrs. Compson's bedroom establishes more than a dramatic polarity between child-mother and non-mother; it is related once again to a symbol of religious and archaic value. In the fourth section, long after Caddy's dismissal from the family, Dilsey takes Benjy with her to the Easter service in the Negro church. There, the Reverend Shegog preaches a sermon on the dying son, the Lamb who shed his blood. But the dying god actually pictured is the infant Jesus, the child dragged from his mother by King Herod's soldiers: "Listen, breddren! I sees de day. Ma'y settin in de do' wid Jesus on her lap, de little Jesus. Like dem chillen dar, de little Jesus. I hears de angels singin de peaceful songs en de glory; I sees de closin eyes; sees Mary jump up, sees de sojer face: We gwine to kill! We gwine to kill! We gwine to kill yo little Jesus! I hears de weepin en de lamentation of de po mammy widout de salvation en de word of God!" (p. 369). Through her weeping, Dilsey is identified with Mary; sitting with Benjy in her lap, Caddy is also linked to the mother of God; Caroline, however, betrays herself fully and finally as an anti-madonna. In due time, it must be asked whether Faulkner's image of the Holy Mother is Christian or pagan; for the moment, it is enough to recognize Mrs. Compson's dissociation from both the Madonna (the mother of life enfolding her son) and the Pietà (the mother of death mourning her son). Her influence upon her children is injurious, but it is consistently represented in anti- or non-symbolic terms. Some other element, then, is present in her characterization.

Almost the first narrative words out of Caroline Compson's mouth are " 'You, Benjamin.' Mother said. 'If you dont be good, you'll have to go to the kitchen' " (p. 3). Benjy's unreflecting sensory experience will take some time to build a fuller portrait of her; but the suddenly revealed stridency in her address to the idiot child anticipates the coldness and rejection she will display toward him. Her motive for rejection is soon apparent; when Caddy calls the boy "Benjy," she is chided by her mother: " 'Nicknames are vulgar. Only common people use them. Benjamin.' she said" (p. 78). The woman's social correctness seems no more at first than a mere excuse; the real truth is that she would scotch all tenderness in "Benjy" because the child is an affront to her family dignity. At birth he was named Maury, for his maternal uncle Maury Bascomb, but when at five years of age his evident idiocy cast a slur upon "Bascomb," Mrs. Compson changed his name to Benjamin. Dilsey indirectly provides the same explanation for the boy's repudiation: " 'You know how come your name Benjamin now.' Versh said. 'Your mamma too proud for you. What mammy say' " (pp. 85–86). One cannot help noticing at this moment the implicit contrast between "mamma" and "mammy."

The consistent non-symbolic element in Mrs. Compson's depiction is a sort of twisted societal ambition. Even in the scene where her real motive for forbidding Benjy's being carried might go very deep (as suggested by the urgency of "No, no. Not in my lap"), her objection has a class emphasis. "All our women," she says, "have prided themselves on their carriage. Do you want to look like a washerwoman." There is a note of false pride, of uneasy affectation, in her warning, as though she (and not her daughter) must rise by precept above the condition of low birth. The social standing of the Bascomb side of the family is not defined explicitly; Uncle Maury's parasitism and Caroline's oversensitivity suggest they have less than aristocratic origins. Perhaps, as a parvenu Bascomb,

Caroline has reason to feel defensive, faced with the complacent irony of her husband and with a gallery of planter-Compsons (of whom one has been a governor and one a general):

"Shoot who, Father." Quentin said, "Who's Uncle Maury going to shoot."

"Nobody." Father said. "I dont own a pistol."

Mother began to cry. "If you begrudge Maury your food, why aren't you man enough to say so to his face. To ridicule him before the children, behind his back."

"Of course I dont." Father said, "I admire Maury. He is invaluable to my own sense of racial superiority. I wouldn't swap Maury for a matched team. And do you know why, Quentin."

"No, sir." Quentin said.

"*Et ego in arcadia* I have forgotten the latin for hay." Father said. "There, there." he said, "I was just joking." He drank and set the glass down and went and put his hand on Mother's shoulder.

"It's no joke." Mother said. "My people are every bit as well born as yours. Just because Maury's health is bad."
(pp. 52–53)

Neither the assumed conventions of ladydom nor the stiff ego-centricity of pride can permit her to see her brother as even his idiot nephew is able: "Uncle Maury was putting the bottle away in the sideboard in the dining-room" (p. 4). Each time Benjy passes, without understanding, through the room, Uncle Maury confirms his own dipsomania; the reader knows, though Caroline Compson does not, must not, why Uncle Maury's health is bad.

If Mrs. Compson's societal ambitions are twisted, it is because they are self-centred; she rejects her Compson offspring, excepting Jason whom she describes as a "true Bascomb." "Jason," she says, "was the only one my heart went out to without dread" (p. 126). Incapable of love herself, she favours her one unloving child. "Bascomb-ness" is in reality for her a matter of pervasive ego-centricity; she dignifies the Bascombs (her brother Maury, her son Jason) at the Compsons' expense because she is self-aggrandizing. Through her deadly hypochondria, she preys on the decency and sympathy of those around her; she is thus able to exercise power in a cold and ruthless way, all the while preserving her self-engendered image of a lady. " 'I know I'm nothing but a burden to you.' Mother said. 'But I'll be gone soon. Then you will be rid of my bothering' " (pp. 75–76). With her maudlin phrase, "I'll be gone soon," she subjugates in turn her husband Jason, her daughter Caddy, her sons Quentin and Jason, and the Negro servant Dilsey. The irony of her threatened martyrdom is that she outlives at least two of the enslaved by several decades.

Again, Mrs. Compson betrays this tendency toward self-aggrandizement in relation to Caddy. Though she is much more concerned with social appearance than with her daughter's welfare, she speaks with coquettish delicacy to Sydney Herbert Head on the subject of losing her "little daughter" (p. 117). The adjective itself reveals her desire to be more important—in her own eyes if in no one else's. When Herbert brings to Caddy as an engagement gift the first automobile the town has ever seen, Mrs. Compson, who has hardly had the opportunity to see one either, says "Country people poor things they never saw an auto before lots of them honk the horn Candace so . . . they'll get out of the way . . . your father wouldn't like it if you were to injure one of them" (p. 115). She must hold herself above peasantry, of course, even after she learns that her daughter has spent time in the woods and in ditches like "nigger wenches." Accordingly, she secures the match with this eligible son of an Indiana industrialist; she makes a strained and nervous attempt to preserve not only the conventional proprieties but her acquired standing in the community. When the marriage is dissolved through an unusually premature birth, Mrs. Compson makes her daughter promise never to come back again (p. 251). The only thing she seems ever to have cared about is her own image in the community. The pronunciation of this social accent must be remembered in her rejection of Caddy.

Perhaps it is Quentin, however, who realizes most poignantly the family difficulty. On the afternoon of the day he commits suicide, he sums up his life with the words *"if I'd just had a mother so I could say Mother Mother"* (p. 213, Faulkner's italics). There seems to be no reason for his rejection beyond his mother's hatred of the Compsons, beyond the ironic abnegation in her feeling that "I have not suffered enough I see now that I must pay for your sins as well as mine what have you done what sins have your high and mighty people visited upon me" (p. 127).

This almost inexplicable condition of mother-rejection in the novel warrants a more speculative investigation. Caddy's place in the family is evidently imaged in the figure of the Madonna; she is at least tentatively invested with archetypal powers, with the positive elementary functions of the Great Mother. It might then be expected that Mrs. Compson (the anti-Madonna) is an incarnation of the negative elementary aspect of the archetypal feminine. Rejection is characteristic of the feminine in this phase; it occurs whenever containment ceases. On a personalistic plane, birth is experienced as the first form of rejection, though its upshot is growth; on a purely archetypal level, withdrawal of love becomes a painful (though positive) factor promoting male (that which is begotten) self-reliance. Most noticeably in the animal world, young males at a certain stage of development are driven away by their mothers; the elementary maternal function seems designed to nourish offspring toward independence. Psychologically speaking, Quentin's rejection would be viewed as the immemorial pattern of response between mother and son, except for one thing: there can be no withdrawal of love in his experience where love has not originally existed. Quentin recalls having been driven away by his mother not for the sake of transformation (growing into adulthood and independence) but almost before he had been borne and nourished. The agony of his cry *"if I'd just had a mother"* points up his initial motherlessness; Mrs. Compson has never had any part in the positive functions (or negative functions resulting positively) of the Great Mother.

Mrs. Compson's non-rational behaviour seems nonetheless to cast her entirely in the role of the terrible mother. Certainly the total repudiation of her idiot son might be looked upon as the instinctual mammalian tendency to abandon all deformity, a trait found even among domesticated animals. Such a characterization is capable of achieving numinosity as the terrible and inexplicable face of the feminine—beyond any semblance of reason, felt only in a profound way as "the wrath of God (the Goddess)." Her undisguised revulsion at holding Benjy comes near to participating in this wrath. Nevertheless, Faulkner does explain the mother's predisposition; that is, he socializes it in terms of her conceit about a name. Dilsey, on the other hand, is beyond even comprehending such affectation: she says, "*Name aint going to help him. Hurt him, neither. Folks dont have no luck, changing names. My name been Dilsey since fore I could remember and it be Dilsey when they's long forgot me*" (p. 71, Faulkner's italics). There is a stolidity in Dilsey, a rock-like security born of the simple acceptance of a name and an identity, that is desperately lacking in the wife of Jason Richmond Compson III, unable to rest in any name.

If Caroline Compson can be thought of even as a partial incarnation of a daemonic archetype, she is not so much represented as a numinous figure, inspiring fascination and awe and dread, as she is pictured as a weak, indecisive, and whimpering human failure. On a ride to the cemetery, she displays the wide range of her neurotic insecurity:

> "Turn around." Mother said. "I'm afraid to go and leave Quentin."
> "Can't turn here." T. P. said. Then it was broader.
> "Cant you turn here." Mother said.
> "All right." T. P. said. We began to turn.
> "You T. P." Mother said, clutching me.
> "I got to turn around somehow." T. P. said. "Whoa, Queenie." We stopped.
> "You'll turn us over." Mother said.
> "What you want to do, then." T. P. said.
> "I'm afraid for you to try to turn around." Mother said.
> "Get up, Queenie." T. P. said. We went on.
> "I just know Dilsey will let something happen to Quentin while I'm gone." Mother said. "We must hurry back." (p. 11)

Perhaps her indecisiveness is only a superficial trait. The real measure of her insecurity is taken when they drive through the town square just to say to Jason, " 'I know you wont come.' Mother said. 'I'd feel safer if you would' " (p. 12). It is suddenly apparent that none of her talk is aimed at influencing decisive action; it is done only in a petulant attempt to make her presence felt—in a sense, to confirm her own existence.

That Mrs. Compson ultimately is a terrible mother deserves to go unquestioned; but for some reason yet to be discussed, Faulkner accentuates her social motivation and her human ineffectualness in an attempt to prevent her full emergence as the "terrible mother."

It has been observed, contrarily, that at least one image associated with Caddy has a sacred and numinous significance; she is identified with the Virgin Mother. Similarly, the picture of the girl hugging the child to her as she walks gives every indication (like the Madonna) of the positive elementary character of the feminine, the body-vessel which shelters and contains with its palpability. The image is heightened by her tiny strength, by her childish encompassing arms. Within Benjy's field of vision, she is a vessel of warmth and containment, not so much personalized—made individual—as she is a faceless presence, both comforter and preserver. In the Appendix prepared for *The Portable Faulkner* (1946), the author said that Benjy, who loved Caddy, did not forfeit her "because he could not remember his sister but only the loss of her."[7] It is characteristic of man's experience of the woman in this primordial phase of the unconscious that her representation should be featureless and transpersonal, remembered only through her absence.

Caddy continues throughout Benjy's childhood in this elementary character as his sole protectress. When Jason cuts up the child's dolls, she offers in a moving way to "slit his gizzle" (p. 79). She will not suffer her idiot brother to be demeaned, or even to be treated hypocritically. After Mrs. Compson has kissed "Benjamin" and called him "My poor baby," Caddy says to Benjy, "You're not a poor baby. Are you. You've got your Caddy. Haven't you got your Caddy" (p. 8). She reacts doubly, it would seem, to the belittlement implied in "poor," both in the sense that Benjy through his handicap is humanly impoverished, and in the corollary meaning which Caddy seizes upon—that he is motherless. Because of course he cannot be impoverished within the Great Round of the sheltering and encompassing feminine.

Nevertheless, the more profoundly sacred identification of Caddy with the mother goddess is given in her association with trees. No full study has undertaken to explain the dynamic and ambivalent presence of the symbol in her characterization. Benjy is the reiterant voice in this identification; just before Caddy denies, for example, that he is a "poor baby," Benjy's narration relates how "we stopped in the hall and Caddy knelt and put her arms around me and her cold bright face against mine. She smelled like trees" (p. 8). Upon first mention, "Caddy smelled like leaves" (p. 5), but immediately and thereafter, "Caddy smelled like trees" throughout the first section. Nor can the germinal image, the one from which the novel was said to have grown, be forgotten: the mental picture of the little girl climbing a tree to look in the window upon her grandmother's funeral.

From the time of Faulkner's earliest work, young girls are associated with tree images in a conscious and allusive manner; the faun-speaker of "L'Apres-Midi d'un Faune," his first known published poem, pursues a girl "through the singing trees" until, in conclusion, the trees themselves are become sad, sighing nymphs who "dance, unclad and cold."[8] The poplars of "The Marble Faun" are "Like slender girls"; in the poem addressed to "A Poplar," the speaker says

> You are a young girl
> Trembling in the throes of ecstatic modesty,
> A white objective girl
> Whose clothing has been forcibly taken away from her. (p. 60)

The tree-maidens of the early poetry share an epicene virginity; they often participate in a state of reluctant undress. It has been noted previously, in the discussion of the apprentice novels (chapter 2), how Faulkner's early symbols fail to be archetypal; he is over-conscious of them—they are borrowed definitions instead of self-contained experience—and he has failed to resolve them thematically. Nevertheless, when he links the coy and insincere Cecily Saunders of *Soldiers Pay* to Hamadryads and to poplars, he is at least attempting to convey an arboreal image of the voluptuous and eternal Virgin. By the time of *The Sound and the Fury*, the perfected craftsman has distilled a similar yet more profound import into a hauntingly ambivalent image; the image takes on a life of its own, acquiring definition from within (within character experience and within thematic structure) instead of from without.

To Benjy, Caddy smells like trees only to the moment of her deflowering. Yet because of his ubiquity in time, her arboreal fragrance can be re-actualized at any moment, as, at the close of his day in 1928, he drifts into the sleep of thirty years ago, being held by Caddy and smelling the "something" of the trees, seeing "the windows, where the trees were buzzing" (p. 92). As a consequence,

Caddy's virginity (her smelling like trees, like the girl-poplars of the early poetry and fiction) is preserved in Benjy's desire for stasis. Paradoxically, however, the girl's vital life-giving sexuality takes place in the woods, beneath the trees. So the fixity of Benjy's mind gives rise to a tension which persists throughout his section; Caddy is at once virgin and not-virgin, like the Holy Mother of God; the symbol contains a functional antinomy.

The ambivalence of the image deepens when one realizes what Benjy cannot: that the pear tree leading to the sight of the forbidden funeral is the tree of death, both in its literal significance as the avenue opening out upon the prospect of death, and symbolically as the forbidden tree in Eden which "Brought Death into the World, and all our woe" (*Paradise Lost*, I, 3). If one should happen to miss its manifold nature in relation to the girl, Faulkner gives it a technical underscoring in one of Benjy's time equations: "The room went black. *Caddy smelled like trees.* We looked up into the tree where she was" (p. 54, Faulkner's italics). These three sentences bring together three distinct aspects of the tree symbol; Caddy is the eternal Virgin, giver of life; she is Eve, the giver of death; beyond either, she is the mother archetype, the agent of growth and change. For Caddy is unable to rest in fixity. She is possessed of an inner dynamism which propels her to discover death and change and, symbolically, female sexuality, the matrix of them both (pictured in the image of the muddy drawers; this soiling in the sexual regions being the prerequisite for participation in the forces of the feminine). It is this image complex of the tree which invests Caddy with full numinous meaning.

To a significant extent, the archaic context of the symbol should point up the manner in which Faulkner's image complex holds a spontaneous relation to the meaning and movement of Benjy's story. The archetype of vegetation is, of course, the great Earth mother who brings forth all plant life from herself; the tree stands at the center of her vegetative symbolism. Egyptian mythology records the birth of Osiris out of a tree; it is but one early instance out of many in which the Tree Goddess is revealed as the mother of life. The infant Jesus, lying in his wooden manger, also has archaic connections with the "vegetation gods"—the Babylonian grain god, for example, the virgin-born ear of corn; as the crucified God, Jesus becomes the fruit of the Tree of Life. Ovid, among classical writers, betrays a genuine primitivism in his reverence for the tree as a principle of the community of all living things. He relates a number of stories in *The Metamorphoses* of goddesses and women changed to trees. Peneian Daphne, who flees from the burning love of Apollo (Phebus), is enabled to save her maidenhead by asking succor of the earth in Diana's name; she takes root on the spot in her beloved forests and, in the form of a laurel, she preserves her virginity in perpetuity. Ovid also tells of the birth of Adonis out of a tree, recalling Osiris; although Ovid's story is overlain with a patriarchal consciousness of incest, Adonis's Myrrh-mother reconfirms the generative principle inherent in the tree symbol.

Hathor, the sycamore goddess of ancient Egypt who in some accounts gives birth to the divine son Horus, bears as well the sun upon her head. A parallel of sorts is found in the sun dance mythology of the North American Indian; the buffalo skull placed atop the sacred tree represents the sun: symbolically, it is "borne" by the tree. Both instances suggest the birth of consciousness (the principle of light) out of the matriarchal unconscious; they reveal the feminine in her transformative phase. Another central figure in Egyptian art is the date-palm goddess who confers nourishment upon souls; this nourishment likewise leads to spiritual transformation. Analogously, the art of medieval alchemists points up the transformative character of the "Alchemical Tree"; its trunk is a nude woman, with the "tree" branching and blossoming above her. The alchemists, of course, were partly concerned with material transformation, with the transmutation of base metals into gold. Their philosophy, however, has the deepest psychic origins; in this century, Jung has found the tree symbols of alchemy to be produced spontaneously and unconsciously by many dreamers. He relates them to the psychic process of individuation, the modern equivalent of spiritual transformation.

Ovid's story of the mother Dryopee suggests a further type of transformation under the aegis of the goddess. As Dryopee's body, then her face, are slowly overgrown with bark, she asks that her infant son be raised to revere the following advice:

But lerne him for to shun all ponds and pulling flowres from trees, *the "Great mother"*

And let him in his heart beleeve that all the shrubs he sees,
Are bodyes of the Godesses.[9]

Since Dryopee is, in effect, dying by her transformation, one then
expects the tree to be more than the divine mother of life: somehow
she is deeply linked to death as well. The wood of coffins possesses
this maternal character, as the word "sarco-phagus"—devourer of
flesh—suggests. Tree burial has been known throughout the primitive world; the Wagogo of Tanganyika and the Cree of northern
Canada are two tribes who have sheltered their dead in the maternal
tree. Even in death, however, the great tree goddess has not
finished her inexorable processes. Egyptian Nut, who in the character of a coffin enclosed the dead, was also the goddess of rebirth.
In Germanic cosmology, the rebirth of the sun at the winter solstice
was marked by the Festival of the Trees; it is observed unwittingly
(and in debased form) each year at Christmas. The gallows-tree on
which the Norse god, Odin, hung and the tree-cross on which
Christ was crucified, are likewise symbols of death and rebirth; the
maternal tree brings death but it in turn gives immortality. This
is the highest development in the spiritual transformative phase
of the archetypal feminine.

The most inclusive symbol, however, of the tree's maternal
character occurs in Yggdrasill, the all-dominating world tree of
Norse myth. It is related to destiny, with its crown spreading
throughout the heavens and its roots burrowing into the underworld of the frost giants. As Fate, it is the mother of life and the
mother of death. So the tree becomes another aspect of the Great
Round, bearing that life which it takes back into itself.

Benjy's perception of Caddy is as complex as the image-constell-
ation of the great tree goddess. Although she does not give birth to
him, she is his true mother. The Caddy who smells like trees is
identical with the tree goddess who confers nourishment on souls.
Her over-spreading love is very much the positive elementary
character of the great mother, nourishing, containing, and protecting. As a mental "primitive", Benjy is content to live in this
deepest stage of the matriarchal unconscious; he is happy to be
contained by the Great Vessel which engenders its own seed in
itself. So long as the girl remains a child, he does not even have to
preserve the elemental state of virgin mother and son; he lives in a

safely closed universe. Caddy, however, is unable to stand still;
unlike each of her brothers, she must grow and change. The tree
which she climbs leads to her own transformation; climb it she
must, for it is integral to her feminine nature. The life force is her
real dynamic, and growth is her true mystery; of necessity she
experiences metamorphosis (death, sex, pregnancy, birth) and
because of it, she produces change around her.

It is this transformative character seated (quite literally) in
Caddy which Benjy fears, the shocking new perfume which blocks
out the odour of the trees. His outrage checks Caddy on her initial
foray into womanhood; she washes off the perfume and gives the
bottle to Dilsey. Then "Caddy smelled like trees. 'We dont like
perfume ourselves.' Caddy said. *She smelled like trees*" (p. 51). She
can't prevent herself, nevertheless, from growing toward sexual
experience. When Benjy finds her in the swing with Charlie, a
potential lover, he bellows until she retreats once more into promised stasis:

> "Caddy." Charlie said.
> Caddy and I ran. We ran up the kitchen steps, onto the
> porch, and Caddy knelt down in the dark and held me. I
> could hear her and feel her chest. "I wont." she said. "I wont
> anymore, ever. Benjy. Benjy." Then she was crying, and I
> cried, and we held each other. "Hush." she said. "Hush. I
> wont anymore." So I hushed and Caddy got up and we went
> into the kitchen and turned the light on and Caddy took the
> kitchen soap and washed her mouth at the sink, hard. Caddy
> smelled like trees. (p. 58)

Shortly thereafter, Caddy goes beyond kissing; Dalton Ames fulfils the image of the muddy drawers.

So the Caddy who was brave enough to climb the forbidden tree
becomes for Benjy the mother of death as well as of life. Because the
rudimentary male consciousness he possesses has refused alteration
of his inflexibly conceived order, he is destroyed when Caddy
climbs whatever tree of change she must. Perhaps this makes Benjy
sound more volitional than he really is; the point to be emphasized
here is not that he wilfully, rationally, refuses change, but that
there exists even in the elemental masculine mind an innate
deficiency and an inherent disability to cope with what, for the

female, is completely natural. He contends desperately with the forces of transformation after she is gone, striving to deny them, but he grieves continually for the absence of her love. Finally her absence brings about his gelding and, some time later (as we learn in the Appendix) his committal to the State Asylum in Jackson. Finally, in *The Mansion*, Benjy returns from Jackson to set both himself and the house aflame and he dies at last in the swirling shapes of the fire he has always loved. It is worth noting that this element of fire also belongs to a feminine symbology in both its destructive and transformative aspects. So Benjy is fully absorbed within the totality of the Great Round, taken back again into the bosom of the great mother. If Benjy is, in part, destroyed by the daemon he loved, he is doomed in greater measure by the very urgency of his resistance to life and change. Caddy becomes his fate; he is absorbed at last into the madness and death of that symbolic power which once invigorated him with the value of existence.

The remaining Compson brothers, though by no means limited to the sensory consciousness of Benjy, react similarly—if on a higher plane of mind—to the primordial feminine in Caddy. It is evident, for example, that Quentin's elementary experience of motherhood has been negative. Since he lacks the protective and nourishing maternity of his sister, his experience of the mother archetype is determined entirely by its transformative character; he repudiates it as desperately and violently as Benjy before him.

Quentin's hatred of time is one measure of his fanatical opposition to the archetype of life; his act of tearing the hands from his watch is for him a despairing attempt to arrest the forces of growth and change inherent in time itself. Yet even when he has placed the crumpled hands in an ashtray—and so relinquished "that constant speculation regarding the position of mechanical hands on an arbitrary dial which is a symptom of mind-function" (p. 94)—the little wheels go on clicking and clicking behind the blank face. He cannot stop it, in the same way that he cannot stop Caddy's steady swelling into motherhood. He cannot turn the clock back to beyond her marriage or beyond her meeting Dalton Ames beneath the trees. Caddy is identified with processes underlying mind-function, with movement that cannot be halted.

In the archetypal world, it is the female who is the goddess of time; she is the mover of its cyclic processes. Since the primordial era, she has been worshipped as the moon goddess; the moon, not the sun, has archaic recognition as the true chronometer of the cosmos. Menstruation and pregnancy, in their supposed relation to the moon, leave woman dependent on and regulated by time. So it is she who determines time—more so than man whose maddening desire for fixity, for the permanence of eternity, provokes him toward the conquest of time.

Quentin fails, on the morning of 2 June 1910, to achieve his conquest of time. He tries to stop that watch inherited from his father's father even though, on the day of its bequeathal, he has accepted with it cynical and despairing counsel:

> Quentin, I give you the mausoleum of all hope and desire; it's rather excruciating-ly apt that you will use it to gain the reducto absurdum of all human experience which can fit your individual needs no better than it fitted his or his father's. I give it to you not that you may remember time, but that you might forget it now and then for a moment and not spend all your breath trying to conquer it. Because no battle is ever won he said. They are not even fought. The field only reveals to man his own folly and despair, and victory is an illusion of philosophers and fools. (p. 93)

Quentin spends the rest of his day trying to relinquish the battle he could not have won. Yet he cannot escape from it. As he walks through Harvard Yard, he is tormented by the chimes of the half- and quarter-hours. He passes a jeweller's window in Cambridge, "but I looked away in time" (p. 102). Further out in the country he faces a church spire, "the square cupola above the trees and the round eye of the clock but far enough" (p. 149); it is far enough so that he cannot see it. As the day wears on, however, and the shadows lengthen, we find that he has not surrendered the struggle. His every mind-function fastens onto time; he is obsessed with a last strategy for its annihilation.

Quentin's assault on time, of course, is essentially directed at Caddy. His only hope of preventing her transformation finds sharp focus in a vision (Paolo- and Francesca-like) of eternal stasis: "*If it could just be a hell beyond that: the clean flame the two of us more than dead. Then you will have only me then only me then the two of us amid the pointing and the horror beyond the clean flame*" (p. 144,

Faulkner's italics). Quentin wants, like Benjy, to have Caddy all to himself—the eternal virgin and son—though he wants her on an unearthly plane. His deeper yearning is to go permanently beyond the world of flux, to transcend even the earthly flame that will someday consume Benjy, so that he may be more than dead, dwelling wholly in the world of the spirit, amidst the pointing and the horror of eternal damnation—itself a creation of a patriarchal consciousness which seeks the spirit's self-sufficiency alone.

Even damnation is preferable, in Quentin's agonized conscious-ness, to being subject to the physical tumescence of growth and the foul putrescence of decay. For damnation is at least ethereal; it is also clean. This desire for purity betrays a second crucial element in Quentin's opposition to the archetype—his hatred of mater-ial. On the day of his suicide, he walks along the streets of Cambridge, "Trampling my shadow's bones into the concrete with hard heels" (p. 118), and he goes on into the country, "tramping my shadow into the dust" (p. 138). His shadow is an affront, a persistent outrage, to him. For at every step it denies that he is pure spirit; it is the grievous sun-blotting proof of his corporeal existence. It also holds for him (as for primitive peoples) some deep mystical connection with the body; his obdurate pursuit of it helps, at day's end, to accomplish the violence done upon his flesh.

Quentin hates more than his own flesh, however. There rages within him an actual horror, similar, as shall be seen, in kind and degree to Joe Christmas's loathing of the sexual engendering principle enfleshed in woman. His response to the blood mysteries of the feminine is one of acute physical nausea: "Because women so delicate so mysterious Father said. Delicate equilibrium of periodical filth between two moons balanced. Moons he said full and yellow as harvest moons her hips thighs. Outside outside of them always but. Yellow. Feet soles with walking like. Then know that some man that all those mysterious and imperious concealed. With all that inside of them shapes an outward suavity waiting for a touch to. Liquid putrefaction like drowned things floating like pale rubber flabbily filled getting the odour of honeysuckle all mix-ed up" (p. 159). Mr. Compson's observations constitute a sort of initiation rite for Quentin, like the adolescent ceremony in which Joe Christmas learns of menstruation and is sickened by it. The clear identification, in Quentin's stream of consciousness, of Caddy's thighs with yellow moons stresses his incipient awareness of the great mother in his sister's sexual being. She is that goddess of moons and menstruation who determines the flow of time that he would reject. She is also the creatrix of the filthy world of flesh he hates.

This hatred is typical of the male spiritual principle; it is an antivital fanaticism directed against life itself. Whatever creates, sustains, and increases life—and the feminine is its archetype—is regarded negatively because male consciousness desires permanence not change; it wants eternity and not transformation, law and not creative spontaneity.

It is specifically this absolutism of consciousness in Quentin which elects eternal death over life and change. His choice encompasses all that lives beneath the moon, not the engendering filth of woman alone, but plant life—the whole fetid world—as well. Thus even the pasture, equated by Benjy with Caddy, is sold for the aggrandizement of Quentin's intellect at Harvard. And the odour of honeysuckle, sensed simultaneously with Caddy's "wild unsecret flesh" being embraced by a lover in the grass, becomes imprinted in Quentin's consciousness as the sexual scent of earth itself. He would repudiate all that is engendered; in the monastic spirit of most patriarchal religions, he turns his face irrevocably from the world. He begins (though in a manner less physical than Origen) by refusing the sexual principle:

> Versh told me about a man mutilated himself. He went into the woods and did it with a razor, sitting in a ditch. A broken razor flinging them backward over his shoulder the same motion complete the jerked skein of blood backward not looping. But that's not it. It's not not having them. It's never to have had them then I could say O That That's Chinese I dont know Chinese. And Father said it's because you are a virgin: dont you see? Women are never virgins. Purity is a negative state and therefore contrary to nature. It's nature is hurting you not Caddy and I said That's just words and he said So is virginity and I said you dont know. You cant know and he said Yes. (p. 143)

Quentin wants to make his virginity retroactive, to have it antedate his conception. He wants to deny that he has ever taken part in a sexed world; he tries to forget that even he is dependent at last on the female for being.

Mr. Compson's counter-affirmation is surprising, on the one hand, since it is his cynical and patriarchal intellect which has tutored Quentin in a life-negating nihilism (perhaps for the very reason that in his era the Compson patriarchal aristocracy is in its death throes): " 'Of course.' Father said. 'Bad health is the primary reason for all life. Created by disease, within putrefaction, into decay' " (p. 53). On the other hand, the father's analysis is profoundly accurate; it is, in fact, a full admission of the pervasiveness throughout all existence of the feminine principle. For physical purity and a state of pure consciousness are contrary to nature, to the earth archetype, and to the archetypal feminine. In the physical world, virginity implies sterility and death; in the world of the psyche, an absolute consciousness spells the mind's severance from the life-giving fecundity of the maternal unconscious.

So Mr. Compson, even out of his own near-dereliction, affirms the necessity of his daughter's action; for confined as she is by social codes and by her brothers' terrific resistance to motion, she yet bears within her an irresistible flow of motion which carries her through windows and into woods and ditches. Caddy is the archetype of life; she is nature, trees, honeysuckle, earth; and like the seasons she cannot be stopped.

Quentin does his best to restrain her. Like Benjy before him, he challenges the presence of her lover; yet unlike Benjy, he loves only a word—"some concept of Compson honor" (*Portable Faulkner*, p. 743)—so he fears not material loss but the ruin of an idea. His concept of honour is drawn from the traditional code of patriarchy: that a woman, whether sister, wife, or mother, is the monogamous instrument of patrilineal succession, she is the bearer of the male name in all its self-sufficiency. But he is not man enough to duel, as that code demands, with the despoiler of his sister's virtue. When he demands of Dalton Ames that he leave town, the man says, "listen save this for a while I want to know if shes all right have they been bothering her up there" (p. 198). Dalton seems to care genuinely about the girl where her brother cares only for some abstraction of consciousness, some concept of male identity. Ironically, Dalton is the true male; he is a primitive frontiersman: a horseman, a good hand with a gun, a man capable of proving his words with his hands. This mythic male—the one true mate to the goddess—abbreviates Quentin's hopeless though frantic reliance on words:

> did you ever have a sister did you
> no but theyre all bitches. (p. 199)

Quentin is so stung by what his mind cannot admit that he strikes out in opposition to what his fists cannot hope to oppose. The scene is both lyric and comic. Quentin faints in Dalton's arms, and Dalton lies to save the pride of his assailant. The man then rides away; one assumes that he does not see Caddy again. But Dalton, the vital male, has pointed to something which must at last be accepted or the consequences faced. There are bitches, and there are *bitches* in the world; yet in the final analysis, all womankind are such. The world, in reality, is one great life-giving bitch. The word has for Dalton a positive accent, for Quentin a negative.

So Quentin turns away from bitchery to his little sister death, echoed in his mental refrain, "And the good Saint Francis that said Little Sister Death, that never had a sister" (p. 94). He is neverthe-less distressed by Saint Francis because the friar's little sister is only a figure of speech; Quentin feels he is faced with a living sister death. When he learns that Caddy has lost her virginity, he says "I wish you were dead" (p. 195). She does not die by his wish; she continues, instead, to bear life. But it is life which drives him into death. He goes to his end (like Fitzgerald's Gatsby) seeking his little sister, the virgin, the unbegot and unbegetting; it is the other, changing Caddy who becomes his death.

Along the route he takes to his self-appointed doom, he meets a little Italian girl whom he addresses as "sister"; he finds a momen-tary way of arresting time through her—by projecting her young virginity upon Caddy. The child is lost and he tries to restore her to her family. Her brother Julio mistakes Quentin's intent, in a moment of high irony, for meditated criminal assault. The scene parodies Quentin's own defense of his sister's honour; yet Julio is much more successful than he, knocking him down, jabbing at his face. (On another occasion in childhood, Caddy had torn at his face with her fingers; symbolically, Quentin's mind is identified as the antagonist.) Julio's fists also shatter the composite image Quentin holds of the little-girl-virgin-Caddy; he must now acknowledge his momentary use of "sister" as no more than a figure of speech. He is forced to retreat finally into his wished-for, though un-happening, idea: "Nobody else there but her and me. If we could just have done something so dreadful that they would have fled hell except us. *I have committed incest I said Father it was I it was not Dalton Ames*" (pp. 97–98). Except that to make the idea happen, to make Caddy eternally dead with him, he must put the idea itself to death. He can only do that by killing himself.

His absolutism leaves Quentin no alternative but to assert the omnipotence of thought. He has to avow that his idea of incest is more real than the deed: "And he did you try to make her do it and i i was afraid to i was afraid she might and then it wouldnt have done any good but if i could tell you we did it would have been so and then the others wouldnt be so and then the world would roar away" (p. 220). This is his ultimate affirmation of the intellect as the shaper and sustainer of whatever is; it is also his last maddened attempt to live in the world of spirit alone, uncorrupted by, but corrupting what is horribly alive. The unacknowledged irony of his situation, of course, is the possibility that there is no spirit realm in which to live; his end (death) might mean extinction, not damnation.

A darker irony, however, clouds his choice of a means. Quentin's conceptual act of incest does not corrupt the female element; it draws him unwittingly back into her power. For the tendency toward incest is the trend toward self-dissolution in the primordial feminine; the "son" is reabsorbed within the maternal Uroboros which has given him life. Thus, for example, in the Aztec myth of Quetzalcoatl, the son-god is enticed by his sister-beloved into drunkenness and physical incest. He laments that he is borne away by "Our mother . . . as her child"[10]; yet even he—the solar deity, the light of consciousness—cannot withstand her dark power.

Since the transformative character of Quetzalcoatl's sister is still latent, it is her elementary figure which lures him into *physical* incest; she becomes the terrible mother who is death. Quentin's seduction, however, is merely an abstraction; he wants to believe he has been the "son-lover" of his sister so that her bodily trans-formation might never have been. It is precisely because Quentin rejects Caddy's transformative figure that he regresses into the spiritualized incest of a higher plane. Though unbeknown to him,

Quentin is finally overwhelmed by the mother archetype of the unconscious; its fascination leads him to the uroboric incest of madness and the urge for death. He seeks the quiet of the water, the clean male-named river (Charles), though (and this is the final irony) even it is "heading out to the sea and the peaceful grottoes" (p. 139). If one misses the symbolism of where Quentin is headed, Faulkner repeats it at the end of the section: "Caddy said in the caverns and the grottoes of the sea tumbling peacefully to the wavering tides" (p. 217).

Benjy and Quentin are two brothers confronted with tremendous and dangerously decisive psychic experience. Benjy, who is incapable of spiritual development, need only respond to Caddy's natural transformation to permit his spirit to become nature. He rejects it, clinging desperately to his memory of the virgin "trees"; but his resistance (which is hardly volitional, since he doesn't have the equipment for volition) dooms him. Quentin, on the other hand, is compelled to spiritual transformation by the anima, but consciously refuses change. The result is negative transformation, downward into madness, dissolution, and death. So Caddy, in every sense a human incarnation of uncanny factors beginning as the mother of life, is forced in the end to become as well the mother of death. In this way, the story of *The Sound and the Fury* becomes her personal and human tragedy.

Jason's section seems to be quite a different story from his brothers' impotence of consciousness. For Jason would appear to have succeeded as the coldly victorious male intellect, retaining in triumph the subjugated feminine, turned now completely to his own ends. Faulkner accents this rationality of Jason's character in the cameo portrait of the Appendix: "The first sane Compson since before Culloden and (a childless bachelor) the last. Logical, rational, contained and even a philosopher in the old stoic tradition" (*Portable Faulkner*, p. 750). Contrary to Quentin, Jason has a coldly realistic outlook on woman; he noisily opens his section with the words "Once a bitch always a bitch, what I say" (p. 223). Rationally, he comes to the same conclusion about women as Dalton Ames does; only his tonal response is different.

Having lost, through Caddy's untimely and inconsiderate whelping, a job promised to him in Herbert Head's bank, Jason takes his revenge on her through a very clever fraud. He accepts unacknowledged support from Caddy for her daughter, Miss Quentin; he then deposits it directly into his bedroom savings account. He also outwits Caddy early in her banishment, accepting one hundred dollars in advance for what she does not know will be but a passing glimpse of her infant daughter. Jason would seem to put the patriarchate in its ascendancy once again, the principle of "light" arising out of darkness.

Even in this latest episode, however, there are anticipations of another outcome: "And so I counted the money again that night and put it away, and I didn't feel so bad. I says I reckon that'll show you. I reckon you'll know now that you cant beat me out of a job and get away with it. It never occurred to me she wouldn't keep her promise and take that train. But I didn't know much about them then; I didn't have any more sense than to believe what they said" (p. 255). His cold and logical justification notwithstanding, Jason is hotly in error with his implication that he knows more "about them" now than before. For "them"—womankind, the female element—embody all the forces of irrationality which will outface him in the end.

To Jason's sense of rational order, the world is a predictable place. So he is outraged when Miss Quentin steals his embezzled savings; he is appalled because she does it blindly, on impulse, leaving his logic no defense against it. He is literally maddened at the thought that his niece's probable accomplice is the circus huckster, the man in the red tie. The tie goads him, like the proverbial flag before the bull, because it sums up for him all the forces of illogic which oppose him: "The fact that he must depend on that red tie seemed to be the sum of the impending disaster; he could almost smell it, feel it above the throbbing of his head" (p. 384). His rationality is enmeshed in an especially desperate anomaly when he now must trust, depend, subject himself to irrationality in the hope of tracking down the fugitives.

Most of all, it is the condition of being thwarted by the female which drives him closest to despair, and most nearly forces him to the thought of locking up his shop of consciousness: "If he could just believe it was the man who had robbed him. But to have been robbed of that which was to have compensated him for the lost job, which he had acquired through so much effort and risk, by the very symbol of the lost job itself, and worst of all, by a bitch of a girl" (pp. 383–84). Bitchery to him is that ever present unpredictability which in one afternoon can ruin a family reputation (so he holds, publicly at least) and in one night can spoil the careful hoardings of a lifetime.

Jason is no abstractionist like Quentin; bitchery threatens social and material ends. The paralysing thing about bitchery's latest onslaught against him, however, is that Jason is prevented by his own logic from any form of satisfaction; he is left as impotent as Benjy and Quentin have been. He cannot tell the police the real amount he lost, and he cannot force the sheriff to go after them, else his criminal embezzlement will come to light. So of course Jason would prefer to believe it was the man who robbed him; that way his loss would be due solely to superior brains. This other way, he is made to acknowledge his unending submission to feminine indiscriminacy. And his rage against chaos makes that about as easy to accept as Benjy's bellowing non-acceptance of the wrong way taken round the courthouse. Jason is ultimately incapable of transformation, yet somehow, in his cold, sane (or maybe totally insane) way, he manages to live with his defeat.

Jason's tone, in comparison to his brothers', is finally the best index of his response to the woman within. Through a kind of sensory voice we feel the response of Benjy to the great mother; in a poetically frenzied voice, Quentin's response is heard; but in Jason's case, it is perhaps the voice of wit—a chiselling of cynical and caustic conceits out of the lifestuff of his fellows—which is the fullest measure of his reaction to the life-giving daemon. For he, like Quentin, is ultimately in love with death; worse, he wants to deny all existence except his own. His humour is sardonic, sadistic, and self-righteous, so much so that his dark laughter becomes fully as destructive of life as his instrumentality in the literal gelding of Benjy:

> I could hear the Great American Gelding snoring away like a planing mill. I read somewhere they'd fix men that way to give them women's voices. But maybe he didn't know what they'd done to him. I dont reckon he even knew what he had been trying to do, or why Mr Burgess knocked him out with the fence picket. And if they'd just sent him on to Jackson while he was under the ether, he'd never have known the difference.

But that would have been too simple for a Compson to think of. Not half complex enough. Having to wait to do it at all until he broke out and tried to run a little girl down on the street with her own father looking at him. Well, like I say they never started soon enough with their cutting, and they quit too quick. I know at least two more that needed something like that, and one of them not over a mile away, either. But then I dont reckon even that would do any good. Like I say once a bitch always a bitch. (pp. 328–29)

Jason's section closes on its opening keynote of universal bitchdom, adding to it only a now futile hope of spaying the female (Caddy and Miss Quentin). His loathing for life, quite as intense as Quentin's, does, however, find narrow release within the wittily defensive turnings of his consciousness. So he survives (perhaps because in her warped way his mother singled him out for some sort of love) but he will not endure. For this one "sane" Compson male since Culloden is a childless bachelor. The terms of his sexual relationship are cash on the barrelhead—money becomes a surrogate for male consciousness, for controlling and defending oneself from the anima: mythographically, Zeus descending on Danae in a shower of gold—and his issue will be only a sterile childlessness, the patronym of Compson blotted from the earth with his death.

Then only the girl, the fatherless Miss Quentin, will remain, lost but living, like her mother, in the wide world. Perhaps it is Faulkner's way of restoring the matriarchate to culture, to civilization. If so, he finds it imperative that the old order should crumble; he places Caddy in a Nazi staff car with the powers of twentieth-century destruction ranged around her.

Miss Quentin starts out by embodying some of the same life-force of her mother (the capacity to go through windows and climb down trees), and she is symbolically linked to Caddy by "a soiled undergarment of cheap silk a little too pink" (p. 352)—the soiled loins motif extending as a female prerequisite throughout the novel. But her potentially positive character has been stifled by the last of her mother's brothers, and she becomes the witch not alone to Jason, but even to poor witless Benjy ("You old crazy loon,[11] Quentin said" [p. 58]. In the same way as for her mother Caddy, Miss Quentin's story then becomes what Faulkner claimed the novel to be, "the tragedy of two lost women: Caddy and her daughter."[12]

The shift which takes place in the fourth section—from a narrow subjectivity to a wider objective view, from the moribund minds of male consciousness to the enduring being of the Negress Dilsey—is a measure of the great mother's continuance in the Compson household. Dilsey has long been regarded as a vital presence in the totality of the novel, but never for the fullest and most satisfying reason. Admittedly, her patient endurance is a strong stabilizing influence in a family where there is so much wrong-headedness. She is a keeper of the peace, a protector and constant nourisher. In a very practical way, she (like Caddy) is a true mother to the Compson children, more so perhaps because of her timelier maturity. With reason, she says of the infant girl Quentin, " Who else gwine raise her 'cep me? Aint I raised eve'y one of y'all? " (p. 246). She is also chief antagonist to Jason (he dare not fire her), the champion of humanism in conflict with inhumanity. If this, however, were the sum of her presence in the novel, there could be no justification for identifying Dilsey with the archetypal feminine.

The truly numinal world is revealed, in Caddy's absence, during the primitive ritual of the Easter morning service in the Negro church. There, a form of communion is established in the chanted sermon, where the monkey-faced little preacher tramps back and forth "while the voice consumed him, until he was nothing and they were nothing and there was not even a voice but instead their hearts were speaking to one another in chanting measures beyond the need for words" (p. 367). It is perhaps Faulkner's finest expression of the ritual experience where man is made one with his fellows in communion with the deity. The god whom Reverend Shegog speaks about is the dying son, as has been seen, the infant Jesus snatched from Mary's lap. He pictures Mary's fright in the face of the soldiers; he describes "de weepin en de lamentation of de po mammy widout de salvation en de word of God!" (p. 369). Then, with the mother of God still weeping for the baby Jesus, the preacher sweeps into the stunning sorrow of Good Friday, almost as if

Herod's slaughter and Golgotha were happening on the same day. And although the father God, Jehovah, is portrayed as looking down from Heaven on the conclusion of these events, still the narrator follows immediately with a portrait of the mother in the congregation, weeping beside her son: "In the midst of the voices and the hands Ben sat, rapt in his sweet blue gaze. Dilsey sat bolt upright beside, crying rigidly and quietly in the annealment and the blood of the remembered Lamb" (pp. 370–71).

Once again, as he did in *Sartoris*, Faulkner uses a Christian Holy Day to great effect. But the final result should not be called Christian, for the abiding emphasis rests not on Jesus, but on the eternal mother of the dying god. Thus when Dilsey says, "I seed de beginnin, en now I sees de endin" (p. 371), she has seen clearly into the matrix of existence, and has learned that motherhood begins in life and ends in death, that the feminine encompasses both; but she has also seen clearly into time, and has discovered that "de beginnin" and "de endin" are the same. In the beginning, the son died, and now it is down to that again, the old myth repeated in history once more. Except that the son, "rapt in his sweet blue gaze," has not seen at all; he must merely sit there, blind and idiotic and knowing not what he does. It is the mother alone who sits outside of time, who in the symbolic sense comprises it.

There is only the single poetic theme, as Robert Graves says, of life and death. This "single grand theme of poetry" is "the life, death and resurrection of the Spirit of the Year, the Goddess's son and lover" (*White Goddess*, p. 422). Although the eunuch is obviously not Dilsey's lover, Faulkner's symbol nonetheless encompasses, as it has throughout the story, life and death. The dying son is a particular symbol of the fate humanity is subject to, while the mother goddess is that which is transcendent and always numinous.

Faulkner's Negro church—while nominally, though neither biblically nor theologically, Christian—is not exempt from the compelling force of the eternal feminine. There is no theology whatsoever in Reverend Shegog's sermon; there is only the ritual story of the dying son. And the experience carried in this religious primitivism is a final affirmation of the mother archetype in its endless domination of life and death. For it is the Compson males who perish in the narrative of *The Sound and the Fury* (Quentin and his father, literally, and Benjy in his gelding); yet nowhere in the "Doomsday Book" (*Lion*, p. 255) of Yoknapatawpha County do Caddy, her daughter, or Dilsey die. The last word, in fact, on Dilsey is, "They endured" (*Portable Faulkner*, p. 756).

Dilsey vivifies the fourth and final section of *The Sound and the Fury* just as Caddy animates the whole of the first three sections; literally and symbolically, Dilsey takes up where Caddy leaves off. She raises Miss Quentin and she mothers Benjy; " 'Hush, now,' she said, stroking his head. 'Hush. Dilsey got you' " (p. 395); she protects and shelters them both from Jason. Yet in the moving icon of the Pietà, she becomes, like Caddy, the sorrowful mother of death.

In connection with these two women, the reversion, on Faulkner's part, to the symbols of primitivism marks his attempt to return to the source and value of existence. For the Compson world of this novel is a clear expression of the cultural failure of Faulkner's own South. The modern Christian form of sacrament can be no more authoritative to him than to Mrs. Compson who whines about having "tried so hard to raise them Christians" (p. 351), and who then bumps her Bible with complete indifference onto the floor (p. 374). Otherwise he would not have created in Benjy an idiot Christ. Nor would he have dislocated the Easter dates.

There are two reasons to doubt that Faulkner intended a serious re-presenting of the Christ-myth (these in addition to the Nativity irony of *Sartoris*): First, if the thirty-three year old Benjy is a Christ figure, he is witless and gelded; he is not only un-resurrectable, but he bellows in despair. So he represents a powerless form of sacrament, not at all the hope of Christianity, at best, perhaps, a symbol of mankind's suffering. Second, the symbolic focus of the Easter morning service is on the mother goddess and not on her son. It seems that the purpose of Faulkner's archetypal art is to incarnate the female deity as she is defined by her son. In any event, the feminine is the archetype of primitive feeling and the emotive life; she is the restored means of sacramental experience.

The Easter dates offer two final caveats, perhaps conclusive ones, against too easy an acceptance of the structure of Christian myth in the novel. It has been said that the very device of the dates seems to suggest the lost soul (the unredeemed Benjy) in hell on Saturday, the crucifixion of the god of love (through Jason's hatred) on Friday, and the resurrection with its implied hope on Sunday.[13] But on Easter morning, "The day dawned bleak and chill, a moving wall of grey light out of the northeast which, instead of dissolving into moisture, seemed to disintegrate into minute and venomous particles, like dust that, when Dilsey opened the door of the cabin and emerged, needled laterally into her flesh" (p. 330). Shortly thereafter, "A pair of jaybirds came up from nowhere, whirled up on the blast like gaudy scraps of cloth or paper and lodged in the mulberries, where they swung in raucous tilt and recover, screaming into the wind that ripped their harsh cries onward and away like scraps of paper or of cloth in turn" (pp. 331-32). The violence of the inclement weather, and the echoes of raucous screaming carrying down the windy Sunday sky, seem a deftly pointed irony to the brilliant and glorious dawning of that other Easter morning. Nature itself appears to deride the Resurrection on this eighth day of April, 1928. And not least, these dates of Easter are themselves disrupted, running initially from Saturday to Friday with an eighteen-year hiatus between them. This presentation would seem to be as muddled and as thoroughly recalcitrant as Benjy himself is, taken the wrong way round the square in the novel's final scene.

The fragmenting, the distorting, and the ultimate frustrating of the Christ "myth" in *The Sound and the Fury* serves once again, and in deeper measure, to deny that the full accent of that myth rests squarely on the dying son. Far more fully and profoundly than he had done in *Sartoris*, Faulkner brings an incarnation of a pagan deity, the great mother, into this present world. She is formed in all her significance by the symbols of authentic primitivism.

Nonetheless, the form of her narrative epiphany was never fully satisfying to the author. He consistently stated that, though he felt *The Sound and the Fury* was his best work, it was a failure. He linked "part of the failure" on one occasion to its structure: "It seemed to me that the book approached nearer the dream if the groundwork of it was laid by the idiot, who was incapable of relevancy. That's—I agree with you too, that's a bad method, but to me it seemed the best way to do it, that I shifted those sections back and forth to see where they went best, but my final decision was that though that was not right, that was the best [sic] to do it, that was simply the groundwork of that story, as that

idiot child saw it" (*University*, pp. 63–64). The temporal dis-
locations do not, as any undergraduate will testify, make for coherent
reading. Yet Faulkner found it best for his purposes first to transcribe
the "dream" in the fluid time of the idiot. Benjy does not in and of
himself make Caddy's story timeless, but the symbols encompassing
him do achieve the resolution of time and timelessness. In a structural sense, the icon of the Madonna and the icon of the Pietà contain
the whole of the narrative between them; they give it its "time"
but they also surround that time. In a strictly archetypal sense,
they evoke non-historical figures embracing creatures who are
fully temporal. This quality of timeless femininity is, if anything,
heightened by Benjy's, Jason's, and especially Quentin's frantic
efforts to stop time. So the temporal aspect of the work cannot be
the major failure in its technique.

One might conjecture that the only failure in the mythos of this
novel is the uncertainty as to where suprapersonal authority resides.
The defect in *The Sound and the Fury* is the absence of Caddy
throughout its later portions; ostensibly beginning as the story of
the sister and her numinous influence upon her brothers, the novel
in conclusion becomes the story of the Negro servant. The nature
of the archetype (what the "dream" is about) does realize its
potential in this transference, but the figure of the feminine is
split. This splitting is caused literally, of course, by Caroline
Compson's refusal to allow her dishonoured daughter to return
home. Yet Caroline is also an integral facet in the character of the
great mother. Perhaps she is represented as a social and human
failure rather than as a numinous and archetypal figure because
Faulkner could not yet bring himself to accept the goddess as the
inexplicable cause of death. The fascination which he admits to in
the character of Caddy seems to represent his commitment to the
positive presence of the primordial mother; concomitantly, there is
a marked emphasis on the inner failings of the brothers as the
source of self-destruction. This emphasis is fortunate insofar as it
reinforces the element of free will in male survival, unfortunate in
that it is not yet quite willing to accept the "terrible" powers to
which mankind is subject.

The tone of pessimism which is left as a kind of residue at the
conclusion of *The Sound and the Fury* means only that at this
particular point in his development, Faulkner reacted to the

negative and destructive aspect of the archetypal feminine with a negativity of his own. How he began to overcome that feeling not unakin to despair shall be examined in the writing of *As I Lay Dying*.

4

As The Mother of Death Lay Dying:

As I Lay Dying

The pairing of *As I Lay Dying* with *The Sound and the Fury* in the Modern Library Edition (1946) is more than the binding in one volume of temporally adjacent works; the theme of the former is also, in part, the lack of mother-love and its consequent impact upon a family. Nevertheless, where the destructive power of Caroline Compson has been accounted for in terms of human frailty and of social incompetence, no equivalent attempt has been made to resolve the character of Addie Bundren. By symbolizing the "terribleness" of her influence very directly, the artist has offered, as it were, mythic amends for his prior "failure."

There are three principal ways by which to approach the story of the Bundrens. One of them is to look upon Addie as the source— despite the dreadfulness of her tale, both by her own account and by report of others—of everything that happens.[1] Another is to regard Anse, the father, as the redeeming figure in the family, the comic antidote to the mother's poison: as one critic remarks, "Since Pa is at the center of the book, the novel could be wholly successful only if he were fully acceptable as a tragicomic figure at the center of a tragicomic action."[2] The final way is the *via media*, discovering in Addie a representation of the victorious power of love, yet finding Anse to be "exempt from moral condemnation, so comically and affectionately is he treated by his creator."[3] In the first two instances, the narrative outcome of the novel is thus viewed (for very different reasons) as the triumphant merger in Cash of the deed with the word, in the last, as the replacement of Darl and words by Jewel's action: as the discovery through love of the power to act (Backman, pp. 65–66). Whatever construction is placed upon the narrative conclusion, the symbolic polarity of the novel then oscillates between the deeds of an awesome mother and the words of an amusing father.

Anse is given the first word in establishing this structural antinomy:

Durn that road. . . . A-laying there, right up to my door, where every bad luck that comes and goes is bound to find it. I told Addie it want any luck living on a road when it come by here, and she said, for the world like a woman, "Get up and move, then." But I told her it want no luck in it, because the Lord put roads for travelling: why He laid them down flat on the earth. When He aims for something to be always a-moving, He makes it longways, like a road or a horse or a wagon, but when He aims for something to stay put, He makes it up-and-down ways, like a tree or a man. And so he never aimed for folks to live on a road, because which gets there first, I says, the road or the house? Did you ever know Him to set a road down by a house? I says. No you never, I says, because it's always men cant rest till they gets the house set where everybody that passes in a wagon can spit in the doorway, keeping the folks restless and wanting to get up and go somewheres else when He aimed for them to stay put like a tree or a stand of corn. Because if He'd aimed for man to be always a-moving and going somewheres else, wouldn't He a put him longways on his belly, like a snake? It stands to reason He would.[4]

Anse divides roads, wagons, horses, snakes, and woman from trees, corn, and man because the former are all horizontal (earth-bound), the latter vertical (sky-directed). In his view, the female symbols are negative (even evil) because they move; the male ones are positive because they stand still. Though Anse is personally inert to the point of being grotesque (in the comic sense of "exaggerated," as in a tall tale), his symbology is more than a device of personal characterization; it is the index of opposed states of being.

At first sight, Addie seems to contradict her husband absolutely: "And so when Cora Tull would tell me I was not a true mother, I would think how words go straight up in a thin line, quick and harmless, and how terribly doing goes along the earth, clinging to it, so that after a while the two lines are too far apart for the same person to straddle from one to the other" (p. 165). The story of the Bundrens is, in fact, the record of "how terribly doing goes along the earth"; *As I Lay Dying* creates a kind of continuous image of a mule-drawn wagon crawling terrifically through the dirt with a yellow box and a family squat upon it and with buzzards wheeling high in the horrid stench above it. Though she is dead, Addie continues in motion, and she draws her immobile husband with her.

The proof of the inefficacy of Anse's symbols consists in the fact that he does not remain rooted; he is drawn to the road and to the wagon (which he himself has identified for us as being feminine) by the strength of Addie's will. The source of that symbolic weakness lies, it seems, in his misunderstanding of two elements within his own image complex: First, he does not admit that corn and trees and (symbolically) men are dependent for their rootedness upon the earth. For if the earth-bound symbols of motion are feminine in being, the static masculine images are feminine in origin. Second, although Anse has appropriated the tree image to represent a male condition, he has not perceived its dynamic ambivalence. Dr. Peabody gives him his initial arboreal characterization: "He stands there beside a tree. Too bad the Lord made the mistake of giving trees roots and giving the Anse Bundrens He makes feet and legs. If He'd just swapped them, there wouldn't ever be a worry about this country being deforested someday. Or any other country" (p. 41). Yet before Peabody has finished speaking, the image has become maternal: "The path looks like a crooked limb blown against the bluff. Anse has not been in town in twelve years. And how his mother ever got up there to bear him, he being his mother's son" (p. 41). The miniature road is not only likened to a tree which has been moved, it also is (literally and comically) the path which Anse's mother traversed in order to bear him. So when Anse steps aboard the wagon, he consequently forsakes his terrific stasis and heads out horizontally in the "doing" that goes terribly along the earth. Even in death, Addie's earthbound impelling is reaffirmed as she rides in horizontal repose on the wagon.

The reasons why these images of motion are true symbols and not mere signs must of course be considered. That discussion depends, however, on the acknowledgement of a peculiar force in Addie, and on the awareness of a particular form which that energy assumes. An estimation of her power might be approached first by relating her story to the title of the novel.

The phrase "As I Lay Dying" raises a very interesting problem. Addie Bundren is the only person in the novel who dies, yet the past tense of the intransitive verb "to lie" suggests that she goes on speaking. The mind of a decaying corpse, in other words, looks back upon the story of its own life as an already completed action; Addie Bundren speaks to us from beyond the bound of death. Proof positive that the "lay" of the title is not mere grammatical error comes from Addie herself; in her monologue she speaks in the past tense of holding the baby Jewel "and I lying calm in the slow silence, getting ready to clean my house" (p. 168). Addie would know grammar, of course, having been a schoolteacher.

If a literary source for the title exists, Carvel Collins seems to have ferreted out the single possibility—Homer's *Odyssey* in several of its little known English translations.[5] Particularly, Collins cites the 1925 Oxford University Press translation by Sir William Marris, which is timely enough for Faulkner to have encountered it sometime between his joining the Sherwood Anderson circle (where he read *The Golden Bough*, among other things) in New Orleans during the first half of 1925 and his Autumn 1929 composition of *As I Lay Dying*. The phrase occurs in the Eleventh Book of *The Odyssey* where, at the bidding of Circe, Odysseus seeks out the spirits of Erebus in order to be advised of a safe route home to Ithaca. In a succession of moving passages, he speaks with the shades who have recovered, for the moment, living voices by drinking of the dark blood Odysseus sacrificed and spilled in the earth. Agamemnon's spirit, in deploring the faithless treachery of Clytemnestra, says

". . . I, as I lay dying

Upon the sword, raised up my hands to smite her;
And shamelessly she turned away, and scorned
To draw my eyelids down or close my mouth
Though I was on the road to Hades' house"
                                        (p. 195)

Collins explains the contextual import of the Homeric passage in the following manner: "Darl Bundren, with open eyes staring and open mouth foaming, comes to his end in *As I Lay Dying* locked in the hell of the Jackson madhouse thinking of his faithless mother" (p. 123). The title gets twisted in making it refer to Darl; only Addie dies in the story, and she, like Agamemnon, alone seems to speak from beyond the grave. Here, it seems, the direct correlation of Addie and Agamemnon ends. Addie is a woman brought to death seemingly (from the absence of any explanation, even a medical reason from Peabody) by her own commanding will and she speaks not, like Agamemnon, of the perfidy of woman but of the terribleness of living and of the process of violation and becoming whole again. So if Faulkner echoes Agamemnon in the title phrase, he appears to suggest a larger correspondence between woman and death than the individual slaying of a spouse by a mate. In the most explicit sense, Faulkner uses the phrase to raise an old ghost, to evoke a power of awareness that reaches beyond life itself.

This power of Addie's continuing awareness is referred to in several ways within the novel. Anse finds no difficulty after Addie's death in accepting what by logic his son Darl is not able to see: " 'It's Addie I give the promise to,' he says [to Samson]. 'Her mind is set on it' " (p. 109). This unreflecting confidence he displays in the persisting *is* of his wife contrasts significantly with Darl's syllogistic straining to keep his mother's *was* alive:

Beyond the unlamped wall I can hear the rain shaping the wagon that is ours, the load that is no longer theirs that felled and sawed it nor yet theirs that bought it and which is not ours either, lie on our wagon though it does, since only the wind and the rain shape it only to Jewel and me, that are not asleep. And since sleep is is-not and rain and wind are *was*, it is not. Yet the wagon *is*, because when the wagon is *was*, Addie Bundren will not be. And Jewel *is*, so Addie Bundren must be.

And then I must be, or I could not empty myself for sleep in a strange room. And so if I am not emptied yet, I am *is*. (p. 76, Faulkner's italics)

Existence for Darl depends, as for Quentin Compson, upon its logical confirmation; his desperate argument for is-ness spells out his rational absolutism and its impending disaster.

Dr. Peabody offers the better gloss on is-ness and death as he enters the room where Addie lies dying:

When we enter she turns her head and looks at us. She has been dead these ten days. I suppose it's having been a part of Anse for so long that she cannot even make that change, if change it be. I can remember how when I was young I believed death to be a phenomenon of the body; now I know it to be merely a function of the mind—and that of the minds of the ones who suffer the bereavement. The nihilists say it is the end; the fundamentalists, the beginning; when in reality it is no more than a single tenant or family moving out of a tenement or a town. (pp. 42–43)

Faulkner upsets most conventional opinions about death through placing this speech in the mouth of his country doctor, precisely because the man who, limited by practice to physical cause and effect, should be affirming a more scientific outlook, contrarily asserts a mythic and poetic view of dying as a form of movement. Since an underlying theme of the novel is the opposition between stasis and movement, Dr. Peabody's words shall bear repeating. More immediately, however, it is important to recognize the premise on which the whole story might well be constructed: that in death there lies neither end nor beginning. For if death is merely a function of mind, or more specifically a mind-function of the bereaved, then only the mind conceiving of cessation suffers loss. Addie, of course, would remain pre-eminently unaffected by her changing state even should her mind cease to be. If, however, her power of awareness continues, then in reality (Dr. Peabody's terms) she experiences neither beginning nor end but a setting out, like the tenant moving out of a tenement. Symbolically, the story of Addie's burial journey entails this setting out, and she takes her family with her.

The horrorific tale of the funeral cortége then suggests four things about death: it is neither end (of the body) nor beginning (of the spirit); it is motion-transformation for both the bereaved and the "departed"; it is vitally associated with maternal being; and it participates in the numinous world. Because Addie endures both as an active force and as a perceptive faculty after she is dead, the mythos of *As I Lay Dying* offers a unique literal-symbolic rendering of the presence of the "non-historical" in human time. The dead woman embodies something which is suprapersonal, which extends beyond mere ephemeral consciousness of the individual, and which sums up the potentiality of death. Far from explaining the dreadful character of the human mother, "As I Lay Dying" abruptly proposes her numinous representation; it makes the woman not only "larger than life" (Faulkner's description of Eula Varner) but larger than death as well. Faulkner, in the characterization of Addie Bundren, turns deliberately and even candidly to an evocation of the mother of death, to an aspect of the archetypal feminine which he seemed at pains to modify in *The Sound and the Fury*.

Addie speaks directly only once in *As I Lay Dying*. The location of her soliloquy heightens, if anything, the effect of her voice. For it is given after Mrs. Bundren has been dead some five days. Critics are faced with the choice of saying that it is ironically placed after her coffin has been fished from the river,[6] or arguing that it occurs when the bier has been floated across the dreadful stream, immediately after the dead woman has crossed the Styx.

Addie's favourite son, Jewel, offers a clue leading to the second alternative. He draws a graphic image of his desired relation to his mother: "It would just be me and her on a high hill and me rolling the rocks down the hill at their faces, picking them up and throwing them down the hill faces and teeth and all by God until she was quiet" (p. 15). If an echo out of Classical myth is heard in Jewel's thinking, it would seem to be from Hesiod's *Theogony*, where Mother Earth advises her earth-born sons to enlist the rock-hurling Hundred-Arms in their war with the sky god, Cronus.[7]

Jewel's hill might literally be the cliff on which the Bundren house is set, but it recalls additionally the home of the "awful goddess," Styx, dwelling (in Hesiod's cosmos) among high rocks towering up to the sky (p. 75). Hesiod makes the goddess Styx a collaborator with Zeus in his war with the sons of Earth, but in another version of the Giants' Revolt, Apollodorus says the assault on Olympus begins with an oath made to the river Styx.[8] The river Styx, of course, is the province of the death goddess (bearing the same name), but it is also associated with Demeter, the loving mother, who cursed it to escape the unwelcome attentions of Poseidon (*White Goddess*, p. 367).

Graves quotes Pausanias as well to show that Demeter is identified more positively with the deathly goddess. Near Nonacris, the high cliff where Styx originates, Melampus, son of a mare-mother "purged the daughters of Proteus with black hellebore and pig-sacrifices, and afterwards washed away their madness in a stream. . . . The three daughters were the triple goddess, the Demeter of the Styx, who must have been mare-headed, else a horse's hoof would not have been proof against the poison of the water" (p. 368). In a limited sense, Jewel, whose "mother is a horse," purges his mother in a stream down which a dead pig floats (p. 148), for he washes away her "mad" fear of old that she will not get to Jefferson. Likewise, if Jewel's literal horse panics in the current, his symbolic mare-mother is proof, in the coffin Jewel floats to shore, against the water and the log which stands "for an instant upright upon that surging and heaving desolation like Christ" (p. 141). Darl, who makes this identification, hopes beyond all hope to see the "Christ" whelm an emergent (and threatening) pagan goddess, but the heroic efforts of Jewel as the son who defines the loving mother lead irrevocably to the expression of her deathly power. So it is fitting that Addie should speak out the moment her body has crossed the river; she has entered her own realm. To the extent that she is figured actively in her deathly power, in her war with the celestial principle of thought (words), and in her maternal love, her son's allusions are more than arbitrary parallels. The temporal context of Addie's speech then seems less indicative of irony than of something quite as noumenal as the title suggests.

In structure, Addie's monologue is a recapitulation of her womanhood. It recounts her life in the past tense, beginning with her earliest tie to children as a schoolteacher—"I would go down the

hill to the spring where I could be quiet and hate them" (p. 161)—
and ending with the balanced fulfilment of her maternity and the
cleaning of her house—"And then I could get ready to die" (p. 168).
Yet even as "there was no beginning nor ending to anything
then" (p. 167), so there is neither end nor beginning to her influence now, even in death. Addie's father helps to underscore
this theme of her speech both at its start and at its finish: "I could
just remember how my father used to say that the reason for living
was to get ready to stay dead a long time" (p. 161). The Compson
father instilled the same life-denying attitude in his son Quentin.
In Addie, however, the male principle becomes transformed: "She
knew at last what he meant and that he could not have known
what he meant himself, because a man cannot know anything about
cleaning up the house *afterward*" (pp. 167–68, emphasis mine).
Though her father offers no more hope than the nihilistic Mr.
Compson, Addie carries motion into death as a sort of life-in-death:
capable of acting afterward. The focus of her action in both life and
death is the house, the female domain.

Context and structure aside, the content of Addie's monologue
is the key to the novel. Much in the manner of Milton's council
in Heaven (*Paradise Lost*, Bk. III) where God defines the criteria
by which the poem and all of its actors are to be judged, so too
Addie defines her nature in relation to her family and to all of life.
Her character also contains as does the Old Testament Jahweh, the
same inexplicable blend of love and destruction.

The reiterant theme of her monologue is "that living was
terrible" and that "words are no good" (p. 163). Addie says she
learned the terribleness of living when she knew that she had Cash,
but the quality of "terrible" is not reserved for childbearing alone.
It has been sensed already in her central symbolic statement that
"doing" goes terribly along the earth; she refers also to "the old
terrible nights," to "the terrible blood," and to "sin the more utter
and terrible" (p. 166). Certainly Darl, in his agony and extremity
of consciousness, would agree that living is terrible; of her pregnancy, Dewey Dell admits that "the process of coming unalone is
terrible" (p. 59); and no "doing" ever goes more terribly along
the earth than the journey of the Bundren family to Jefferson.
Addie gives a special valence, however, to "terrible" in its relation
to living, to blood, to sin, and to doing.

The woman defines "living" by the perspective of the matriarchate:[9]

> Cash did not need to say it to me nor I to him, and I would say, Let Anse use it, if he wants to. So that it was Anse or love; love or Anse: it didn't matter.
> I would think that even while I lay with him in the dark and Cash asleep in the cradle within the swing of my hand. I would think that if he were to wake and cry, I would suckle him, too. Anse or love: it didn't matter. My aloneness had been violated and then made whole again by the violation: time, Anse, love, what you will, outside the circle. (p. 164)

Addie claims as mother to participate in the primordial Great Round of being, the containing feminine circle of all that lives and dies; the father, in terms of this view, has no part in the waxing and the waning of life. A word like "love," then, is vitally alive for Addie within the maternal round of mother and child, but it consists in doing (being), rather than in saying; it has no abstract existence. Anse is alive (by her standards) only if and when he should be son-like (capable of being suckled, dependent on the woman for life). Insofar as he depends on words, he is dead like they are; for words are an abstraction of consciousness, removed from the *mater* of material and devoid of intrinsic life. Addie says that when Cash was born, she learned "that words dont ever fit even what they are trying to say at . . . that motherhood was invented by someone who had to have a word for it because the ones that had the children didn't care whether there was a word for it or not. I knew that fear was invented by someone that had never had the fear; pride, who never had the pride" (pp. 163–64). She then claims explicitly that Anse has died in his "words":

> He did not know that he was dead, then. Sometimes I would lie by him in the dark, hearing the land that was now of my blood and flesh, and I would think: Anse. Why Anse. Why are you Anse. I would think about his name until after a while I could see the word as a shape, a vessel, and I would watch him liquefy and flow into it like cold molasses flowing out of the darkness into the vessel, until the jar stood full and motionless: a significant shape profoundly without life like an empty door

frame; and then I would find that I had forgotten the name of the jar. (p. 165)

Whether Addie is right or not about Anse remains to be seen; but his inertia, the male resistance to motion, is perfectly figured in the slow thickness of cold molasses pouring into the shape of a motionless and profoundly lifeless jar.

Living (and promoting life), on the other hand, exacts a terrible price from the woman. Addie says her aloneness had never been violated in the nights by Anse, it had never been violated at all until Cash came and made her violation whole again. This reference to the mother's "aloneness" figures beautifully in the mysteries of Isis where "the Mother of all things in the universe"[10] is sought, as Plotinus says, in "the flight of the alone to the Alone" (p. 160). The violation of the human mother not only emphasizes her aloneness but, in Addie's case, makes her the Alone, the mother like Isis of the very earth ("hearing the land that was now of my blood and flesh"). Her assimilation of the land links her to Dr. Peabody's assessment of its formative power in the human world: "Like our rivers, our land: opaque, slow, violent; shaping and creating the life of man in its implacable and brooding image" (p. 44). For she and the earth are fused as the *magna mater* of all life: "My children were of me alone, of the wild blood boiling along the earth, of me and of all that lived; of none and of all" (p. 167). She is the sole, violent shaper of life.

Addie's mythic identity is not complete, however, in her earth-mothering capacity to give life. Blood is her most vital symbol (just as it was the quickening element to the dead spirits whom Odysseus met), but it also signifies the terrible flow of motion which is alive, and the involuntary pulse of doing. Again and again she speaks of "the wild blood boiling along the earth"; it seems to be her element, the most characteristic revelation of her nature, because it is in ceaseless and inexorable motion. Even before she has had children of her own and knows what "blood" means, she is obsessed with making it flow. In the schoolhouse, facing the children, she says "I would look forward to the times when they faulted, so I could whip them. When the switch fell I could feel it upon my flesh; when it wetted and ridged it was my blood that ran, and I would think with each blow of the switch: Now you are aware of me!

Now I am something in your secret and selfish life, who have marked your blood with my own for ever and ever" (p. 162). The whippings seem to be a monstrous perversion of childbearing—an attempt by unnatural means to make blood other than her own flow. Addie's hatred stems, of course, from stasis, from being confined within the schoolhouse and within the rudimentary life of the intellect. That is why she seeks comfort, at the close of each day, by the foot of the hill where the spring bubbles up and away; the spring is at once her attribute and her personal release, emblematic of feminine motion. Unconsciously, however, she is also seeking the source of motion and of life; she attempts to become the source of that motion among schoolchildren.

In the spring season, she can no longer bear this inert living, with the geese streaming high and faint and wild up the northern sky. So she takes Anse, whom she first sees sitting atop his moving wagon like a tall humped bird. It is only after she has discovered in Anse the deadness of words that she understands her schoolhouse dilemma: "I knew that it had been, not that they had dirty noses, but that we had had to use one another by words like spiders dangling by their mouths from a beam, swinging and twisting and never touching, and that only through the blows of the switch could my blood and their blood flow as one stream" (p. 164). She is seeking a kind of sacramental union (mother with child) not available to consciousness (which can only abstract and differentiate); but she employs terrible and sacrificial means until she can discover the deeper meaning of blood in motion: transformation. Through childbirth, her blood not only begins to flow with another blood, but it shapes, begets, transforms that other blood. Addie's blood-element is really the central symbol of the feminine transformation mysteries; from menstruation through pregnancy to feeding and death, woman reveals her numinous power to create and destroy in this her element. Lifeblood is then both emblem and essence of her awesome domination in the human world. Addie contains an ambivalent female capacity to create or to destroy.

The final "terrible" entity to which Addie gives a complex valence is her adultery with the preacher, Whitfield. Having learned of the generative capacity of blood, of the identity she shares with earth, and, most of all, of the deadness of words, she goes to the man believing "that the reason was the duty to the alive, to the terrible blood, the red bitter flood boiling through the land" (p. 166). The word "terrible," it seems, is carrying throughout a double valence (aweful/ghastly) even as Addie's attitude is maintaining her symbolic ambivalence (hating life/committing herself to it). For when Addie meets her lover, as Caddy Compson meets hers, in the woods, their sin is "terrible" for opposite reasons: his "since he was the instrument ordained by God who created the sin, to sanctify that sin He had created" (p. 166), hers since their act must transport the preacher beyond the lifeless realm of a patriarchal god where sin is sanctified merely by words. She says, "I would think of the sin as garments which we would remove in order to shape and coerce the terrible blood to the forlorn echo of the dead word high in the air" (p. 167). "Sin" marks her vital battle with the male concept; she attempts to make the word one with the deed, for she has heard "the dark land talking the voiceless speech" (p. 167), a "dark voicelessness in which the words are the deeds," utterly remote from "the other words that are not deeds" (p. 166). She seems to be successful in the attempt, for Jewel is begot of her effort, the son who not only defines her as the good mother, but who "will be my salvation. He will save me from the water and from the fire. Even though I have laid down my life, he will save me" (p. 160).

After Addie dies, she draws Anse into this same terrific struggle to coerce the terrible blood into a high, dead, nigh-unreachable word. In her lifetime however, she is betrayed first by her husband, then by her lover, both of whom retreat into the refuge of words (love, safety, what you will). She is left alone then with her "wild blood," transforming the "doing" beneath the trees into the nourishing and protective warmth of mothering: "And so I have cleaned my house. With Jewel—I lay by the lamp, holding up my own head, watching him cap and suture it before he breathed—the wild blood boiled away and the sound of it ceased. Then there was only the milk, warm and calm, and I lying calm in the slow silence, getting ready to clean my house" (p. 168).

In the icon of a blood-generating madonna and in the symbol of a blood-shedding priestess, Addie Bundren configures the totality of the archetypal feminine in human form. The content of her monologue creates an antimony which is reflected in the course of her burial journey. While she is alive, she is accented negatively in

her "hatred" of life, but she is also empowered to bear life; after
she is dead, she is projected as Demeter-Styx, the terrible goddess
of death, but also the life-giving mother by the process of her death.
This ambivalence is the life of the myth.

The final task which Addie sets herself before she dies is "cleaning
up the house afterward" (p. 168). It is an action which she commences in life and continues in death. The moment her intention
is out, she says "I gave Anse Dewey Dell to negative Jewel." She
means literally, of course, that her husband's daughter is a kind of
balancing for the child with which Anse has been cuckolded;
"housecleaning" results initially in the increase of life. In a
broader sense, however, Dewey Dell reflects the negativity of her
mother in the act of conception. For although the girl has on
occasion been identified as an earthmother,[11] it is equally true that
her obsessive desire on the trip to Jefferson is to find the means for
an abortion.

Dewey Dell is the one family member who says almost nothing
about her mother. She is preoccupied, of course, with a problem
more urgent to her than her mother's death; but that explanation
belies the basic artistic reason for this silence. She is the mirror
image of her mother. Her hatred for the male consciousness of Darl
which probes and violates her privacy, her *"agony and the despair
of spreading bones, the hard girdle in which lie the outraged entrails of
events"* (pp. 114–15, Faulkner's italics), and her assertion that "the
process of coming unalone is terrible" (p. 59) all parallel or echo her
mother's hatred of life. Nevertheless, her name and her deterministic
posture toward her lover in the woods put her, like Addie with
Whitfield and like the Addie-Jewel-Madonna figure, in possession
of the positive attributes of the primordial mother. Her identification
as well, with the warm, hot, moaning cow (Io was worshipped in
Egypt and in Greece as the cow mother) and with the procreative
powers of earth ("I feel like a wet seed wild in the hot blind earth"
[p. 61]) links her to life forces which are both part of and beyond her.
Dewey Dell is then mythically ambivalent in a way similar to her
mother. Although she is disposed toward destroying incipient life,

she learns on the course of the journey that, for her at least, abortion is impossible and she must now reconcile herself to the forces of life, sitting atop the wagon and awaiting the return journey home. She too is drawn into motion and change by Addie's continuing act of cleaning her "house." So in a natural and a symbolic manner, life is maintained through the bitter and terrible movement of the burial journey. In a mythic sense, the daughter becomes the mother, and the death goddess reveals her disposition toward the renewal of life.

The final matter which must be considered, then, is the effect which this mythic mother has upon the male life around her, for, like Caddy, she prompts them to speak out. Before examining, however, the composite picture projected by Darl, Jewel, Cash, Vardaman, and Anse, it is revealing to note how a social characterization of woman is counterpointed to the symbolic presentation of Addie. In *The Sound and the Fury* the terribleness of the mother was explained in social terms. In *As I Lay Dying*, however, the suprapersonal character of the terrible mother is dissociated from the personalistic portrait of a terrible woman. For Cora Tull, that domestic fishwife and neighbouring busybody, appoints herself as the judge of Addie's life and as the janitor of her soul. " 'God gave you children,' " she says, " 'to comfort your hard human lot and for a token of His own suffering and love, for in love you conceived and bore them.' I said that because she took God's love and her duty to Him too much as a matter of course, and such conduct is not pleasing to Him" (p. 158). Despite her presumption of knowledge, her self-assurance, and her fundamentalist self-righteousness, she is absolutely wrong in each of her successive judgements.

When Darl stands in the doorway of his mother's bedroom, Cora says, "He just stood and looked at his dying mother, his heart too full for words" (p. 24). She is superficially correct, but her underlying misperception contributes to high irony. For looking only upon the outwardness of human action, and being predisposed by certain social expectations, she cannot see Darl's heart filled with yearning hatred, nor does she recognize the unfolding of a mythic action before her sightless eyes. Even Darl can see a quiet holiness in the tableau of Addie and the infant Jewel (p. 137), but Cora says "She just sat there, lost in her vanity and her pride, that had closed her heart to God and set that selfish mortal boy in His place.

Kneeling there I prayed for her. I prayed for that poor blind woman as I had never prayed for me and mine" (p. 160). Her husband Vernon has already depicted her, however, as a humorous deistic substitute for the Christian Father God: "I reckon if there's ere a man or woman anywhere that He could turn it all over to and go away with His mind at rest, it would be Cora. And I reckon she would make a few changes, no matter how He was running it. And I reckon they would be for man's good. Leastways, we would have to like them. Leastways, we might as well go on and make like we did" (p. 70). Tull's view of his wife, though speaking more fluently of him and his household situation than of a truly numinous female character, proposes the supersedence of a father God in the novel and bespeaks, once again, the extent of the failure of Protestant Christianity to provide a regnant authority in religious symbolism. From Addie's perspective, Cora Tull is but the handmaiden of a god of words, herself a perfect manifestation of his powerlessness. Addie's final renunciation of her is then made on Cora's own grounds, in the light of her social and economic ambitions: "Like Cora, who could never even cook" (p. 166).

Addie's "household" affairs, on the other hand, present a numin- ous picture; her impression upon a male world of husband and sons (like Caddy Compson's impression upon her brothers) is profoundly inexplicable. The manner of Addie's presentation is also similar to Caddy's; excepting her single monologue, she too exists as an oblique presence in her own story, seen while still alive through other eyes, and felt when dead as a continuing force.

Since a full third of the narrative of *As I Lay Dying* (nineteen of fifty-nine monologues) is conveyed through the consciousness of Darl, he tends to serve as the major narrative index to the figure of his mother. Nevertheless, as one critic observes, "She is the only character watched and remembered by Darl, the artist, whom he does not, in Tull's words, take us 'inside of.' She remains shadowy in all his reflections, ubiquitous and defining but undefined" (Waggoner, p. 83). Considering the intuitive power of Darl to enter into the minds of those about him, Addie's inviolability is crucial; she is beyond the power of his logical consciousness to sift and fathom.

Earlier, Darl's all but mad attempt to found his being in pure rationality was outlined. The crux of his syllogism bears repeating:

"Yet the wagon *is*, because when the wagon is *was*, Addie Bundren will not be. And Jewel *is*, so Addie Bundren must be. And then I must be. . . ." Addie is actually dead now, but the wagon and Jewel (which Darl intuits as his mother's symbolic elements) *are*; if they exist, so does she; then crucially, if Addie *is*, Darl can still exist. Darl betrays three things here about the workings of his mind: Jewel and the wagon have intrinsic life because they are associated with Addie; Darl cannot (though he would like to) exist independently of his mother's being, yet symbolically he has not identified himself with her; the only way Darl can make himself a part of her (and so keep both of them alive) is by logical connection. Nevertheless, he ultimately denies having any dependent association with her as, speaking to Vardaman who is confident of mother-defined relationships, he repudiates his woman-begetting: [Vardaman]: "I am. Darl is my brother. 'But you *are*, Darl,' I said. 'I know it,' Darl said. 'That's why I am not *is*. *Are* is too many for one woman to foal' " (p. 95, Faulkner's italics). Darl's existence is then more real to him after Addie's death since, inversely, her existence now depends upon his syllogisms.

Apparently, this must explain why Darl, in the course of the burial journey, is so desperately concerned that Addie should "lay down her life." For even he is not completely free from a belief in her unremitting, vital presence. With the coffin resting under the apple tree on the Gillespie farm, he shares with Vardaman the impression that their mother speaks in a "secret and murmurous bubbling" (p. 202):

> "What is she saying, Darl?" I say. "Who is she talking to?"
> "She's talking to God," Darl says. "She is calling on Him to help her."
> "What does she want Him to do?" I say.
> "She wants Him to hide her away from the sight of man," Darl says.
> "Why does she want to hide her away from the sight of man, Darl?"
> "So she can lay down her life," Darl says. (pp. 204–5)

Even before his mother's death, however, Darl has been resisting doggedly the movement toward Jefferson. To spite both Jewel and Addie, he takes his brother beyond reach of the dying woman. As the two of them ride the wagon into the approaching storm for a load of wood, Darl says, "Jewel . . . do you know that Addie Bundren is going to die? Addie Bundren is going to die?" (p. 39). Later, he bespeaks the same attitude: "*Jewel, I say, she is dead, Jewel. Addie Bundren is dead*" (p. 51, Faulkner's italics); " 'It's not your horse that's dead, Jewel,' I say. . . . 'But it's not your horse that's dead' " (p. 88). His taunting repetitions, his mockery of Jewel's affections, and his unconcern over Jewel's outrage (" 'Goddamn you,' he says. 'Goddamn you' " [p. 88], all testify to Darl's obsessive hatred; he exults, in fact, gloats over his mother's death, and he goads his brother Jewel unmercifully. His gestures do more, however, than separate the dying mother and son; they delay the journey to Jefferson until the bridge is washed out. The consequent "terribleness" aboard the wagon is accented throughout by Darl's resistance to its motion. When the wagon capsizes in the swollen river, he makes no attempt whatever to save the coffin from the current; Cash breaks his leg, as a result, and Darl "fixes" it in concrete. But Jewel retrieves his mother's casket and the journey proceeds inexorably. So Darl is driven despairingly at last to burn Gillespie's barn, hoping in this way to end the unexpected continuance of his mother's power. As long as the journey continues, Addie is symbolically alive; she is still a reproof to his self-contained consciousness.

Darl's feeling that he is not a part of his mother is more than an expression of sibling rivalry. Addie's rejection of him is absolute; it is the most terrible thing she does. The only reason given is her cryptic statement that Darl was conceived at a time when she believed herself to be beyond further violation: "Then I found that I had Darl. At first I would not believe it. Then I believed that I would kill Anse. It was as though he had tricked me, hidden within a word like within a paper screen and struck me in the back through it. But then I realised that I had been tricked by words older than Anse or love, and that the same word had tricked Anse too" (p. 164). Addie's explanation is clear in the outcome, but quite opaque in the cause; for Darl cannot literally be engendered by a word, yet he is literally made up of words. To the extent that words represent the celestial principle of the Idea, Darl's very countenance reveals his opposition to feminine being; Dewey Dell describes him "at the supper table with his eyes gone further than the food and the lamp, full of the land dug out of his skull and the holes filled with distance beyond the land" (pp. 25–26). Again, just before she has in fantasy killed Darl, she says, "The land runs out of Darl's eyes; they swim to pinpoints. They begin at my feet and rise along my body to my face, and then my dress is gone" (p. 115). Although Darl has expressed woman's true nature in his glimpse of Dewey Dell's leg as "that lever which moves the world; one of that caliper which measures the length and breadth of life" (p. 98), the girl seems justified in her ambivalent hatred of him. His un-earthly "violation" of her repeats Anse's violation of Addie with a word. He may rightly identify her (as Addie too has been identified) with the earth itself: "Squatting, Dewey Dell's wet dress shapes for the dead eyes of three blind men those mammalian ludicrosities which are the horizons and the valleys of the earth" (p. 156); yet acknowledging his own dead eyes, he nevertheless sees only absurdity in the horizons and valleys of that mothering earth. Thus, in his non-earthly identity, through his syllogistic imperatives, in his frequent monologues, and by his resistance to the "doing" of the journey, he emerges as Addie's major antagonist. His eloquent but static rationality is finally engaged in a life-or-death struggle with her forces of motion, development, and change. For what is really at stake along the way to Jefferson is transformation; whether in life or in death, the feminine will not forsake her vital character.

When Addie claims to have been tricked by a word in Darl's conception, she says "that my revenge would be that he would never know I was taking revenge. And when Darl was born I asked Anse to promise to take me back to Jefferson when I died" (pp. 164–65). Literally (and at first, perniciously) she wants to retaliate against the father-son-word the only way she knows how: by discharging herself from the family after death. In time, however, she learns that her "duty [was] to the alive"; symbolically, then, her revenge goes much further than her own self-satisfaction. Anse is now bound—if he values his word—to transform it into the deed; the trip to Jefferson is meant to change what he, at base, *stands* for. He too must finally cast the son most like him ("Darl, the one that folks say is queer, lazy, pottering about the place no better than Anse" [p. 23], the one who most resembles his father "looking out over the land . . . with eyes [that] look like pieces of burnt-out cinder" [pp. 30–31]) out of the maternally active family. In this sense, Addie is the collective anima of the family, the transpersonal

factor in man driving toward growth and permutation; the transformation she brings about in each male will be positive or negative,
depending on the attitude of consciousness toward her.

As Darl sits atop the wagon bound inexorably for Jefferson, he
at one point acknowledges his mother's absolute ascendancy. While
they approach the sign reading "New Hope Church. 3 mi." (where
Addie would be given Christian burial), he thinks, "It wheels up
like a motionless hand lifted above the profound desolation of the
ocean; beyond it the red road lies like a spoke of which Addie
Bundren is the rim" (p. 102). It is a statement at once painful and
profound. For Addie, in a symbolic sense, is the rim of the flat land
containing all life; she is also the rim of the vertical wheel (of
which the red road is only a spoke) which has trundled the entire
family into motion. Darl glimpses the meaning of her Great
Round, yet he cannot understand why he is shut "outside the
circle"; he senses the cortège as his final repudiation, but he does
not recognize his word convolutions as the reason. For he refuses,
despite his recognition, to move; he is committed to the permanence
and self-sufficiency of thought. It is he, then, more than his father,
Anse, who is most accurately depicted in the image of cold molasses
and a motionless jar. His last desperate attempt to stop the journey
ends not only in failure (Jewel rescues the coffin from the fire) but
in downfall; on reaching Jefferson, Addie's burial ground, he is
thrown down from the wagon (significantly, it is Dewey Dell who
is on him first) and packed off to the Jackson madhouse. So the end
of the road for Darl leads to the breakdown of his logically conceived order (madness) and to individual dissolution (he speaks
throughout his final monologue in the third person).

The artist, it should be remarked, is not antipathetic to Darl's
predicament of consciousness; his quandary seems, symbolically,
to be the artist's own dilemma, for Darl is a poet both in his lyric
utterance and in his intuitive capacity to enter the minds of other
characters. Even his hatred cannot exclude him from our sym-
pathies; at one point Darl says, "I cannot love my mother because
I have no mother" (p. 89). His situation and his poignant expression
of despair are deeply reminiscent of Quentin Compson's *"if I'd just
had a mother so I could say Mother Mother "* (Faulkner's italics).
Faulkner's own struggle with the anima, however, does not permit
him to stop with Darl in the latter's desperate quest for spiritual

autonomy. The transformations which occur in his art are the record of Faulkner's private coming to terms with an archetypal factor.

It is Cash who takes over from Darl the role of narrator in the conclusion of the novel. Entirely taciturn, pragmatic, and rational at the outset (the first of his five monologues is a kind of carpenter's syllogism; the next two are only a few concerned sentences on coffin balance), he is greatly changed in the course of the journey. His fourth monologue marks the extent of the transformation which is now taking place in his thinking. Although the sympathy he expresses for Darl is couched in the practical, common sense terms of the old Cash, he has abandoned the unfeeling world of "things" and of rigid logic. He still cannot justify the deliberate destruction of another man's labour, but he says "I aint so sho that ere a man has the right to say what is crazy and what aint. It's like there was a fellow in every man that's done a-past the sanity or the insanity, that watches the sane and the insane doings of that man with the same horror and the same astonishment" (p. 228).

Cash, as much as Jewel, however, has been throughout a beloved son of the Mother—Addie, speaking of love, says "Cash did not need to say it to me nor I to him" (p. 164); the infant loved by his mother grows to be a man of deeds; and Addie, in the absence of Jewel, calls out to him at the moment of her death—and he continues that relationship in his silent agony on the wagon. He is not resistant, like Darl, to the process of change; his quiet acceptance of the furthering journey, whatever pain its continuance will cost him, earns him a share in the praise his mother has been given already by Anse: "But couldn't no woman strove harder than Addie to make them right, man and boy: I'll say that for her" (p. 37). His final two monologues then complete a triumphant union of deeds (his mother's sphere) with words (the male element); his practical wisdom together with his deepening humanity recapitulate Addie's recognition that her real duty is "to the alive." Perhaps Cash seems less obsessed than Addie with the terribleness of living, but his cited observation speaks of the terrible sanity-insanity of the entire journey. If what Darl has done seems hardly more horrific than what the rest of the family have done in staying with the stinking wagon, Cash offers a concluding remark on Darl which uncovers his pathology: "This world is not his world; this life his life" (p. 250). For Darl, like Quentin, is thoroughly committed to an anti-maternal world of pure spirit. Whether these identical dispositions are caused by or provoke a lack of mother-love, they are subject to the same "terrible" fate. To accept Darl's point of view, then, as the narrative centre is to miss the significance of the novel's outcome. The climax of his resistance to the mother archetype is psychic death; it is this "I" of consciousness which, like his mother's "I," lies dying at the story's end. In this sense, Addie has accomplished the negative side of cleaning her house; it only remains for her to bring the dependent "we" (the feminine "we" of mother and child) within her defining limits.

Jewel is the son of Addie's attempt to make the word one with the deed; as such, he is the one family member predisposed to continuing his mother's life and love for him in her own medium of doing. His furious and relentless energy overcomes the river, the roaring flames, and Darl's inertia, while bringing the journey to its promised issuance.

By all appearances, Jewel has gone beyond the transformative sphere of the goddess; he is more the agent than the object of her influence. Nevertheless, two image complexes bespeak her continuing transformative effect on him while further reinforcing his identity as the beloved son of the good mother. Most frequently, these images are evoked by Darl (although Dewey Dell makes the same connections on occasion), and they occur as early as the novel's opening monologue: "Still staring straight ahead, his pale eyes like wood set into his wooden face, he crosses the floor in four strides with the rigid gravity of a cigar store Indian dressed in patched overalls and endued with life from the hips down . . ." (p. 4). When Jewel approaches his horse, "they are like two figures carved for a tableau savage in the sun" (p. 12); and when he returns to the wagon, having sacrificed his horse in payment for the mules, he comes "up the road behind us, wooden-backed, wooden-faced, moving only from his hips down" (p. 198). Initially it might seem as if Darl is trying to deaden Jewel's furious, passionate nature by encasing it in the fixity of carven wood. If so, Darl does not perceive the self-same identity in his mother's body, however altered now by death; Peabody says, "Beneath the quilt she is no more than a bundle of rotten sticks" (p. 43). It is Jewel too, and not Darl, who pictures "her hands laying on the quilt like two of them roots dug up and tried to wash and you couldn't get them clean" (p. 15). Faulkner returns to the maternal tree symbol here (recalling Caddy Compson), except that now "wood" is also son to the feminine, and her transformative power over it is stamped into the material as though it were shaped from her own substance.

Perhaps tree-transformation mysteries also account for a similar tableau elsewhere in the book where Cash, the mother's other well-beloved son, stands in front of her window, fashioning the wood for Addie's coffin. Since the containing character of the tree as coffin is a central symbol of the mother of death, it is fitting that one of her sons should assist its coming into shape. So in this context, the carpenter might be likened to a priest of the Great Mother, ritually performing her mysteries.

Jewel, however, is deeply angered by the "One lick less" of the carpenter's adze. In his brief monologue, the only time he expresses himself in words, he registers his furious and violent desire to isolate his mother and himself out of the loud world: "It would just be me and her on a high hill and me rolling the rocks down the hill at their faces, picking them up and throwing them down the hill faces and teeth and all by God until she was quiet . . ." (p. 15). We have noted Jewel's allusions here to mother earth and to the goddess of death; there are equally resonant echoes, however, from Faulkner's previous work. Jewel's vision seems remarkably similar to Quentin's fantasy of incest with his sister Caddy, intended "to isolate her out of the loud world so that it would have to flee us of necessity and then the sound of it would be as though it had never been" (SF, p. 220). Upon further consideration, though, Jewel's intention is seen inversely; for where Quentin would deny by intellect the sexual principle of life and so negate living in a static concept of eternal punishment, Jewel would by his desperate energy save Addie from the necessity of dying. He would thus affirm the undying sexual bond of mother and child: he would make it as though it had always been, the two of them enclosed in a world of their own. This tableau of Jewel's exclusiveness in Addie—as the pure expression of mother and son—is recalled by Darl (and then intuited by Cash) while they yet face the river crossing: "When he was born, he had a bad time of it. Ma would sit in the lamp-light, holding him on a pillow on her lap. We would wake and find her so. There would be no sound from them. 'That pillow was longer than him,' Cash says" (p. 137). Addie herself, in the only other Madonna portrait in the book, reaffirms the unique and living bond with the son of her wild "doing"—with Jewel taking the warm milk from her breast "and I lying calm in the slow silence, getting ready to clean my house" (p. 168). In each of the three monologues, the finally dominant impression is of silence and a kind of wordless communion flowing between mother and child. Thus, "lying calm" to give life to the infant, Addie prefigures the lying she will do on the wagon to renew the life of the family.

The other symbol configuration which helps to shape Jewel's relation to his mother lies in his association with his horse. We have already seen the two of them, man and beast, identified in wooden tableau, carved "savage in the sun"; Darl, after professing that he has no mother, says "Jewel's mother is a horse" (p. 89). Anse also gives an indication that the horse, in its "longways" relation to the earth, is symbolic of the female element. Like roads, wagons, and woman, the horse is an agent of motion. Motion and life, for Faulkner, are identical energies;[12] one is inconceivable except in terms of the other. Then what is found in Jewel's horse is an equation of motion, life, and the transforming power of the mother archetype. The horse which he has earned by "terrible" doing—cleaning forty acres of new ground through five months of sleepless nights—becomes Addie's means of inner motion in her son. When the flooded river turns the team of mules belly up, Jewel gives up the horse without a word so that the journey might continue. It is, as one critic says, "the most heroic thing he does" (Brooks, *Yoknapatawpha Country*, p. 162). Jewel, in this pure expression of selflessness, is revealed as utterly unlike Jason, that other beloved son of a destructive mother; his transformation is part of the supreme achievement of the feminine. For Jewel has surrendered his individual propensity for motion to his mother's need to continue the journey; he moves from the dead world of "I" to her living world of "we." When Darl says "Jewel's mother is a horse," he says quite poetically that the Addie Jewel knows is the positive aspect of the goddess, the mother of life and not, as for him, the mother of death.

To Vardaman as well, Addie and the horse are an equatable life force. The moment the woman dies, the young boy runs, crying, to the barn where Jewel's horse becomes a ritual solace to him through the stroking and smelling of its skin. In a sense it is one confirmation of the ongoing character of his mother's life: "The life in him runs under the skin, under my hand, running through the splotches, smelling up into my nose where the sickness is beginning to cry, vomiting the crying, and then I can breathe, vomiting it. It makes a lot of noise. I can smell the life running up from under my hands, up my arms, and then I can leave the stall" (p. 53). Vardaman also ratifies Dr. Peabody's notion that death is a form of movement, "no more than a single tenant or family moving out of a tenement or a town." The boy says, "And now she is getting so far ahead I cannot catch her" (p. 52). It is rather appropriate that he should run to the horse, the representative of motion and the carrier of men; symbolically, it is his only hope of overtaking her.

Likewise, the fish which Vardaman catches and chops up on the afternoon of his mother's death becomes for the boy an important corroboration of Addie's continuing life. It is so emphatic, in fact, that the single sentence, "My mother is a fish," (p. 79) constitutes one terse chapter of the novel. In his anguish of mind, Vardaman thinks of the fish in sacramental terms; it too appears to be a giver of life, or, when ritually eaten, to be metamorphosed into the lives of its partakers: "It's laying in the kitchen in the bleeding pan, waiting to be cooked and et. Then it wasn't and she was, and now it is and she wasn't. And tomorrow it will be cooked and et and she will be him and pa and Cash and Dewey Dell and there wont be anything in the box and so she can breathe" (pp. 63–64). Faced at last with the physical stench and the social realities of death, the boy denies the evidence of his senses, holding doggedly to the mythic belief that his mother will appear again: *"Darl says that when we come to the water again I might see her and Dewey Dell said, She's in the box; how could she have got out? She got out through the holes I bored, into the water I said, and when we come to the water again I am going to see her. My mother is not in the box. My mother does not smell like that. My mother is a fish"* (p. 187, Faulkner's italics). And when the coffin does get away in the stream, he sees her in motion as a fish, the natural reason why "in the water she could go faster than a man" (p. 143). His relentless belief, then, in the mythic efficacy of the fish becomes a moving affirmation of life in the face of actual death.

At one point in the narrative, the affinity of horse and fish is accentuated by juxtaposition:

"Jewel's mother is a horse," Darl said.
"Then mine can be a fish, cant it, Darl?" I said. "Jewel is my brother."
"Then mine will have to be a horse, too," I said. (p. 95)

There is no certain difference in Vardaman's mind between them, although they give Darl a chance to play upon the truth of differing paternities. To Vardaman, they are both life-giving mothers, so he is not disturbed very greatly at the prospect of choosing; they share the same totemic function. For in the child-mind of a ten-year-old boy and in the unconscious passions of the man Jewel, Faulkner does seem to have evoked totems—"natural objects bearing deeply felt relations to human beings"[13]—by which each feels his individual kinship to and his private unity with the goddess. Among primitive peoples, totemic sacrifice is the most effective means of achieving oneness with what is sacred; it most often entails a communal killing, a feast of flesh, and a mimed resurrection—as though what dies is never really dead (*Themis*, pp. 141–43). Vardaman, bedaubed with fish blood and fish guts, enters more literally than Jewel into totem sacrifice; but for both of them, the horse and the fish operate as symbolic extensions of their mother's life, admitting no division between the living and the dead.[14] The totem symbols abrogate the boys' aloneness after their mother's death; they serve to hold splintering "I's" together in the feminine and family "we."

Addie completes the cleaning of her house by uprooting Anse and by placing him aboard a wagon. For Anse, who has hated even the rain "a-coming up that road like a durn man" (p. 36), gives in at last to the very naturalness of roads; he moves from the stasis of word-consciousness to a state where the word and the deed are one. He goes to Jefferson ostensibly to keep his promise to his dead wife— to prove that words have a binding life—yet the stress of the journey proves that words are lifeless unless they are continuously translated into action. By his own admission, Anse enters into the doing that goes terribly along the earth because Addie's "mind is set on it"; her effect upon him is the fullest testimony to her positive, life-giving power.

In some quarters, Anse has been the subject of critical abuse for his platitudinous acceptance of Addie's death, for his refusal to buy a shovel with which to dig her grave, for his self-indulgent desire to finish the trip so that he can get new teeth in Jefferson. It is said that "Cushioned by words and conventional sentiments against the harsh impact of reality, he is the only one of the Bundrens completely unchanged by Addie's death or by the funeral journey. The horrors which drive Darl into insanity and leave their mark on the others pass him by so that he avoids agony and insight alike."[15] This is to mistake, it seems, Darl's insanity for change that has been effected by his insight into the journey, where his madness is actually occasioned by his stasis of mind and by his inability to bring the cortège to a standstill. It is also to mistake Anse's sayings for the inner man. The following portrait, which gives him the deepest and most touching sort of contradictory humanity, is narrated by Darl *in absentia*:

Pa stands over the bed, dangle-armed, humped, motionless. He raises his hand to his head, scouring his hair, listening to the saw. He comes nearer and rubs his hand, palm and back, on his thigh and lays it on her face and then on the hump of quilt where her hands are. He touches the quilt as he saw Dewey Dell do, trying to smoothe it up to the chin, but disarranging it instead. He tries to smoothe it again, clumsily, his hand awkward as a claw, smoothing at the wrinkles which he made and which continue to emerge beneath his hand with perverse ubiquity, so that at last he desists, his hand falling to his side and stroking itself again, palm and back, on his thigh. The sound of the saw snores steadily into the room. Pa breathes with a quiet, rasping sound, mouthing the snuff against his gums. "God's will be done," he says. "Now I can get them teeth." (p. 51)

The man's hands give evidence of a restrained pathos, and his continuing, yet pathetic, ineffectualness to perform some act, some moving tenderness toward his dead wife, heightens his terribly effectual action on the road to Jefferson. When he gets to town, Anse will certainly "get them teeth," but it is absurd to suggest he has spent nine days in the company of a rotting corpse for that purpose; there are easier ways to get to town. The apparent crassness of his present statement serves as admirable personal and narrative restraint on what might have become mere sentimentality. So it is of the utmost importance to weigh Anse's conventional words against the inarticulateness of his movements.

Private motives for the trip do heighten characterization and lend variety and humour to the story, but these personal issues do not detract from the seriousness of the ritual procession to Jefferson. For no matter how leech-like Anse may be in his seemingly astonished self-pity, and notwithstanding his perennial willingness to let his neighbours wade so deep in his aid that "Returning were as tedious as go o'er," there is still his dogged and heroic insistence in this one instance to bear Addie in their wagon with their own team because *"She'll want it so"* (p. 87, Faulkner's italics). Nor can one ignore his unquestioned imperative that the deed be confined within the family; for Anse refuses all offers of assistance, bartering his cultivator and seeder, his false teeth fund, Cash's "graphophone" money, and even Jewel's horse in exchange for a gaunt team of mules from trader Snopes. His claim that "she wouldn't have us beholden" (p. 186) points up his commitment not to self but to the family "we" as it still relates to Addie. His unaccustomed determination to be independent of the Tulls and Samsons and Armstids is the fullest measure of his novel dependence on the woman's will. Nevertheless it is also Anse's will which is literally responsible for the fierce pride displayed by the Bundrens on the exacting road to the Jefferson cemetery.

The nervous witticisms of Anse's neighbours offer final proof that a different and more ominous Anse has been drawn into motion. Samson says, "I notice how it takes a lazy man, a man that hates moving, to get set on moving once he does get started off, the same as he was set on staying still, like it aint the moving he hates so much as the starting and the stopping. And like he would be kind of proud of whatever come up to make the moving or the setting still look hard" (p. 108). Anse is comically translated into a physics textbook definition of inertia, though as a body in motion he is much more awesome and frightening than he is funny. Laughter is a rather uneasy defense mechanism in the face of those powers which have put him in motion; lampooning is perhaps the only means the "sensible" people have of coming to terms with the man or with his motives. Vernon Tull, Bundren's one faithful and committed friend, would laughingly disparage Anse's critics, yet his ambivalent jest serves in its own way to caricature the man, to tag him with a monstrous shadow: "If it's a judgment, it aint right. Because the Lord's got more to do than that. He's bound to have. Because the only burden Anse Bundren's ever had is himself. And when folks talks him low, I think to myself he aint that less of a man or he couldn't a bore himself this long" (p. 70). The irony of Tull's character recommendation is that the burden Anse now bears is different in kind from "himself"; the impetus of the dead woman behind him and the living anima inside him make him a thoroughly redoubtable man. He is at last representative of the dark and terrible voicelessness in which the word and the deed are one; he, like Cash and Jewel, has become living testimony to the trans-formative power of Addie.

The last word on Anse, however, must be about his "doings" when the outbound journey is ended. Having refused assistance all the way into Jefferson, the first thing he does upon arrival is to borrow a set of spades. He stops at a Mrs. *Bundren's* house (p. 225); the woman cannot be kin to him, because he takes her back with him as his bride in conclusion. This "duck-shaped woman" is by no means Addie (even if Addie's yearning for life and motion is greatly intensified by the sound of wild geese overhead), and yet this nominal identity suggests that the first wife also undergoes a type of symbolic transformation. This new Mrs. Bundren who returns from Jefferson has already been anticipated in the "old" Mrs. Bundren who lies reversed in the coffin, wearing "her wedding dress [that] . . . had a flare-out bottom" (p. 83); Addie, as well as Anse, has gone to town to be "married." In other words, it appears that Anse, in laying Addie to rest, has exorcised the "terrible" side of his anima; he returns home with his wife and family to a scene of idyllic contentment, "setting in the house in the winter" (p. 250), and listening to the music from the graphophone which, as Cash says, is "about the nicest thing a fellow can have" (p. 248).

In overview, several things remain to be said about the particular expression of the myth of woman in *As I Lay Dying*. The wagon which configures Addie's transformative power is not, like the mare-fish mother, historically recognizable as an archaic symbol; nonetheless it is an authentic symbol because something inexplicable looms behind the dead woman's identification with its motion. Dr.

Peabody's glimpse of death as no more than a family moving out of a town makes the wagon lead at last, like the road, into mystery. Likewise, the mythos of the novel suggests the presence of a numinous power in human (though decaying) form. For Addie's burial trip to Jefferson is both a death-dealing and a life-giving journey. The image antinomy of her monologue has already established the pattern for her active ambivalence; her inexplicable will to die results in the casting out of the male principle of absolute death—the static intellect of Darl—and in the bringing of new life and harmony into the family. In this respect, Addie is one with the sacrificial goddess of archaic myth who, by her death, brings "Cosmos" once again out of "Chaos."[16] She is not, as has been suggested, the inversion of the Demeter-Kore myth of fertility,[17] but its supreme triumph; for the profound truth of the Eleusinian mysteries is that the mother and daughter are one, that the mother of death is the same person as the mother of life.[18]

One is led at last to conclude that *As I Lay Dying* is not in any sense a mock epic as some commentators have claimed,[19] that Faulkner is, in fact, writing about the very wellsprings of heroic action, maybe more truthfully even than those ancient poets who long have sung of Helen as the mother of the siege of Troy, of its terrible and glorious feats. At the same time, the novel is comic if not mock: comic in the larger sense of being fully optimistic. For although Caddy has received positive emotional emphasis in *The Sound and the Fury*, and Addie is more negatively accented in the present novel, yet Addie's transformative power in death has positive results while the thwarting of Caddy's power in life has a negative effect. Where the stasis of male consciousness and social prescriptions have redirected the feminine will in the prior work, Addie's will in this book is absolute and irresistible; it triumphs over the deadness of the intellect and conventional social forms. *As I Lay Dying* is a novel of full cosmic optimism because it affirms the encompassing mother of death, this time as an archetypal figure who must die herself to bring new life into the world. One critic has remarked that the theme of this book "would seem to invite the dividing of people into those who accept the bitterness and violence of living and those who do not."[20] However accurate this may be, Faulkner himself in *Dying* accepts the bitterness and violence of living, in fact, celebrates the deathly aspect of his muse.

5

The Profaned Temple

Rational Crime and Draconian Justice in *Sanctuary*

Literary estimates of *Sanctuary* have invariably been influenced by one of two questions (even where these questions have not been asked directly): first, how far did the revisions of a "cheap idea"[1] go toward redeeming it as a work of art; and second, in what sense is the final version of a heretofore "horrorific tale"[2] pessimistic. Faulkner raised the first question himself in a notorious preface to the 1932 reprint of the novel, but he also set the standard for serious evaluation when he wrote that, in tearing down the galleys and in rewriting the book, he tried "to make out of it something which would not shame *The Sound and the Fury* and *As I Lay Dying* too much and I made a fair job. . . ." (p. vii). Recent criticism is generally agreed that early antagonists of the book never read the latter half of Faulkner's introduction, and that *Sanctuary* ranks deservedly alongside the two works published immediately prior to it. The first full study of the galley revisions, however, reverses the accepted estimate, claiming that "far from reworking a lurid sex story into a more significant work, Faulkner seems to have had a single practical purpose—to turn a slow-moving psychological study into a streamlined drama ready for the cameras of Hollywood. The intricate pattern of flashbacks and shifting perspectives was discarded for a chronological presentation that plays down the impact of events on Horace and thus highlights the sensationalism of the story of Temple Drake."[3]

This judgement renews some of the oldest potboiler suspicions about *Sanctuary*, except that now the published novel—not the unrevised galley-version—is said to be the more vulgar work. It can be readily admitted, even from a cursory collation of the novel with the galleys at Virginia,[4] that "the story as Faulkner first wrote it was unmistakably focused on Horace as the protagonist" (*Revision*, p. 8) and that the effect of the revisions is to focus the whole more sharply on Temple as a kind of protagonist-antagonist. It is less certain, however, that the novel is marred by a structural split between these two characters, or that the story of the coquette is exploited for its lurid sensationalism. The plot has been streamlined in explicit contours of cause and effect precisely because new lines of force are thereby revealed; the horror of Temple's story is heightened for a reason which grows directly out of this force field.

Those critics who have recognized in Temple Drake a central character and a serious purpose are mutually concerned about the pessimism of the work. Melvin Backman does not state his concern over Temple quite forcefully enough when he says, "In her own way she proves as destructive as Popeye: she is instrumental in killing four men, Tommy, Red, Goodwin, and even Popeye himself. Like her rapist, she knows neither truth, justice, nor morality; she shares his childish but deadly egoism. This child-bitch is one of the primary degenerating forces in the world of *Sanctuary*" (p. 44). Such dual emphasis on gangster and child-bitch as the equal agents of an inexplicable presence of evil in the novel seems a diminution by division of the horror the story engenders. A crucial explanation is given for Popeye's character; yet Temple's motivation grows more obscure with the progress of the tale. We are never told why she does not simply leave the Old Frenchman place before her rape and the related murder of Tommy, why she does not escape from the bordello before Red is killed, why through an act of perjury she condemns Goodwin to trial by gasoline-fire, or why in conclusion Popeye's curious will-to-hang is just as mysteriously juxtaposed to her callous ennui in the Luxembourg Gardens. On the contrary, the symbols associated with Temple Drake suggest a more-than-human dimension.

"She closed the compact and from beneath her smart new hat she seemed to follow with her eyes the waves of music, to dissolve into the dying brasses, across the pool and the opposite semicircle of trees where at sombre intervals the dead tranquil queens in stained marble mused, and on into the sky lying prone and vanquished in the embrace of the season of rain and death":[5] Campbell and Foster are disturbed enough by the novel's final sentence to view the events of the story as finally determined and to extend what they regard as the symbolic ambivalence of the passage into a realm where human conduct is not divisible from cosmic influence, arguing that "from another standpoint it is symbolically 'the season of rain and death' which has had Temple from childhood under its control and which is the cause, and not the pathetic fallacy result, of her folly."[6] From a limited human viewpoint, *Sanctuary* is undoubtedly the most horrorific, and perhaps the most despairing, narrative Faulkner ever published. It is difficult to doubt, by story's end, that its female protagonist has substance in a cosmic and inhuman dimension: the repetition of the three variants of "dying" in the concluding sentence, the final widening perspective which opens out from Temple through the marble queens onto an all-encompassing season of doom, and the weight of the story's final word falling on "death" all contribute markedly to a tone of cosmic annihilation. Each of the men who figures importantly in the novel's opening scene at the Old Frenchman place has by now met with violent destruction or utter defeat while the focal point of the completed action sits in sullen discontent in Paris, pruning herself in a small vanity mirror, at the same time that the narrator is linking her to powers which would seem to lie beyond her, causes which are large enough to be allied with Earth herself.

That Temple's symbolic attributes are no mere fortuitous circumstance nor a late and gratuitous addition to the narrative seem to be borne out by certain recurrent images, the most notable of which is the penultimate clause, "the dead tranquil queens in stained marble mused" (p. 380). Much earlier in the story, while Temple yet maintains a fascinated equipoise between inviolacy and violation, she is described as lying on the chattering cornshuck mattress, "her hands crossed on her breast and her legs straight and close and decorous, like an effigy on an ancient tomb" (p. 84). The "effigy" is of course identified with "the dead tranquil queens in stained marble," who in turn participate, symbolically at least, in the "cosmic season of rain and death." Nonetheless, Faulkner can hardly be said to be creating only mood by his imagery (although he does so very skilfully). He is also representing the ancient death goddess in maternal form: in the feminine season which holds the masculine sky "prone and vanquished"; in the stained marble statues which muse above the gloom of the trees; in the figure of an earthly woman who presides indifferently and without regard over the demise of her would-be lovers and over the wane of the moribund year.

I suggest that the rearrangement in plot in *Sanctuary* is governed by the artist's deeper sense of the implications of his symbols—that the reduction in the role of Benbow both clarifies the meaning of Temple's presence and qualifies the pessimism of the prior account. It should be clear from the symbol complex already referred to that Temple Drake, like Addie Bundren before her, configures the deathly visage of the archetypal feminine, but that the outcome of their two stories is remarkably different. I intend, then, to demonstrate not only that *Sanctuary* fits the perspective and expression preceding it, but to establish the manner in which it makes a vital contribution to that perspective.

Although it has been suggested that the published version of *Sanctuary* is the sequel to *Sartoris* (Adams, p. 57), Millgate rightly points out that the effect of Faulkner's revisions is to reduce the role of Horace Benbow and consequently the subservience of the work to the Benbow family of an earlier novel (pp. 115–16). Alternatively, the various threads of the novel are now drawn through the loom of the Temple Drake story. This altered form can be observed even from the greatest distance; in the galley proofs, Temple's existence is not even hinted at until page 85 (approximate page proof),[7] whereas in the published version of *Sanctuary* she is met on page 31, running that much earlier toward a would-be lover. The effective restructuring of the novel breaks down the insularity of Temple's presence, confined as it virtually is to the middle third of the galleys,[8] and redistributes it in more forceful juxtaposition to the ineffectual intellect of Horace Benbow. Millgate's suggestion that Horace is retained "more firmly and specifically" as the central intelligence of the novel (p. 117) is sensible, but it must be further argued, in view of Langford's contention that Horace is depersonalized in the reworking (pp. 10–20), that his real function as a monitoring intelligence is to serve as a spokesman for the four men who die by Temple's influence. Horace, in other words, becomes a kind of composite and metaphoric mind configuring the male dilemma in relation to the dominant feminine archetype.

Before Faulkner's editing receives closer examination, however, the outline of the abandoned narrative provides a clearer indication of the kind of story the artist first set out to tell. The sandwiching effect of the initial triadic structure (Horace-Temple-Horace) strongly suggests that the Temple-plot is developed more for the sake of Benbow's criminal case than vice-versa. The opening chapter, in fact, strikingly anticipates one of Faulkner's later novels, *Intruder in the Dust* (1948), a story told quite frankly in the detective mode. The galley-*Sanctuary* begins with Horace questioning Goodwin and Ruby in jail, attempting to piece together the events leading to Tommy's murder, just as *Intruder* opens upon the Negro Lucas Beauchamp being led to jail while Charles Mallison sets about discovering the true murderer of Vinson Gowrie. In other words, the unrevised work reveals what Faulkner later told us in his introduction: that *Sanctuary* was originally intended as a popular novel, one which would make him some money. At this point, it is fascinating and deeply revealing to see how Faulkner commences to fall back on family precedent.

A half-century earlier, Colonel William C. Falkner, Faulkner's great-grandfather, published *The White Rose of Memphis*, a prose romance which proved to be tremendously popular.[9] Apart from sartorial differences in the two works (differences of manner, characterization, and social tone), *The White Rose* and the galley-*Sanctuary* appear to be deeply related. Both are primarily murder mysteries relying heavily upon devices of sleuthing, jail cell interviews, and courtroom drama. It would seem that William Faulkner did not have to look beyond family tradition to gain insight, when he most needed it, into the literary-economic way of the world.

A number of important parallels—points of correspondence which disclose something about the final effect of the rewritten novel—persist right into the published edition of *Sanctuary*: elements, for example, of judiciary satire. Chapter thirty-two of *The White Rose of Memphis* sardonically portrays a double miscarriage of justice: a destitute father who has several minutes too prematurely carried home a side of bacon promised to him is given a "lenient" two-year prison sentence, while a public administrator indicted for the embezzlement of three hundred thousand dollars in widows' trust funds is exonerated after his battery of lawyers points out that the letter "t" has not been crossed on the bill of indictment. Far more savagely and grimly in *Sanctuary*, a double miscarriage of justice occurs. In the first trial resulting in the death of the innocent Lee Goodwin, "The jury was out eight minutes" (p. 349). Very pointedly, "The jury was out eight minutes" (p. 373) in the Alabama trial which convicts Popeye of one murder which he did not commit. Vickery has suggested that the real pessimism of *Sanctuary* consists in Horace's recognition of this separation of justice and law, truth and belief, dream and reality in the world and his inability to reunite them (p. 114). From this standpoint, Temple's rape is merely the first act in a chain of events leading to Benbow's high-intentioned though hopeless quest for justice in his world; he is condemned to living with ironies of justice that he cannot hope to change because the social and conventional mode of response to violence is far more powerful and prevalent than his personal and exploratory way of reacting.

The failure of Horace's quest notwithstanding, ironies of social and legal justice must be relegated to a secondary level when it becomes evident that Popeye could be acquitted on appeal, yet he acquiesces to the death knell of an unheard bell. For he is subject in the same mysterious way as Goodwin to the influence of Temple Drake; he is at the mercy of some higher form of feminine justice. In a minor way (in which the differences are more important than the similarities), the travesty of legal proceedings in *The White Rose* also serves as a foil to another woman's ultimate mastery of a situation where justice sits in decision. Lottie Wallingford, the heroine of Colonel Falkner's romance, plays the unaccustomed role of an attorney to thwart the intrigue of a murderess (a woman who has been seduced and carried off to New Orleans, then Memphis, and who confesses likewise to having left "the temple of honor" [*White Rose*, p. 486]). To the wonder and pride of a male court, the Portia-heroine triumphs over evil and death. But the forces of control she represents are social and legal; she is the rational master of evidence and argument, she works within humanly contrived forms of order, while the "dark woman" she defeats is the agent of nothing more than a man's ambition. The twentieth-century Faulkner, on the other hand, has been freed by changing taste to focus on the debauchee and her "reiteration of an old story" (*White Rose*, p. 486), though concerned not so much this time with a "temple of honor" as with a temple of a different order.

Although elements of the murder-detective novel do remain in the finalized *Sanctuary* of 1931—justifying André Malraux's celebrated comment that the book "demonstrates the intrusion of Greek tragedy into the detective story" (cited by Millgate, p. 118)—it is the Greek sense of tragic inevitability which contrasts most significantly with the type of legal order asserted in *The White Rose of Memphis*. Temple's very surname seems a comment on the ordinary law, "Draco" or "draconian" suggesting a code which by its very harshness—exacting death for the most trivial crimes—goes outside of the social good and hence the legal order. For the forces of control represented in Temple Drake partake of a wholly other symbolic dimension, reaching far beyond the laws and prescriptions of a social contract. The specific kind of *hybris* or tragic flaw—more critical than the physical rape of a feminine "temple"—which provokes this other judicial dimension and its sense of tragic inevitability cannot be overlooked. But for the moment, it is enough to recognize that the social law fails in *Sanctuary*, and the violent form of social order which lynches Lee Goodwin is itself subservient to the will of the "tragic inevitability." This is where the revision process, by which *Sanctuary* ceases to be a murder mystery as it comes more fully under the control of a woman identified with mythic powers, becomes vitally important.

Extensive deletions (more than 1100 lines out of an opening 3000) serve as the primary indicator of a radical alteration of focus taking place in the story. These excisions affect the narrative meaning largely through a shifting emphasis on Horace Benbow. The attorney had once been developed for his own sake in *Sanctuary*; six beginning chapters had formed a kind of portrait gallery, detailing his character and family background, confirming him as the novel's protagonist. The new opening, however, swiftly establishes in three chapters the more vestigial character of an idealistic though vapid man attempting to flee from his wife, at the same time that it sketches contrapuntally the relationship of Lee Goodwin-Ruby Lamar, and introduces the setting of the Old Frenchman place, the stage upon which Temple Drake is about to perform for the next eleven chapters. The lawyer's subsequent attempt to defend Goodwin from the law and Ruby from the moral code of the Baptist Church is recurrently played off against Temple Drake's not-altogether-unwilling sojourn in a Memphis whorehouse, until at last the two converge in a meeting held in one of Miss Reba's business rooms. Here (chapter 23), Horace faces for the first time Temple's story of the night leading to her rape and Tommy's murder. The confrontation of these two, approached as it is in a deliberate contrapuntal manner, becomes of climactic significance to the theme of the work, especially in the resultant expression of Benbow's nauseous despair. The action, however, must still proceed from this moment through a series of culminating events, including the murder of Red (occurring offstage but tensely and dramatically led up to), Goodwin's furious though peaceful lynching, and Popeye's starkly nonchalant hanging.

Another kind of structural change is noticeable in the conclusion —minor in technique but major in effect. It involves the transposition of one sentence, *"Sure, the sheriff said, I'll fix it for you; springing the trap"* (galley version, Faulkner's italics), from its location as the concluding statement of the story to its proper chronological position at the end of Popeye's scene on the gallows, before the Temple episode in the Luxembourg Gardens. The result, of course, is that the "season of rain and death" sentence is promoted to the status of last word, and stands now in its ever-widening significance, unconstricted by the impact of one man's death, referring not to victim finally but to agent—to that which is eternally recurrent and consequently archetypal. Faulkner's incisive rearrangement at this moment is one index of his artistic subordination, however bleak his feelings, to an evocation of the dominant archetype of the anima.

One more revisional process should be considered before the subject is dropped: the addition of new material. Most frequently, the published interpolations in *Sanctuary* are simply transitional sentences or paragraphs, intended to bridge a reordered chronology. But the final three chapters are new almost in their entirety except for the latter half of chapter 31. They deal, directly or indirectly, with Temple's impact upon three male characters: Goodwin, Benbow, and Popeye. Nearly eight new pages of the final chapter, for example, chronicle Popeye's history in terms of his parentage and early childhood, yet thematically they offer far more than a standard explanation from heredity or environment. Important new information is given about his sexuality, what might be termed his "sexual determinism" in a contextual, more than a genetic, sense; this, in itself, has a profound connection with Horace's reaction to Temple's story. The twenty-ninth chapter, which vividly relates the nightmare lynching of Goodwin, is likewise new; it replaces a letter from Narcissa to her brother, informing him of Lee's removal from the jail to prevent the lynching, if only to preserve him for legal hanging (galley 101). Violence is thus accelerated in the novel, carrying the reader to an emphatic climax.

Chapter 30, for the first time as well, dramatizes Benbow's return to a woman from whom he had tried to free himself, to a wife whose last indifferent, yet peremptory, word is, "Lock the back door" (p. 360). Horace's moral collapse is now absolute, issuing directly out of his unresisting defeat in the courtroom. Unlike the case in *The White Rose*, the attorney's mastery of logic here wins him no victory. Precisely because of this failure, an innocent man dies in a blaze of gasoline; but ultimately, both the lawyer and the bootlegger are destroyed by a force before which they are impotent. Horace divines that power before he ever suffers its effect: " 'I know what I'll find before I find it,' he said. 'She will have on a black hat' " (p. 339). Neither Horace nor Faulkner offers any further explanation, yet the man's despairing fatalism proves justifiable in view of what follows, not only for him but for Goodwin and Popeye as well. This Hecate figure whose imminence Benbow heralds seems the only necessary, indeed the only adequate, explanation for the helpless, even nihilistic, response of the two men. Positive proof must lie in the narrative caesura, in Benbow's sudden, enigmatic paralysis; at the full height of his fledgling confidence shown in, "But today will be the last. By noon he'll walk out of there a free man: do you realize that?" (p. 336), he unexpectedly looks upon the hideous aspect of the archetypal feminine, and in that glimpse he is transfixed.

Linton Massey's claim that "with a minimum of effort, Faulkner altered the entire focus and meaning of the book" (p. 204) is evidently ratified. The paring out of extraneous material, the incisive rearrangement of already existing material, and the radical increase in Temple's violent impact upon a male world invests her with an unlimited numinous power that she did not formerly possess. Her Hecate visage is explanation enough for the tragic inevitability with which each of the men is hedged about; what is not yet clear, however, is the precise nature of the crime by which this death-dealing power is unleashed.

On a simply popular level, *Sanctuary* appears to fulfil a public appetite for tales of sex and violence. Indeed, sexuality seems throughout this novel to be the mother of violence, in both act and progeny. The story hinges on a shockingly brutal rape; the fruits of the act are murder, lynching, and execution. So far, there is nothing to indicate that these events are more than the stock ingredients of a lurid bestseller. But when Horace listens to Temple's account of the night leading to her violation, his response illuminates the wider meaning of a number of incidents in the narrative. Returning from Memphis late in the night,

> He walked quietly up the drive, beginning to smell the honey-suckle from the fence. The house was dark, still, as though it were marooned in space by the ebb of all time. The insects had fallen to a low monotonous pitch, everywhere, nowhere, spent, as though the sound were the chemical agony of a world left stark and dying above the tide-edge of the fluid in which it lived and breathed. The moon stood overhead, but without light; the earth lay beneath, without darkness. He opened the door and felt his way into the room and to the light. The voice of the night—insects, whatever it was—had followed him into the house; he knew suddenly that it was the friction of the earth on its axis, approaching that moment when it must

decide to turn on or to remain forever still: a motionless ball
in cooling space, across which a thick smell of honeysuckle
writhed like cold smoke. (pp. 266–67)

The cataclysmic imagery of his despairing thought is most significant in its relation to his sexual revulsion. For the scent of
honeysuckle evokes in him the same suffocating sensation of female
sexuality, of cloying fertility, that it does in another of Faulkner's
anti-vital intellectuals, Quentin Compson. But where Quentin
dreams only of a private, etherealized incestuous destruction in
response to honeysuckle, Horace envisions an entire world destroyed
and wound in the writhing coils of sexual provocation. The ball
of earth, which has become masculine for the moment in his
agonized mind, is seen as finally burned away by feminine heat,
motionless, dead now and cooling, though held still in the embrace
of an insatiable power. All the concrete symbols of Benbow's nighttime world coalesce to produce his prophecy of cosmic annihilation:
the moon rides darkly overhead, the goddess in her waning and
destructive aspect; the furious seethe of insect sound drops off, life
stranded and spent on a shore from which the moon-driven tide has
ebbed. Ephemeral, then, as gnats and no more than insect-sized,
the dependent world of masculine life is conceived as being at the
mercy of a dominant and perhaps capricious goddess. So Temple
Drake, who has functioned as the catalyst of this male response, is
more vitally connected to an awesome force.

Nevertheless, the dying ebb of insect sound still carries for
Horace the capacity of choice. Proleptically, he imagines that before
the globe ceases to spin on its axis, it voluntarily succumbs to its own
inertia and friction: it longs (Darl Bundren-like) to abandon the
terrible effort of motion. The male principle thus relinquishes, of
its own accord, its source of life in the daemonic archetype. Horace,
as even his name suggests the book-learned man, would call that
decision a legitimate response to evil: "Perhaps it is upon the
instant that we realise, admit, that there is a logical pattern to evil,
that we die, he thought, thinking of the expression he had once
seen in the eyes of a dead child, and of other dead: the cooling
indignation, the shocked despair fading, leaving two empty globes
in which the motionless world lurked profoundly in miniature"
(p. 266). Death without the indignation and despair of evil, he

implies, is better than life intertwined with vice. His dictional choices, however, expose in "logical pattern" and "shocked despair" his own blighted roots; he is a rational idealist who must impute his own logical absolutism to evil as abstract order rather than accept the indissoluble unity of good–bad, life–death, virtue–vice, in the very tissue of living.

Evil is more to Horace than an aberration from a moral code; it is a function of the engendering flesh. His very reflection on evil is prompted indirectly by the sight of two figures standing face to face in an alley, "the man speaking in a low tone unprintable epithet after epithet in a caressing whisper, the woman motionless before him as though in a musing swoon of voluptuous ecstasy" (p. 265). In a direct sense, of course, his concept of evil is rendered more actual by the story of sexual horror he has just heard in Temple's bedroom. But his horror is not occasioned alone by Popeye's unnatural act; on an elemental level, Horace is appalled by natural sexuality because it is life-promoting. To him life is bad, for in its absence, evil would cease to exist. "Better for her if she were dead tonight, Horace thought, walking on. For me, too. He thought of her, Popeye, the woman, the child, Goodwin, all put into a single chamber, bare, lethal, immediate and profound: a single blotting instant between the indignation and the surprise. And I too; thinking how that were the only solution. Removed, cauterised out of the old and tragic flank of the world" (p. 265).

Fertility itself, then, is what Horace is spiritually at war with: the sex act as the giver of life and death. Inevitably, the unattainable desire of the male intellect is to be beyond the female cycle, which for him is inherently evil; and that is why his nihilism can be so strong. That is also why Horace, who prefers eternity to change, law to life, cessation to creation, rejects the sexual principle and the numinous feminine as utterly daemonic. Nonetheless, Benbow's view of the sex act as negative and destructive, while still the predominant outlook of the novel, is significantly qualified in the course of the narrative. In this modification lies the meaning and theme of *Sanctuary*.

Obversely, a part of the horror engendered in Benbow's consciousness is the result of his unconscious fascination with the instinctual drive of life. He is fully representative of the divided mind, the male principle of light straining toward self-sufficiency, and the feminine principle of darkness spiralling steadily downward into light's extinction. The circumambient life of the anima will permit consciousness to emerge into light, insofar as it acknowledges its source. But where the male consciousness pursues too strongly its spiritual independence, a counterbalancing tendency in the feminine unconscious seeks to subvert its rival, drawing it into self-destructive drunkenness. Negatively, the maternal unconscious reasserts its dominance in various forms: madness, incest, impotence, stupor. All lead inexorably to ego-annihilation. Benbow's impotence of intellect, his being cut off from the creative sources of life has been noted before. But there exists in his psyche's darker half an actual impulse toward destruction. Incest lurks there, at best half-hidden, although his conscious mind is struggling to repress that desire by projecting his guilt—the intellectual construct of sin—onto the object of provocation, his stepdaughter, Little Belle.

> He was thinking of the grape arbor in Kinston, of summer twilight and the murmur of voices darkening into silence as he approached, who meant them, her, no harm; who meant her less than harm, good God; darkening into the pale whisper of her white dress, of the delicate and urgent mammalian whisper of that curious small flesh which he had not begot and in which appeared to be vatted delicately some seething sympathy with the blossoming grape.
>
> He moved, suddenly. As of its own accord the photograph had shifted, slipping a little from its precarious balancing against the book. The image blurred into the highlight, like something familiar seen beneath disturbed though clear water; he looked at the familiar image with a kind of quiet horror and despair, at a face suddenly older in sin than he would ever be, a face more blurred than sweet, at eyes more secret than soft. (p. 200)

Little Belle's symbolic association with the vatted liquid of the seething grape anticipates the description of Eula Varner in *The Hamlet*: "Her entire appearance suggested some symbology out of the old Dionysic [sic] times—honey in sunlight and bursting grapes, the writhen bleeding of the crushed fecundated vine beneath the hard rapacious trampling goat-hoof." But where Eula Varner is become little more than an emblem of mammalian fecundity—the glandular love goddess made over into the chattel of Flem Snopes—Little Belle vitally represents for Horace the creative and destructive goddess out of the old Dionysiac times, the bearer of the mad frenzy. For the grape symbology implicitly suggests his intoxication with her dangerous beauty, his desire for uroboric incest leading to a self-destructive drunkenness. He is saved momentarily by consciousness; he displaces all the evil outside of himself, recognizing in the girl, and perhaps in all womankind, agents rather than victims of the world's sin. By the time he has heard the story of Temple's rape, however, his intellect is convulsed and rendered useless by nausea. He looks at his stepdaughter's photograph once again, and he slips back unwittingly into what has been persistently half-hid: "The face appeared to breathe in his palms in a shallow bath of highlight, beneath the slow, smoke-like tongues of invisible honeysuckle. Almost palpable enough to be seen, the scent filled the room and the small face seemed to swoon in a voluptuous languor, blurring still more, fading, leaving upon his eye a soft and fading aftermath of invitation and voluptuous promise and secret affirmation like a scent itself" (pp. 267–68). The same honeysuckle smoke in which he has seen the world perishing now licks at him with "smokelike tongues" of incestuous invitation.

Finally, crucially, Horace's continuing unconscious fantasy identifies Little Belle and Temple Drake,[10] the two of them brought together by a photograph and the recollection of rattling shucks, and focused now into one composite image, "bound naked on her back on a flat car moving at speed through a black tunnel, the blackness streaming in rigid threads overhead, a roar of iron wheels in her ears. The car shot bodily from the tunnel in a long upward slant, the darkness overhead now shredded with parallel attenuations of living fire, toward a crescendo like a held breath, an interval in which she would swing faintly and lazily in nothingness filled with pale, myriad points of light. Far beneath her she could hear the faint, furious uproar of the shucks" (p. 268). Only now, Horace has himself become the terrified victim, a supine sacrifice to the destructive sex goddess. As he retches in the lavatory, he literally assumes a feminine identity, at once suggested by the change in pronoun genders. The act of vomiting his own bile is transformed into "she watched something black and furious go roaring out of her pale body" (p. 268).

The racing tunnel of blackness, whether it signifies uterine regression or regression into the life of the unconscious, still marks
the rape of Horace's consciousness by the violent sexual force of the
feminine. It seems, in other words, that the place of intellect in his
psyche has been usurped by a controlling anima. For in a curious
reversal, he has become passively feminine, reverting into darkness
from light, taking the place now of Temple and Little Belle, himself assaulted by the dangerous potency which is borne within them.
His immediate sexual horror then has a double origin: the incestuous promise leading into dissolution and death, and the forcible
rape of intellect quashing his ego-identity. Either way, he is left
subject to the dominant power of the archetype and its sexual
principle. This horror exhibited by Horace must not be thought of
as mere empathy for Temple in her ordeal; Temple's "terror,"
as we shall see, is qualitatively different. Horace's collapse, on the
other hand, is the precursor of his acquiescence beneath the horrible
visage of the black-hatted woman; it is further evidence too of her
long-standing control.

After the failure of law and the male intellect in Lee Goodwin's
trial, Horace reaches the nadir of his anti-vital despondency:
"There was still a little snow of locust blooms on the mounting
drive. 'It does last,' Horace said. 'Spring does. You'd almost think
there was some purpose to it' " (p. 350). The last we see of him, he
has relapsed into the pull of the incestuous promise, listening first
in vague disquiet to Little Belle's breathing on the telephone, and
then to the breathlessness of her sexual scuffling. Horace has been
brought back fully within the encompassing life of the feminine
now, but only to be devoured by it. For in Benbow, the male
spiritual principle has lost its proper right to participate in the
creative life of the anima; he is psychically doomed to continuing
sterile desire. Irrevocably, then, consciousness has lost its struggle
with the negative elementary character of the Great Goddess; the
Little Belle-Temple figure awaits him finally as a spiritless and
incestuous womb of death.

It is no accident that Benbow's final role should be that of a
central intelligence vanquished by supra-intelligent forces. The
violent destruction, however, of the four other men—Tommy and
Popeye included—can hardly be said to be caused by their participation in a male spiritual principle. The only apparent relation

they have to Horace is a common attitude toward sex, and therein, the female principle. Popeye's physical sterility, for example, is the perfect correlative to Benbow's sterility of consciousness, his corncob rape the counterpart to the other's anti-vital despair. Horace sums up this mutual male dilemma in purely intellectual terms; the other men express their attitudes in action, and they in turn are acted upon by the woman. From the inclusive male point of view, then, sex might appear to be the real antagonist of the story, while from the finally dominant feminine perspective, Horace and his alter egos will not even attain to protagonist status. The growth of that feminine perspective toward ascendancy must be explored before turning in conclusion to its effect upon Tommy, Red, Goodwin, and Popeye.

At first sight, Temple Drake appears to be a flapper created out of the last whimper of the Roaring Twenties. She is an overpainted, overdaring, much-sought-after prize in the college dating game, and she is always on the run during week nights—away from the campus and studious men to whom cars are not permitted—toward the town and local boys and the joyrides of the automotive age. These are the predispositions of her character. As for her story, her placement in a narrative development, she is a glittering and hovering coquette who is raped in cringing terror through grossly unnatural means and carried off into virtual prostitution, meanwhile discovering that she has all along consented to it, even enjoyed it, and that her affinity for evil is absolute, to the point of aiding, abetting, and even willing the evil end of men variously involved in her debauching. Presumably, this is the character served up with a garnish of horror to a vague mass audience. In this form, it is a story of sin without redemption, told for the sake of the sin itself.

But the readers of plot alone may have missed the symbolic qualities of *Sanctuary* which transform its meaning and purpose. From the outset, the characterization of Temple proceeds from a readily apprehended social world into a disturbing and not so easily distilled dimension of symbols: "On alternate Saturday evenings, at the Letter Club dances, or on the occasion of the three formal yearly balls, the town boys, lounging in attitudes of belligerent casualness, with their identical hats and upturned collars, watched her enter the gymnasium upon black collegiate arms and vanish in a swirling glitter upon a glittering swirl of music, with her high delicate head and her bold painted mouth and soft chin, her eyes blankly right and left looking, cool, predatory and discreet" (p. 32). Amidst the social swirl and glitter and the conventional obeisance to proprieties, there is a chilling aura surrounding Temple, not contained alone in the carnivorous adjective "predatory," but centred certainly in the blank, cool eyes which look from side to side still seeing.

In a bedroom later on the Old Frenchman place, as Tommy stares through the window at her, "she lifted her head and looked directly at him, her eyes calm and empty as two holes" (p. 82). The effective impression of character, so often conveyed by Faulkner through the quality of eyes, in this case suggests by vacancy or nonpresence the frightening idea that there is no human being, or perhaps something more than human, behind the taut mask of Temple's features. Immediately thereafter, the concatenation of destructive images is renewed: "She rose from the bed and removed her coat and stood motionless, arrowlike in her scant dress" (p. 82); upon reviewing her story in Miss Reba's house, her mouth will be "painted into a savage cupid's bow" (p. 256); but returning to that night spent on the Old Frenchman place, "In a single motion she was out of it, crouching a little, match-thin in her scant undergarments" (p. 82). Soon thereafter, the sound of Popeye's shooting of Tommy will revert to her: "To Temple, sitting in the cottonseed-hulls and the corncobs, the sound was no louder than the striking of a match" (p. 121). Finally, the thinness of her body itself suggests, in psychic terms, her destructive character;[11] the fullness and massiveness of the nourishing good mother, closely identified with earth, is entirely absent from the portrait of Temple. It might appear that she is constitutionally disposed toward the person of the destroying goddess; one wonders then why the negative side of the archetype should be manifest before it is given cause. It is important to remember, at this point, that the symbol complex surrounding Temple is also the product, on every occasion, of a male perceiver; each man who looks at her appears somehow to evoke her dangerous appearance.

The more demanding question is why Temple does not once flee from danger herself, not from the Old Frenchman house, nor from the brothel, nor at last from the nightclub. By failing to exercise her power to absent herself, she leaves a trail of continuous carnage behind her. Without doubt, she is, in her own mind, terrified throughout. But she is also fascinated, poised between inviolacy and violation. The story recounted to Horace in Miss Reba's house returns obsessively to her night of terror before the rape took place: "That was the only part of the whole experience which appeared to have left any impression on her at all: the night which she had spent in comparative inviolation" (pp. 257–58). But "suddenly Horace realised that she was recounting the experience with actual pride, a sort of naïve and impersonal vanity, as though she were making it up, looking from him to Miss Reba with quick, darting glances like a dog driving two cattle along a lane" (p. 259).

This pride of Temple's, or better, her "impersonal vanity" indicates something here that is at first glance unfathomable. It represents more than having been a violent centre of attraction that night on the Old Frenchman place; this much becomes clear during the prelude of the rape itself. Lying in the darkness with Popeye's hand fumbling inside her knickers and her skin jerking ahead of it like flying fish before a boat, she seems driven to the extremity of terror, falling desperately back on fantasy to prevent the advancing encroachment. At first, through the energy of will alone, she seeks to change the gender of her vulnerable female organs, in the confident belief that not even Popeye would have anything to do with a little boy. But when the longed-for penis fails to sprout, she conjures up a self-pitying vision of herself in a coffin, veiled in white like a bride (the matriarchate's vision of the marriage of death—ravishment by the hostile and alien male), crying because "they had put shucks in the coffin where I was dead" (p. 263). A prophetic irony, of course, transforms the cornshucks of the mattress into the corncob of the following morning. Nevertheless, Temple now repeats the silent admonition she had thought to say when Popeye first entered the bedroom: " But I kept on saying Coward! Coward! Touch me, coward! I got mad, because he was so long doing it. I'd talk to him. I'd say Do you think I'm going to lie here all night, just waiting on you? I'd say. " (p. 263). Then, almost proleptically, Popeye is metamorphosed into a tiny "black thing," male and utterly subordinate to a great ogress of a schoolteacher with "iron gray hair," "all big up here like women get" (pp. 263–64).

Unquestionably, the outcome of the narrative suggests that Temple's fantasy at this point is close to prophetic vision. At the very least, her motivation is now ambivalent. On the one hand, it seems that her fear of genital injury is the correlative to a male sense of impotence, of complete helplessness. On the other hand, it is clear that she is also, from her deepest being, tempting Popeye to her violation and the violence that will follow it. The problem, if it is at all a problem, in Temple's characterization is that she is unconscious of herself as an incarnation of numinous forces. Insofar as she participates in the male element of consciousness, she is terrified. On the fundamental level of the unconscious, however, she draws the male world towards annihilation. Her later pride, then, is impersonal precisely because it is unconscious: her ego does not enter into it. This denial of Temple's personal motivation leads directly to her more decisive mythic motivation. Her rape—which is the focal point of her story—is a sort of catalyst precipitating this transition to impersonality; the events leading up to it reduce her part in ego-consciousness and heighten her symbolic characterization.

If one considers Temple's perspective in its developmental stages, it can be said that prior to her rape, her state of consciousness is patriarchal. Put another way, when she privately appeals for help, she tries to pray conventionally to a male deity: "But she could not think of a single designation for the heavenly father, so she began to say 'My father's a judge; my father's a judge' over and over until Goodwin ran lightly into the room" (p. 60). The comedy of an unwitting pagan goddess trying unsuccessfully to recall the heavenly father's name is steel-bladed and double-edged. For the male element of rationality is made ludicrous, caught praying to a human and social father, thus casting implicit doubt on the existence—much less the efficacy—of a "heavenly father." The abject helplessness of the patriarchal power is portrayed even more ludicrously in the moment of the rape—again through Temple's choice of a father to whom she can pray:

She could hear silence in a thick rustling as he moved toward

her through it, thrusting it aside, and she began to say Something is going to happen to me. She was saying it to the old
man with the yellow clots for eyes. "Something is happening
to me!" she screamed at him, sitting in his chair in the sunlight,
his hands crossed on the top of the stick. "I told you it was!"
she screamed, voiding the words like hot silent bubbles into
the bright silence about them until he turned his head and
the two phlegm-clots above her where she lay tossing and
thrashing on the rough, sunny boards. "I told you! I told you
all the time!" (p. 122)

In actuality, the old man sits on the porch of the house, several
hundred feet from the barn where Temple lies thrashing. He
nevertheless becomes transformed in her fantasy to a figure who
looks, god-like, down from above her, sightless, silent, repulsive,
and powerless. The "impotent" old man marks an end of a pa-
triarchal-psychic situation in Temple; the forces of the matriarchate
begin from this moment henceforth to grow into final dominance,
until the male world is held totally thrall. And Temple is in fact
given justifiable sway over that masculine element, beyond even
her natural proclivities as a destroying goddess.

   Tommy is her earliest victim. He tells Temple, ". . . Lee says
hit wont hurt you none. All you got to do is lay down . . ." (p. 118,
Faulkner's ellipses). "Then she felt his hand clumsily on her thigh.
'. . . says hit wont hurt you none. All you got to do is . . .'" (p. 118,
Faulkner's ellipses). His slow yearning for her is easily converted
into protectiveness, without ever lessening the sluggish fire of his
desire: "He squatted there, his hip lifted a little, until Goodwin
went back into the house. Then he sighed, expelling his breath, and
he looked at the blank door of the crib and again his eyes glowed
with a diffident, groping, hungry fire and he began to rub his hands
slowly on his shanks, rocking a little from side to side. Then he
ceased, became rigid, and watched Goodwin move swiftly across the
corner of the house and into the cedars" (pp. 119–20). Not even the
mindless Tommy is free of a kind of conscious lust. Popeye shoots
him because of his quietly possessive passion.

   Red, the nightclub bouncer, furnishes stud service for Popeye
on demand in a Memphis brothel, itself a kind of comic adjunct to a
patriarchal world. Minnie, a maid in the house, provides us with an

unforgettable tableau: "the two of them [Temple and Red] would be nekkid as two snakes, and Popeye hanging over the foot of the bed without even his hat took off, making a kind of whinnying sound" (pp. 311–12). This obscene portrait must be examined apart from Red's personal part in it. Once Red grows warm in his work, however, Popeye drills a bullet hole in his forehead. The mortal Temple, who has turned "wild as a young mare" (p. 311) under the bouncer's good offices, says quite the wrong thing to Popeye in a frenzied attempt to preserve her lover: " 'He's a better man than you are!' Temple said shrilly. 'You're not even a man! . . . Don't you wish you were Red? Dont you? Dont you wish you could do what he can do? Dont you wish he was the one watching us instead of you?' " (pp. 278–80). In spite of her physical desire for Red, the undercurrent of her passion is revealed in not-surprising terms: "He came toward her. She did not move. Her eyes began to grow darker and darker, lifting into her skull above a *half moon* of white, without focus, with the *blank rigidity* of a *statue's eyes.* She began to say Ah-ah-ah-ah in an expiring voice, her body *arching* slowly backward as though faced by an exquisite torture. When he touched her she sprang like a *bow,* hurling herself upon him, her mouth gaped and ugly like that of a *dying* fish as she *writhed* her loins against him" (p. 287, emphasis mine). The point of the italicized words is to recall their previous symbolic use in connection with Temple's character-disposition, and with Horace's vision of the destructive power of the archetypal feminine. Their renewed orchestration at this point, where even Temple supposes that she supports the man, only underscores her hidden but controlling motives.

Lee Goodwin, the third victim in chronological sequence, gets drunk on the Old Frenchman place and, stealing into the woods, looks (Actaeon-like) upon Temple's excremental nakedness. Later, he stalks barnward through the trees with rapacious intent. It is obvious what is on his mind; he has slapped Ruby down for standing in his way, and he has spelled out the nature of the act to Tommy who gives his mental assent. Goodwin is destroyed finally in terrible fury, and it seems now that there is a mythological reason for it.

Each of these interlocked instances is of one piece with Popeye's pressing a corncob into sexual service. They all are emblematic of a sort of sex which has gotten into consciousness and turned male, unnatural, infertile.[12] The physical sterility of Popeye's unnatural implement serves supremely as an objective correlative of Benbow's sterile understanding. In different ways, they share the same disease of intellect—mind dissociated from its creative source. Correspondingly, Popeye leaning over the foot of the bed and whinnying in impotence is only one more example of head having usurped the sexual principle of life.

This mythic reason for the violent destruction of four men and the moral-intellectual collapse of another is stressed in the novel by an interesting reinterpretation of the myth of the Fall—itself related to Minnie's image of Popeye watching (Teiresias-like) the man and the woman "nekkid as two snakes." Temple, in the darkness of her Memphis bedroom, is reviewing the hour for dressing for a dance back in her college dormitory:

> The worst one of all said boys thought all girls were ugly except when they were dressed. She said the Snake had been seeing Eve for several days and never noticed her until Adam made her put on a fig leaf. How do you know? they said, and she said because the Snake was there before Adam, because he was the first one thrown out of heaven; he was there all the time. But that wasn't what they meant and they said, How do you know? . . . until she told them and held up her hand and swore she had. That was when the youngest one turned and ran out of the room. She locked herself in the bath and they could hear her being sick. (pp. 181–82)

The whole movement of the novel justifies this claim that Adam, not Eve, brought about the Fall. His sin was getting sex into his consciousness, covering up Eve's genitals, and consequently drawing the serpent into the act. The male intellect, then, which violates the naturalness of the conjunctive principle of life, is the first treacherous step into perdition. That, says the artist of *Sanctuary*, is the true version of the myth of the Fall.

Faulkner's account of man's damnation is remarkably close in cause to the rationale of D. H. Lawrence:

> When Adam went and took Eve, *after* the apple, he didn't do any more than he had done many a time before, in act.

But in consciousness he did something very different. So did
Eve. Each of them kept an eye on what they were doing, they
watched what was happening to them. They wanted to KNOW.
And that was the birth of sin. Not *doing* it, but KNOWING
about it. Before the apple, they had shut their eyes and their
minds had gone dark. Now, they peeped and pried and
imagined. They watched themselves. And they felt uncom-
fortable after. They felt self-conscious. So they said, "The *act*
is sin. Let's hide. We've sinned."
   No wonder the Lord kicked them out of the Garden. Dirty
hypocrites.
   The sin was the self-watching, self-consciousness. The sin
and the doom. Dirty understanding.[13]

Interestingly enough, the reaction of the girls in Temple's dormitory—their "dirty understanding," their participation in the
male world of intellect—predicates the same violence, horror, and
nausea found among the men. Through the light powder in the air
the eyes of the girls, which pin back the non-virgin against the
dressing table, look "like knives until you could almost watch her
flesh where the eyes were touching it, and her eyes in her ugly face
courageous and frightened and daring" (p. 182); the youngest of
them, when she understands the truth, like Horace retches in the
bathroom.
   Man, however, attempts to live completely in a world of understanding; so in the "fallen" world of knowledge, it is man who
pays the real price for "sin." The novel is the proof of that: as each
man in turn violates the feminine principle of life (the sanctuary)
by the profane deed of thought, he is harried down and punished
according to the gravity of his sacrilege. Temple, whose name seems
at first subtly ironic, is revealed more and more as a true and
terrible temple; from the moment of her profaning by consciousness, she begins to assume her unconsciously destructive character.
   Before turning to the implications of draconian justice in the
novel, two further matters concerning the male contamination of
sex must be raised. Since appearances such as Temple's in *Sanctuary*
are not what they seem at first, one might better appreciate what
otherwise would be an awkward concluding chapter in the novel,
introducing Popeye's origins only after his life is ended. Most

critics have noted the metallic, machine-like imagery associated with Popeye, "that vicious depthless quality of stamped tin" (p. 2) which so effectively heightens his villainy. Yet in conclusion, new information is given about the man which tends to confirm him as Temple's agent or active element, instead of as the self-willed actor. Popeye's weakness, his ascetic aversion to alcohol, his viciousness, his actual physical impotence, are all attributed to an outrage perpetrated upon his mother: "What with the hard work and the lack of fresh air, diversion, and the disease, the legacy which her brief husband had left her, she was not in any condition to stand shock, and there were times when she still believed that the child had perished, even though she held it in her arms crooning above it. Popeye might well have been dead" (p. 368). We are forced, almost with a sense of shock, to the recognition that Popeye's life has been all along determined. The very act of his existence is retribution for the sexual disease his father has bequeathed to him. And his role is configured from the outset in the icon of the Pietà, in his association with the mother of death.

Even the product of a physically healthy union, Ruby's child fathered by Lee, is contaminated, however, totally blighted: "The child lay on the bed, its eyes shut, flushed and sweating, its curled hands above its head in the attitude of one crucified, breathing in short whistling gasps" (p. 160). The only possible explanation is a mythic one: Goodwin, the child's father, has always regarded woman as the object of lust. Long before he purposes Temple's rape, he has killed a soldier over a black woman in the Philippines. So in a manner similar to Popeye's father (though spiritually instead of physically), he seems to have bequeathed his sexual contamination. The father thus "crucifies," without power of resurrection, his own son.

Accordingly, it must be concluded that the male imbalance of sexual consciousness in *Sanctuary* is responsible for the eruption of the negative side of the archetype. Where the feminine is violated by the prying intellect, where she is degraded into little more than an object of male gratification, there will retribution be meted out in mind-annihilating fury. The justice served upon Tommy, Red, Goodwin, Popeye, and even Benbow is draconian in the sense that it is rigorous; it is not, however, punishment for a trifling crime. However slight the offenses are of every man but Popeye, they represent a sacrilege against the basis of being; they must be punished. In the nemesis which follows, nonetheless, *Sanctuary* approaches the *götterdämmerung* of Faulkner's creation.

We come full circle to the despairing tone of the novel. The outlook propagated by this story is the bleakest, perhaps the most oppressive, in all of Faulkner's work. Even the despondency of *The Sound and the Fury*—the hopelessness which is evident as an aftermath of the blocking of Caddy's transformative character, and of her conversion into the destructive face of the archetype—is at least partially overcome in Dilsey, the finally positive representation of the Great Mother. When, however, in *Sanctuary*, the archetype offers to be similarly split, no amelioration from it is permitted by the all-powerful witch face of the goddess.

Ruby Lamar should configure the symbolic presence of the loving mother in the novel. Her name implies that she is the primordial Aphrodite, the treasure (jewel) of the sea. Time and again, she is almost portrayed as the primitive madonna: "The child whimpered, stirred. The woman stopped and changed it and took the bottle from beneath her flank and fed it. Then she leaned forward carefully and looked into Goodwin's face. 'He's asleep,' she whispered" (p. 329). She is not, however, permitted to breastfeed her son; she can only heat the bottle with her flank. The reason for this symbolic ambivalence is made quite apparent in the narrative. Once, to get her common-law husband out of Leavenworth, she unquestioningly gives herself for two months to a reprobate lawyer. Without hesitation, she expects to pay Benbow in the same currency. Benbow's response says more about himself than about her: " 'Can you stupid mammals never believe that any man, every man—You thought that was what I was coming for? You thought that if I had intended to, I'd have waited this long?' " (p. 330). Her reply is perfectly characteristic: " 'It wouldn't have done you any good if you hadn't waited.' " Horace's refusal, though noble, discloses in "you mammals" his revulsion once more, his disgust for the sexual principle and the primal nature of woman. But that primal nature seems to have atrophied in her destitute prostitution; she has been an all too willing accomplice to Goodwin's degradation of her power.

If the symbols surrounding Ruby tend toward a portrait of the good mother, the mythos projecting her activity does not. The

powers of life she represents are weak. Nothing indicates that more
clearly than her confrontation with Temple on the Old Frenchman
place: "She returned and drew another chair up to the stove and
spread the two remaining cloths and the undergarment on it, and
sat again and laid the child across her lap. It wailed. 'Hush,' she
said, 'hush, now' her face in the lamplight taking a serene, brooding
quality" (pp. 69–70). Despite her spoken scorn for the college girl,
we find in contrast the following forceful image: "A thin whisper
of shadow cupped its head and lay moist upon its brow; one thin
arm, upflung, lay curl-palmed beside its cheek. Temple stooped
above the box. 'He's going to die,' Temple whispered. Bending,
her shadow loomed high upon the wall, her coat shapeless, her hat
tilted monstrously above a monstrous escaping of hair. 'Poor little
baby,' she whispered, 'poor little baby' " (p. 73). On a Saturday
night in May of no particular year, within a gutted farmhouse of a
remote sector of north Mississippi, the artist chisels in a few brief
strokes two figures in cosmic opposition. Beyond all doubt, the
monstrous forces of death shadowed from the outset in Temple
Drake are much more potent than the placid and serene principle
of life flickering on the face of Ruby Lamar. The only explanation
for this given situation seems to be the mythic one: Ruby has
vitiated her own life-giving potency, both in her working out of
legal fees and in her marriage to a culpable husband.

Temple's unconscious motivation, on the other hand, makes her
own object-desirability a plague rather than a payment, a lure
instead of a love bond. She is at once protagonist and antagonist.
Her influence upon the characters who are most sympathetic
(Tommy, Goodwin, Benbow) is devastating, hence antagonistic;
yet her very negativity serves as a mythic redress and a moral
purging. She is also the protagonist in the sense of being the leading
figure of the story; by the end of the novel, she is mistress of both
cosmic and social forces, including the temporal energies of Jefferson,
Mississippi. Narcissa Benbow, for example, shares no symbolic part
in the archetype; but she and her Baptist kind have acted as unwitting instruments of a numinous character they do not even come
in contact with. They drive Ruby in the name of respectability out
of Horace's house, out of the local hotel, and finally out of the town.
Their cohort, Eustace Graham, the corrupt district attorney, utters
conventional, even patriarchal, social platitudes in the prosecution of

his case: " 'You have just heard the testimony of the chemist and the gynecologist—who is, as you gentlemen know, an authority on the most sacred affairs of that most sacred thing in life: womanhood —who says that this is no longer a matter for the hangman, but for a bonfire of gasoline—' " (p. 340). Faulkner's irony is brutally incisive, for womanhood, as we have seen, is the most sacred thing in life. The fathers and brothers responding to Graham's appeal, however, believe they act out of social verities: that the violation of a uterus upsets the law of patrilineal succession and the mores of marriageable virginity. Perhaps the archetypal feminine alone can comprehend their subservience to her darker, unconscious motive-power. In any event, they serve the cause of impotent legal justice, at the same time that they are made instruments of a terrible mythic justice, where even the thought is punished as the deed.

For reasons, then, which must ultimately defy comprehension, it seems that the destroying goddess will vanquish creation. The weakened aspect of the good mother is not able to outface the terrible feminine; Ruby Lamar is in every way overridden by Temple Drake, at last giving up her man to the furious mob. The only concrete hope left for life and continuance lies in the final portrait of her, sitting in the courtroom: "The child made a fretful sound, whimpering. 'Hush,' the woman said. 'Shhhhhhhh' " (p. 348). The more intangible hope of *Sanctuary* must lie in its prophetic warning and its apocalyptic message. The final scene of Temple in the Luxembourg Gardens brings impenitent mankind to the verge—if not the midst—of *götterdämmerung*, the duration of which will be no more than "the season of rain and death." In this limited sense, *Sanctuary* is an instructive and a deeply positive work.

Twenty years later, Faulkner was to renew the story of Temple Drake in *Requiem for a Nun*. The interim change in his handling of meaning and theme is absolute; perhaps only a contrast of the two works can reveal how fully mythic *Sanctuary* is in scope and execution. Nancy Mannigoe, the "nigger dopefiend whore"[14] of *Requiem* who murders Temple's infant daughter, takes human life now for the purpose of forcing the mother to accept social and moral responsibility. Temple, married to Gowan Stevens and mother to a boy and a girl, plans to run away with the brother of Red, her former lover of bordello fame. Nancy's last desperate means of holding the family together is the act of infanticide. As she sees it, "I aint talking about your husband. I aint even talking about you. I'm talking about two little children" (*RN*, p. 184). If it seems Nancy is trying to preserve the elementary character of the mother, no attendant symbols project us into a numinous dimension. Moreover, Temple comes to understand the larger purpose for Nancy's crime as being "to save my soul if I have a soul. If there is a God to save it—a God who wants it—" (*RN*, p. 212). *Requiem* has moved a long way off from the pagan goddess of *Sanctuary*; Temple is now humanized, another Christian soul in search of salvation. It is perhaps significant, in this respect, that the murdered child is a girl, no longer the tiny world of the male dependent in life and death on the Great Mother.

Finally, *Requiem* is now fully dominated, not by the dark forces of the feminine, but by the guiding light of reason. Gavin Stevens, the counterpart to attorney Benbow, controls the narrative outcome, drawing Temple inexorably toward the moral realization that "Temple Drake liked evil. She only went to the ball game because she would have to get on a train to do it, so that she could slip off the train the first time it stopped, and get into the car to drive a hundred miles with a man" (*RN*, p. 135). The instructive quality of *Requiem*, so different from *Sanctuary*, attributes quite an orthodox and social nature to evil. Stevens also indicates a changed conception of the origin of that evil: "Uncheck your capacity for rage and revulsion—the sort of rage and revulsion it takes to step on a worm. If Vitelli cannot evoke that in you, his life will have been indeed a desert" (*RN*, p. 146). A major shift in emphasis has occurred, from Temple as the source of destruction in *Sanctuary*, to Popeye recollected in *Requiem* as a kind of mini-serpent. There is no longer even that sympathy for Popeye once revealed in the last chapter of *Sanctuary*, now only the lofty outrage of violated respectability. The other major index of Faulkner's late social (compared to mythic) art form lies in his prose prologues to the three-act drama of *Requiem*. The progression of "The Courthouse," "The Golden Dome," and "The Jail" takes us more than through the history of Yoknapatawpha County; as one observer says, it establishes the social contract theory of law.[15] Faulkner has at last abandoned the beauties and the terrors of the mythic world, resting now in the comparative security and rationality of the ordinary human world. But if that shift has brought about an increase in private peace of mind, it brings its corresponding decline in art, in both the language and in the driving compulsion of "the heart's desire."

From a final vantage point, one is reminded that the story of *Sanctuary* pivots on a shockingly violent rape. It is very likely, in fact, that never before in the history of the popular imagination had the ravishing of the "flower" of Southern womanhood been told with such a savage twist. The author was never entirely oblivious to the notoriety which his device had earned him: "Years later at a football game when Faulkner shrewdly predicted the right play, Saxe Commins said, 'Now you'll be known as the grandstand quarterback.' Faulkner replied, 'No, I'll always be known as the corncob man!' " (O'Connor, p. 57). Throughout its turbulent history, *Sanctuary* seems indeed to have left an indelible impression as a best-selling narrative of gothic sexual horror. It is at least conceivable, however, that Faulkner could have been parodying that public taste for horror and its titillations, not only in a late extraneous comment, but in the notable excess to which he carried a simple story of rape and murder, surfeiting his audience on its own appetite. But the depth of horror evoked by that story belies a purely satiric intent. Faulkner writes with the greatest competence in the tradition of psychological horror popularized a century before by his countryman and fellow Southerner, Edgar Allan Poe.

Perhaps the greatest tribute accordable to an artist is that he should work at or near the height of his powers and still capture the popular imagination. Axiomatically, one might suggest that the popular mind responds to its archetypes without ever needing to verbalize them as such. Certainly in *Sanctuary*, Faulkner has incorporated the widest possible audience through his choice of matter and his use of more conventional narrative technique. Yet in neither the revised nor the unrevised version has he lessened the intensity of his symbolic medium. The real change in his reworking is in his handling of mythos; by his decisive alteration in the place and effect of Temple Drake, he has come to terms with the implications of his symbols. He has not only tightened the focus of his plot, as is often suggested; he has extended it to its requisite conclusion where all offense is punished and the art itself is subordinate to the archetype evoked. Finally, this subordination is not pessimistic for it exposes the malaise of man with some hope of remedy: destruction will be only for a season. In this sense, the artist, by calling forth the archetype, becomes the physician and the prophet of his culture.

6

Lambence in a Grove

"An Older Light Than Ours"
in *Light in August*

Light in August is a pregnant book; as one scholar remarks, "It has what the Elizabethans called *copia*—an abundance and fullness of life; it bursts at the seams with life."[1] It is so replete a work, in fact, that it often has been thought to rupture (or perhaps brim over) into three distinct stories: the framing episodes of Lena Grove and Byron Bunch, the matter of Hightower, and the tragedy of Joe Christmas. Consequently, even though another Elizabethan concept—that of episodic dramatic structure involving contrapuntal or parallel sub-plotting[2]—was long ago applied to this work, the question of unity has continued to demand analysis from sundry recent commentators.[3] Even now, it is an issue which cannot be ignored, both for its causes and for the method of inquiry it necessitates.

The causes, briefly, are these: the flashback past of Joe Christmas threatens to usurp, in terms of pure length, the narrative present defined in Lena Grove's advent along the road to Jefferson; correspondingly, these two major figures, one dominating the beginning and end, the other most of the novel's middle, do not come face to face in the story, are linked rather by a seemingly arbitrary device of place (they occupy at differing times the cabin on the Burden plantation); and finally, Gail Hightower, the novel's third element, seems largely out of place, lacking crucial involvement in either the action or significance of the other stories. For what internal reasons, one asks, do these three stories at all occupy the same novel? Malcolm Cowley found, when he tried to excerpt the story of Christmas for inclusion in *The Faulkner Reader*, that the various threads of *Light in August* were in fact inextricable. As he said in a letter to Faulkner, "I thought when I first read it that it dissolved too much into the three separate stories of Lena Grove (wonderful), Hightower and Joe Christmas—but I read it [again] with the idea that Lena or Joe might be picked out of the text and found that they were too closely interwoven with the others. It would be easy for you to *write* Joe Christmas into a separate novel, but the anthologist can't pick him out without leaving bits of his flesh hanging to Hightower and Lena."[4] Careful analysis will support in theory what the anthologist felt in practice: that the tale of Joe Christmas is significantly altered by its association with the stories of Gail Hightower and Lena Grove. I propose not only to trace the course of that alteration but to discover the agent of compulsion—the reason for the feeling that none of these stories would be complete without the other.

The method of inquiry which has, in one fashion or another, already been used to establish the homogeneity of *Light in August* is an argument drawn from counterpoint.[5] Since the conventional modes of character interaction and narrative development do not obtain in the novel, the likely alternative is to uncover a compositional structure in the work where plot exists either as a set of variations on a theme (plot as musical score) or as a juxtaposition of response to an internal force (plot as operative theme). The principle of the first approach is to emphasize extrinsic alliances without determining an efficient cause; the identification, for example, of Hightower and Joanna Burden as static and Joe and Lena as dynamic outcasts suggests an aesthetically pleasing symmetry in seemingly fortuitous episodes, but it does little to explain the meaning or inner necessity of that condition. The contrapuntal method in this phase is more mechanical than organic, more extraneous than integral.

The second contrapuntal approach seems better prepared to disclose the rationale governing the whole of *Light in August*; it defines the informing principle of the work by the common agency or internal force which is thought to be operative in the separate tales. The method has the advantage of positing a vital unity within the narrative; its major difficulty is that it has not found an operative theme adequate to the multiplicity of the stories, and, failing to be inclusive, it has raised more questions than it has answered. For example, the contention that the harsh spirit of Calvinism or "punitive religious moralism"[6] is the antagonist of the work explains Hines, McEachern, and Grimm as agents, and to some extent, Hightower, Burden, and Christmas as victims. It does not, however, have anything to say about Lena Grove; she seems to be the pagan antithesis of Puritanism, and as such, to be removed from the central action of the narrative.

Where the community (together with Lena as its life-carrying element) is recognized as the largest unifying principle in the novel—incorporating the powers which at once destroy Joanna Burden, Joe Christmas, and Gail Hightower, and redeem Byron Bunch—one is faced with a three-fold perplexity: First, Byron Bunch is not redeemed back into the community but out of it; he leaves his Sunday church service in the country (that single action shared with the community), and his week-long immunity from evil bought in the town with hard work (that ethic also held in common with the community), to follow after the wandering and anti-communal Lena. Second, Joe Christmas is destroyed by his revulsion from sex and from nature (a condition he shares with Gail Hightower as well as with some of the harshest Calvinists in the story) as much as he is by his alienation from the community; so one must be prepared somehow to impute to "community" a symbolic sense in which woman and nature are united as a single operative force. Third, and finally, while Lena is invested with symbolic powers in creation, she is also linked decisively to Joanna Burden by her death. Millgate calls Lena's presence in the outlying cabin a "substitution" or "replacement of Miss Burden at the plantation after the latter's death" (pp. 133–34). Since neither Christmas nor Joanna ever meets the young pregnant girl from Alabama, this major narrative link between them—involving Lena's giving birth in Joe's (Joanna's) cabin on the day of Christmas's death—might seem artificial, nearing pure *tour de force*. Millgate is justified, nevertheless, in terming the incident a "substitution." Lena not only provides temporal succession to Joanna, she also becomes her symbolic replacement, since, as shall be seen, the two women are identified in terms of "grove." So Lena in creation is somehow related to Joanna in destruction; the one is associated with the renewal of life (childbearing, Bunch's redemption, Hightower's momentary reinvigoration), the other with the violent end of life (her own murder, the lynching of Christmas).

This substitution of the one woman for the other should be taken as a major part of the mythos of *Light in August*; it is at the vital centre of the book, telescoping the characters of two women into a single Janus-face scrutinizing man's attempt to be aloof from the female world. The organic reasons for this arrangement of mythos offer some perspective on the operation of structural factors, assuming that *Light in August* re-enacts, with continued intensity, the controlling presence of the archetypal feminine in the modern world. For the myth of the Great Mother is the only rubric comprehensive enough to contain the interconnections in this novel between a Calvinist rigidity of spirit, man's alienation from nature (concomitant with his sexual revulsion), and the crucial identification of Lena Grove with the murdered Joanna Burden. Ultimately, it can be anticipated that the question of unity in *Light in August* is answerable on the deepest level through an examination of the authoritative conduct of the anima as muse. For the principal male protagonists (three, just as there were three in *Sanctuary*, four in *As I Lay Dying*, and three in *The Sound and the Fury*, though not this time so immediately related by ties of blood or plot) are once again portrayed as being subject, in weal or woe, to the awesome power of woman. It is necessary to work backward, then, from the Lena–Joanna nexus, through the psychologies of sex and Calvinism, toward some kind of understanding of the world in which man must live in this, Faulkner's clearest yet most tranquil book of the Great Goddess.

When asked at Virginia about the title of his seventh novel, Faulkner responded with lyric spontaneity:

In August in Mississippi there's a few days somewhere about the middle of the month when suddenly there's a foretaste of fall, it's cool, there's a lambence, a luminous quality to the light, as though it came not from just today but from back in the old classic times. It might have fauns and satyrs and the gods and—from Greece, from Olympus in it somewhere. It lasts just for a day or two, then it's gone, but every year in August that occurs in my country, and that's all that title meant, it was just to me a pleasant evocative title because it reminded me of that time, of a luminosity older than our Christian civilization. Maybe the connection was with Lena Grove, who had something of that pagan quality of being able to assume everything, that's—the desire for that child, she was never ashamed of that child whether it had any father or not, she was simply going to follow the conventional laws of the time in which she was and find its father. But as far as she was concerned, she didn't especially need any father for it, any more than the women that—on whom Jupiter begot children were anxious for a home and a father. It was enough to have had the child. And that was all that meant, just that luminous lambent quality of an older light than ours. (*University*, p. 199)

Faulkner's beautiful poetic utterance accomplishes two things simultaneously: it evokes an image of suddenly suspended light (and time), as though the world were bathed again in the glow of a Golden Age, and it highlights Lena Grove coming out of and returning into that "luminosity older than our Christian civilization." One recalls the basic thesis of religious primitivism: that the artist who feels impoverished by his Christian symbols will revert to the pagan world, to an older symbolic mode of sacrament, in order to describe the relationship of man to his deities. Certainly the opening scene of the novel, incorporating some of the most resplendent lines in American literature, fulfils the pagan image of the timeless, yet terrestrial, mother goddess journeying not through space so much as through unending time.[7] The language movingly suggests that Lena has come "a fur piece," further indeed than Alabama, as if it were from prehistory itself that she has been travelling, out of earth's archaic past—the road "backrolling now behind her a long monotonous succession of peaceful and undeviating changes from day to dark and dark to day again, through which she advanced in identical and anonymous and deliberate wagons as though through a succession of creakwheeled and limpeared avatars, like something moving forever and without progress across an urn" (p. 5).

One of the things Faulkner accomplishes in this image of motion across an urn is an abrupt resolution of the mythic antinomy of time and timelessness; the personal and human Lena who crosses Alabama and Mississippi in wagons moves through time, yet the dimension through which she moves "forever and without progress" suggests that she belongs to the eternity of Keats's urn without having been frozen into its "Cold Pastoral." The paradoxes of language imply that the non-historical dimension is a living (if symbolic) reality in the world of the mythic artist. It is also worth recalling that the frozen movement across Keats's urn is a religious procession; the living movement across Faulkner's urn will prove as well to be religious, for the urn is the primordial image of the great mother: the body-vessel bearing life out of her sheltering womb and receiving back the ashes of the dead. Both aspects of the body-vessel play their part in the present work; in connection with Lena and with Christmas, there shall be reason to consider the urn again.

Faulkner stated more prosaically on another occasion that *Light in August* "began with Lena Grove, the idea of the young girl with nothing, pregnant, determined to find her sweetheart. It was—that was out of my admiration for women, for the courage and endurance of women. As I told that story I had to get more and more into it, but that was mainly the story of Lena Grove" (*University*, p. 74). It seems reasonable, at least from the extrinsic evidence, to hold that Lena's story is the very stuff of the novel, much more than an ironic frame to the tragedy of Christmas. Nevertheless, as the author begins to "get more and more into" the story of a pregnant girl on the road to no specific place, one starts to see emerging deepseated connections with other characters. Lena passes within sight of the burning Burden house less than twelve hours after the murder of its mistress, Joanna. Though Faulkner threads (unquestionably for the sake of concision) the widest ranging action through a narrow time scheme, he also installs Lena in his county-world-cosmic centre at the virtual moment in which her only other female counterpart is removed.

In this process of replacement, Millgate thinks "that Faulkner may have intended a series of allusions to the goddess Diana and to the sacred groves where she was worshipped. Lena Grove's name is an obvious hint leading in this direction, and the Burden house itself is several times described as standing almost hidden among a grove of trees, a grove which still stands even when the house itself has gone." Millgate goes on to establish a contrast between Joanna and Lena, one likened to the Roman Diana with her masculine qualities and reputation for virginity, the other holding in common with Ephesian Diana an "air of timeless permanence" and attributes of "an earthmother, fertility figure" (p. 134). Whether Faulkner had Diana and her August festival at Nemi specifically in mind, or whether he was re-enacting a more inclusive myth of the goddess (of whom Diana is but one manifestation), it seems fairly certain that he wanted us to see Lena and Joanna identified in terms of *grove*. For when it is remembered that two of three major incidents in the narrative (the slaying of Joanna and the laying-in of Lena) occur in the vicinity of the grove of oaks, that the third event (Joe's murder and castration in Hightower's house) is directly related to the first occasion (and that conversely, most of the "murderers" work in a sawmill), there is cause at least to inquire how far one has been led within the environs of a sacred grove.

Lena rides on the wagon-board of an enigmatic sort of energy. Axiomatically, she seems so at home in wagons and on roads (those twin Furies of Anse Bundren's resistant male world) that the narrator seems driven to adopting both of them as extensions of her—her attributes, in a sense, since for her they form a succession of "identical and anonymous and deliberate . . . avatars" (p. 5). Like Addie Bundren lying in the bed of the creaking wagon, she appears as the agent of pure motion, out on the road at the book's beginning and end, having paused only long enough to give birth in Jefferson. The complex of her wagon-road-movement is given an even wider operative dimension by the narrator as she speaks to Byron Bunch, "telling him more than she knows that she is telling, as she has been doing now to the strange faces among whom she has travelled for four weeks with the untroubled unhaste of a change of season" (p. 47). Through her seasonal vitality, Lena draws at least one male (Byron Bunch) into motion with her, as does Addie. There is only a single important difference between the two females in this respect: Addie is "dead." By dying, the one

constrains a male world (except for Darl, the sole dissenter) to
bend completely within her spiritually transformative power; the
other, by carrying life down "a peaceful corridor paved with unflagging and tranquil faith and peopled with kind and nameless
faces and voices" (p. 4), prompts an equally vivifying response—toward motion, change, and transformation.

Where Addie, however, bears the full significance of the Great
Mother in one person—creating life, compelling its transformation,
calling it back into dissolution—the archetype of the feminine is
split in *Light in August* into good and bad or, more properly, into
benevolent and terrible, creative and destructive. Joe Christmas is
cast out and destroyed, like Darl Bundren, because of his immovable
opposition to woman. In literal narrative terms, he murders Joanna
Burden with whom he has been cohabiting for three years, and for
his crime he is dismembered and slain. Symbolically, however, he is
clearly doomed by his anima (both in the nature of his psychic
responses and in the person of the virgin-succubus) so that when he
does dispatch Joanna, he appears to serve some other preordained
end ("He was saying to himself *I had to do it* already in the past
tense; *I had to do it. She said so herself*," p. 264).

Figuratively, as well, there seems to be a symbolic reason in the
two murders for the specific parts dismembered; Joe's castration, as
shall be seen, is retribution for his offense against the feminine
genetic principle; and Joanna's dangling head becomes Joe's re-
quital for her affront to the male principle of reason. Her non-
rational sexuality, in fact, configures the precise aspect of the
destroying goddess. When she would have herself taken in the
darkness of the grounds, "She would be wild then, in the close,
breathing halfdark without walls, with her wild hair, each strand
of which would seem to come alive like octopus tentacles" (p. 245),
appearing thus as a veritable Gorgon out of classical mythology.
The negative-elementary character of the archetype most often
includes the figure of the Gorgon, and the Gorgon is endowed with
every attribute of masculinity, by which to display her destructive
power. Joanna is several times described as "the calm, coldfaced,
almost manlike, almost middle-aged woman who had lived for
twenty years alone, without any feminine fears at all" (p. 244). In
her actual physical character, then, one meets with adequate symbolic preparation for the face of Medusa; Joe is ultimately destroyed

by this face, though he has safely cut off the head. Medusa is not the extent of Joanna's symbolic character however; the riddance of her terrible aspect links her inexplicably to Lena. Millgate detects a ritualistic fashion in her slaying (he recalls the divesting of woman-sewn buttons and clothing; he might also have mentioned the silent duet of murderous intent in the bedroom, the woman-cocked pistol facing the man-held razor in a kind of motionless dance, as agent and victim become indistinguishable), so he senses that Miss Burden's death "has in some way been a precondition of the rebirth" (p. 135) which seems to follow.

The feeling of life renewed on the arid ruin of the Burden plantation stems narratively from Gail Hightower, and he further implies what the critic claims outright as its precondition: " 'Poor woman,' he thinks. 'Poor, barren woman. To have not lived only a week longer, until luck returned to this place. Until luck and life returned to these barren and ruined acres.' It seems to him that he can see, feel, about him the ghosts of rich fields, and of the rich fecund black life of the quarters, the prolific naked children in the dust before the doors; and the big house again, noisy, loud with the treble shouts of the generations" (p. 385). Since Hightower has been the one man least likely—with the gloom of the past around him and the stench of decay upon him—to be moved by such a prospect, perhaps what he sees might be accepted without irony. Not only has full renewal come, in his foresight, upon the land through Lena's giving birth, but by hindsight "luck and life" have returned with the removal of a previous life. Acknowledging, then, the magical association of life and luck with Joanna's death, it is not untoward to regard her killing as a ritual sacrifice. Here it is Joanna who is tantamount to Addie, fulfilling the primordial role of the sacrificial goddess who, by her death, brings cosmos out of chaos.[8] For in the process of sacrifice, the human victim is rendered coincident with the deity, and life becomes death, death life, each depending on the other. By such means, the face of Joanna begins to coalesce with Lena's figure.

Hightower's poetic glimpse of a former and again imminent fertility is a direct result of his having delivered a man-child out of Lena's loins. The child, nevertheless, is strangely confused by Mrs. Hines with her grandson Christmas in his infancy. Her confusion is so intense, in fact, that even Lena gets "mixed up" enough to believe at times that Christmas—"the one in jail"—is the child's father. One more narrative link is thus forged between Lena and Joanna, between son and lover, birth and death. For in a symbolic sense, it is as if the lover, "father," and son were the same person, identical offspring of that one mother bearing generations in her womb. Conversely, it seems as if Christmas is symbolically destroyed by one aspect of the archetype, while he is renewed by the obverse face. In such a manner, the stories are brought more than figuratively together.

Before one can approach the forces of death and their causes in the novel, a fuller sense of the powers of fertility is required. Hightower's prophecy of renewed life follows hard upon his vision of Lena's future: *"More of them. Many more. That will be her life, her destiny. The good stock peopling in tranquil obedience to it the good earth; from these hearty loins without hurry or haste descending mother and daughter. But by Byron engendered next"* (p. 384). Even at this juncture, more has been mirrored in Hightower's age-ridden eyes than a proleptic belief in human fertility. Lena is glimpsed as the limited embodiment of powers which go beyond her: she not only is affiliated with earth's fecundity, she also lives in obedience to it. Perhaps in some analogous sense, this is what many commentators have meant by the term "earthmother" with reference to Lena. But there is more to Earth herself than simple engendering.

As one observer notes in cogent synopsis, "Faulkner casts the human condition against fundamental processes, the raw common denominator of life on Earth, and it is quite possible that the male's ambiguous fear and hatred and love of woman must be explained in terms of his fear and hatred and love of the old Earth itself, to which Woman is so disturbingly related."[9] Man's ambivalence and especially his hatred, this commentator claims, are aroused by "the female's organic functionalism. The male feels no such deep responsibility to organic process" (p. 146); rather, his quest for rational being lies in the direction of freedom. For the moment, Hightower appears to surrender that terrible freedom; his *fait accompli* reflection upon Lena's childbearing does not for a moment deny the "organic functionalism" of woman or Earth. Yet if such is "the raw common denominator" of the human condition, he perceives it less within the furious tumescent seethe of life than from without—as a serene and abstract overview of woman's part in the processes of Earth. Consequently Hightower maintains, even in the act of material affirmation, a kind of independent ideality.

To Byron Bunch, however, those processes in their actuality are full of terror and a boundless awe. As he runs to the cabin where Lena lies in labour, he does not yet accept her imminent transformation, believing that he will be "met by her at the door, placid, unchanged, timeless." But

> Then he passed Mrs Hines in the door and he saw her lying on the cot. He had never seen her in bed before and he believed that when or if he ever did, she would be tense, alert, maybe smiling a little, and completely aware of him. But when he entered she did not even look at him. She did not even seem to be aware that the door had opened, that there was anyone or anything in the room save herself and whatever it was that she had spoken to with that wailing cry in a tongue unknown to man. She was covered to the chin, yet her upper body was raised upon her arms and her head was bent. Her hair was loose and her eyes looked like two holes and her mouth was as bloodless now as the pillow behind her (pp. 377–78).

What Byron sees in that cabin goes beyond anything perceived by Hightower. In part, most likely, it is due to his less cerebral nature. But the real terror and poignancy of his experience are that he crosses the threshold of a female precinct expecting the immediacy of personal and human contact and he finds, to his dismay, an impersonal—perhaps suprapersonal—being instead. For Lena is aware of nothing in the room—not him nor anything in time or space—"save herself and whatever it was that she had spoken to with that wailing cry in a tongue unknown to man."

If man has fully realized in that moment his exclusion from the crisis of birth, he has also discovered that woman shares citizenship and language with a presence alien and unknown to him. The character of that presence is hauntingly suggested in the portrait of Lena's face; one cannot avoid, especially, her eyes looking "like two holes." In that instant we feel with Byron that Lena does not exist at all in our ordinary sense of the word, that she does not take part in the ordinary scheme of reality but belongs to an absolutely different one. Put another way, it is certain that she is present, yet there is something dreadful about the non-presence, the material unreality in her sight. Everything human and familiar about life seems to centre in the eyes; but in Lena's vision there is nothing mirrored and presumably nothing noted; it is as if the human flesh were only a mask with an abrupt and aweful emptiness behind it. This capacity for emptiness tends ultimately toward negation of space—or something more than space since it is charged with life. If greater than space, however, this life-energy has to be more than organic; it partakes of a different reality, it reveals for an instant the "wholly other."

The identical image—eyes "empty as two holes"—is used in *Sanctuary* to describe Temple; there too the impression of non-physical presence implies the existence of a non-natural or supra-natural potency (see chapter 5). The only difference within this imagistic unity lies in the contrariety of its effect. Where the forces masked by Temple gravitate entirely toward destruction, the non-natural elements glimpsed in Lena are revealed paradoxically in procreation, in the moment of birth. Taken together, then, the images of Byron's experience project female parturition beyond mere "organic functionalism" and beyond even associative dependence on the fruitful Earth. The life-giving, like the life-taking, power is finally something numinous, of which the utmost Earth is only one more phenomenal manifestation. Lena Grove and Joanna Burden, who participate in this same numinous power, ultimately become one person by it; the death goddess is identical to the giver of life.

This, however, is the archetypal perspective of the eternal feminine; the perspective of the limited male life begotten of her is often rather different. The male element must choose whether or not it will cooperate with her; depending on its attitude of consciousness toward her, the aspect of the archetype—the actual sum of the individual condition—will vary. This element of positive choice has enormous implications for the manner of living prerequisite to human survival and endurance.

Joe Christmas does not survive, nor does Gail Hightower endure in any meaningful sense in *Light in August*. But presumably Byron

Bunch will do both (if somewhat awkwardly) and many commentators take that to be the essential point as well about Lena Grove. It must be remembered, however, that Lena is more a mainspring than a model of endurance, and that the bulk of the narrative belongs less to her than it does to three men making or abjuring some form of personal accommodation with woman. In this regard, Richard Chase is not far from the truth when he alleges that "according to Faulkner's gynecological demonology (it constitutes a sort of Mississippi Manichaeism) men are more interesting and valuable than women but the dark or Satanic principle of the universe decrees that they are the weaker sex and are doomed to be frustrated and ephemeral" (*American Novel*, p. 212). Although man may be more interesting because he is doomed, his opposition to woman does not constitute the real "Manichaeism" of Faulkner's universe; that duality resides, throughout the most creative (and likewise most obsessive) period in Faulkner's career, within the archetype alone. Gnostically the myth of the Great Mother encompasses the beatific and satanic principles of the universe.

Whether it is argued that the life of Joe Christmas is shaped from infancy by environment, or whether it is said that he is compelled to certain forms of action by the archetypal content of his unconscious, it is clear that he considers his whole existence doomed and determined. What might be termed his "predestinarianism" is not confined to the approaching crucial event in his life when "he believed with calm paradox that he was the volitionless servant of the fatality in which he believed that he did not believe" (p. 264), nor is it carved on his mind with the ruthless granite chisel of Calvinist election. From almost the outset of childhood, it is the woman he fears, "that soft kindness which he believed himself doomed to be forever victim of and which he hated worse than he did the hard and ruthless justice of men" (p. 158). Even in his desperate attempt to be free of all human moorings, and so running the road (in a manner contrary to Lena), "he might have seen himself as in numberless avatars, in silence, doomed with motion" (p. 213), itself the attribute of that feminine world from which he would flee. Gavin Stevens contributes, as well, to the widening circle of Joe's own fatalism when, in attempting to fathom Christmas's reason for jailbreaking toward Hightower's house, he identifies the old grandmother as the motive power: "I dont think that she knew herself, planned at all what she would say, because it had already been written and worded for her on the night when she bore his mother, and that was now so long ago that she had learned it beyond all forgetting and then forgot the words" (pp. 423–24). The narrator underscores this aura of foreordination in Percy Grimm's inhuman, almost exalted, pursuit of Christmas through the alleys and ravines of Jefferson: "He was moving again almost before he had stopped, with that lean, swift, blind obedience to whatever Player moved him on the Board. . . . He seemed indefatigable, not flesh and blood, as if the Player who moved him for pawn likewise found him breath" (p. 437). The identity of the Player might remain a mystery, linked by name to the game-weary Player—the ideal aristocrat—of *Sartoris*, were it not for the precedence of a woman-derived doom in Christmas's life. Though unnamed and undescribed, the who or what that did the "writing" for old Mrs. Hines seems, by implication, to be the goddess presiding over birth, or the Fate spinning destiny, since the message to the man Christmas was "worded for her on the night when she bore his mother."

In short, Faulkner's evocation of fate is deeply akin to the goddesses of fate in Greece, the *Moirai*, who plaited life and destiny from the temporal moment of birth; and the Fates, in turn, are identical with the spinstress-goddesses of birth in primitive mythology.[10] Throughout the primordial world the great women of fate are the one-, or three-, or nine-fold form of the Great Mother, and the destiny of man spins always from the shuttle of the female. The fate of Joe Christmas, it is suggested, has been threaded on such a woman-shuttle.

Nevertheless, the tragedy of this one man's existence lies in his unremitting struggle to be free of both the loom and fabric of matriarchal destiny. In the largest sense, Christmas rebels against the all-powerful will of an inner feminine being and is ritually destroyed. Should he prove to be symptomatic of the conditioning of his entire culture, the child Christmas still betokens an inherent dilemma in the male psyche. When at the age of five and innocent of knowledge the boy is present at one of the dietician's amours in the orphanage, he reveals something striking about the male mind, something which the half-crazed woman-mind of the dietician could not have grasped: "It never occurred to her that he believed that he was the one who had been taken in sin and was being tortured with punishment deferred and that he was putting himself in her way in order to get it over with, get his whipping and strike the balance and write it off" (p. 115).

Joe's desire for punishment, for a mathematical balance of payment, is very much a part of the hated "hard and ruthless justice of men," possessed long before he met McEachern, and so an innate constituent of his earliest mental processes. But the hard and ruthless principle of men is itself based on abstraction, an attempt of the male spirit to be self-sufficient, free of feeling and the dark world of the feminine unconscious which has engendered it. Thus, when McEachern is about to punish Joe for tardiness at milking time, the narrator says, "Perhaps he was thinking then how he and the man could always count upon one another, depend upon one another; that it was the woman alone who was unpredictable" (p. 149). The irrational element of feminine emotion is, in fact, so hostile to the "male" mind that woman, in her very being, takes on a negative charge: "She had always been kind to him. The man, the hard, just, ruthless man, merely depended on him to act in a certain way and to receive the as certain reward or punishment, just as he could depend on the man to react in a certain way to his own certain doings and misdoings. It was the woman who, with a woman's affinity and instinct for secrecy, for casting a faint taint of evil about the most trivial and innocent actions" [sic] (p. 157). From this "evil" (because unknown and unpredictable) element the ego consciousness must at all costs be free; bodily punishment is a small, if logical, price to pay. As the strap welted his skin, "the boy's body might have been wood or stone; a post or a tower upon which the sentient part of him mused like a hermit, contemplative and remote with ecstasy and selfcrucifixion" (p. 150). The flesh, the body, material itself, are already nothing more for the young man than a stepping-stone for the spirit, whose exaltation the patriarchal religions have always sought.

From the moment of the orphanage incident, then, one realizes that the spiritual principle has not been stamped upon the boy by the puritanical obsessions of McEachern. Puritanism is a capacity innate to Christmas; it is embodied in his creedless subordination of instinctual life to un-life. It is a world view, nevertheless, which is fostered in the McEachern home. When, in a contest of will, the eight-year-old boy refuses to learn his Presbyterian catechism, he is whipped on stern principle (as well as on the dot of every hour). Though the issue of will, rather than intellect, would seem to prevail throughout the incident, in truth the conjunction of these two unyielding intentions produces a conscious result satisfying to both the man and the boy. "When the strap fell he did not flinch, no quiver passed over his face. He was looking straight ahead, with a rapt, calm expression like a monk in a picture" (p. 140). Almost immediately the narrator adds, "It would have been hard to say which face was the more rapt, more calm, more convinced." In its incipience, then, the mind of the child like that of the man maintains a primacy of spirit over matter, preferring death to life, in triumphant denial of the world. What relation this male intellect has to the Christ of Christmas is implied in the previously cited image of "self-crucifixion." If the word, in its religious signification, can refer to the prototypical event in Christian history, then it marks the consummate act of a patriarchal world vying for spiritual autonomy, for the static not-life of eternity. Jesus (apart from the Pietà) and Joe are both antitheses of a matriarchal world view, and the modern "Christ," at least, is crucified against the cross of his own unconscious.

In terms of analytical psychology, Christmas's attitude reveals the ultimate will of intellect to transcend its origins. More revealingly, in mythic terms, his outlook constitutes a denial of the genetic law, itself the *terra firma* of the matriarchal world. Now we might grasp the reason why the child's longing for the abstract principle of punishment is first revealed in conjunction with the female act of copulation. The man's life is heralded in this initial scene: his entire ceaseless effort to be free of the material element, to be free of the murky warmth and enveloping nurture of birth and life, and to live in the clear, unmaterial air of the male spiritual principle is herein contained in embryo. Upon his adult descent into Freedmantown, the narrator describes the man quite distinctly in such terms: "On all sides, even within him, the bodiless fecund-mellow voices of negro women murmured. It was as though he and all other manshaped life about him had been returned to the lightless hot wet primogenitive Female. He began to run, glaring, his teeth glaring, his inbreath cold on his dry teeth and lips, toward the next street lamp" (p. 107). It is not surprising that the woman-voices are "even within him"; they are the anima, the man's inner psychic possession of the female nature. Joe cannot hope, then, to escape from the primogenitive Female: she not only surrounds him in the world of outer experience, but she is within him as well, in his immutable unconscious. He is driven, notwithstanding, to make the attempt. He runs toward the light, looking back at what "might have been the original quarry, abyss itself" (p. 108).

This final effort, occurring on the night he is compelled to Joanna Burden's murder might be viewed as the sum of his entire life, made up of numerous integers of revulsion and repudiation. On that far-away Saturday afternoon of his adolescence, as he takes his turn entering the shed where the Negro girl lies spermfilled, he is outraged by the very nearness of "the womanshenegro" and he kicks out at her in fury. When the other boys rush in to defend the object of their copulation, the girl scrambles away and to Joe, "There was no She at all now. They just fought; it was as if a wind had blown among them, hard and clean" (p. 147). When, on a Saturday afternoon in later adolescence, he hears a hunting companion graphically portray the fact of menstruation, he gives up his weekly hunting camaraderie, and on the Saturday following, he sacrifices a sheep for the filth of womankind. The final episode in the yet uncorrupted ideality of his youth takes place in response to the prostitute Bobbie Allen's confession of her woman's "time":

He went down the road fast and turned from it and sprang over a fence, into plowed earth. Something was growing in the furrows. Beyond were woods, trees. He reached the woods and entered, among the hard trunks, the branchshadowed quiet, hardfeeling, hardsmelling, invisible. In the notseeing and the hardknowing as though in a cave he seemed to see a diminishing row of suavely shaped urns in moonlight, blanched. And not one was perfect. Each one was cracked and from each crack there issued something liquid, deathcolored, and foul. He touched a tree, leaning his propped arms against it, seeing the ranked and moonlit urns. He vomited. (pp. 177–78)

The earth itself is felt now as a larger manifestation of the archetype, and the whole principle, to Joe, is deadly and foul. Trees, which to Benjy Compson carried all the beauty and love and static fertility of his sister Caddy, are in Joe's mind the obverse element of death.

It is apparent, however, that his nausea stems out of more than a physiological disgust with menstrual filth and decay; at heart, it is a disgust with life and with the material-creative principle of life. In a similar vein, Joe's psychic response to trees (the primordial image of the Great Goddess) and to "suavely shaped urns" (the life-bearing body-vessel of the Great Mother) marks his offense against the powers constellated in each of those images.

His nausea notwithstanding, the next Monday night Joe leads Bobbie into those same woods and embarks upon his manhood. It is a road which will lead him to commit murder (as far as he knows) for her and it is a road of uneasy and brittle acceptance which leads him almost a generation later into the house of a spinster who is to become, in a special sense, his own murderer.

Joanna Burden personates, in a curious way, the sexual abnormalities of Christmas together with his puritan or Apollonian intellect. She is, in most respects, his unconscious "soul-figure" or anima (as her surname suggests), re-illuminating the traits which have long been hidden beneath his conscious character as a man. In her nymphomaniacal sexuality, there is reawakened in Joe his old sense of a female "rotten richness ready to flow into putrefaction at a touch, like something growing in a swamp" (pp. 247–48) and once again he begins "to see himself as from a distance, like a man being sucked down into a bottomless morass" (p. 246). Here too, Joanna's wild cries of "Negro! Negro! Negro!" in the embrace of her racially ambivalent lover tend to confirm Joe's fears —granted his identification of the black race with the primogenitive female; of the white race (and light) with the male principle of spirit—that she is making him over in her own image of blackness (the darkness of the maternal unconscious). Likewise, her vision of a black shadow in the shape of a cross upon which the white babies of the world are crucified (p. 239) seems to mirror the man's obsession with self-crucifixion. For it is Joanna's personal part in the element of intellect which trembles at the shadow cast by the mother archetype upon the male spirit (the white race)—the Negro race and womansex for her as well being identified with numinous powers. Joe's indetermination about colour and Joanna's determination to make him black are thus emblematic of "their" divided mind, light striving with darkness, male with female, intellect with unconsciousness, the former never predominating enough to avoid the obsessive confession or testimony of "black-ness."

Joanna's daytime personality as a cold and logical business entity, together with her nighttime aspect as a mind obsessed with the sinfulness of sex, more obviously makes her an objective counterpart to Joe's own psychic life. She personifies, to some extent, the puritanism—or spiritual principle—found in Christmas from the onset of boyhood. Not only in her Protestant ancestry and up-bringing (having forebears with names like Calvin Burden) but finally in her ultimate retreat of consciousness to prayer ("talking to God as if He were a man in the room with two other men," p. 265), she typifies the harshness of spirit and rigidity of principle which has already been identified with Calvinism. The imagery which describes that outlook links her Protestantism with the male postulate (or the a priori belief that spirit precedes matter, that it was created in the beginning by a father God). Joe nevertheless refuses to kneel in prayer, refuses to subordinate himself to even the father God as Joanna commands him, much in the same way he refused as a boy to learn his catechism. His continuing intractability marks at least a tendency of the ego consciousness to acknowledge no allegiance—no dependence—save to the self, as if it held, like Lucifer, that it were self-begot.

Notwithstanding her McEachern-like agency, Joanna's imper-ative is in one significant respect not-male and not-spiritual. She seeks to destroy and dissolve, rather than to mete out spiritual justice. When she aims the monstrously cocked pistol at Joe, she asks for no mathematical concept of payment, but for his reabsorp-tion into the elements out of which he arose. In a way, she is trying to engulf Joe in prayer as she had once done in her gullet vagina. In this sense, she participates in the negative character of the ma-triarchate; her mannishness is only part of that larger symbol complex of the Gorgon with which she has already been identified.

Her further imaging of the archetypal feminine is constantly underscored by the series of phases through which she passes—like the seasons or the moon—and by the images of ebb and flow associated with her life-cycle. She, like Lena, is very much in touch with the forces of earth and instinctual knowledge; she has a pre-monition when full womanhood is about to pass from her: "It was something out of the darkness, the earth, the dying summer itself:

something threatful and terrible to her because instinct assured her that it would not harm her; that it would overtake and betray her completely, but she would not be harmed: that on the contrary, she would be saved, that life would go on the same and even better, even less terrible" (p. 249). Her instinct tells her, of course, that she is entering menopause. The balanced contradictions of the language suggest something more than her sexual ebbing, however; whatever is "threatful and terrible to her" also permits life to go on "even better, even less terrible." Considering her phases and her affiliation with "the dying summer itself," it is possible that the passage forecasts her terrible death by which, symbolically, her life goes on "less terrible." In other words, something dreadful is exorcised by Joanna's death, though she herself is saved by it. She appears as the appointed nemesis to Christmas; she herself is overtaken; then she "reappears" as the mother in the "grove."

Joanna is the fit soul-image for Joe's sterility of intellect, and the final retribution for his resistance to life's creative source. First by prayer, then by the pistol, she threatens to engulf him utterly. On the one hand, Joe's sexual experience of woman (Joanna included) has long been one of confinement and engulfment, of the negative elementary character of the mother goddess. On the other hand, he now experiences in Joanna the more exclusively spiritual character of the anima figure whose whole unconscious function is to lead the male toward transformation. Only this time, he finds something more portentous in her transformative phase. In literal human terms, he kills Joanna before she can destroy him. But in psychic and mythic terms, she makes of him a victim-felon, just as she makes of herself a ritual sacrifice, the precondition of rebirth in the natural world.

Although the psychology of Calvinism has already been considered in passing (and it has been viewed as a derivative rather than a causative function of male spiritual autonomy), its wider manifestations must yet be examined in the world of *Light in August*. In itemizing the Protestant traits of Simon McEachern and Doc Hines, Peter Swiggart observes, "The salient feature of their common puritanism is its abstract or impersonal nature" (p. 132). This puritanism is evidently the outgrowth of the intellect's attempt to free itself by abstract reason from the matriarchal unconscious. Doc Hines, for example, might be observed in the fullest fury of his Jeremian language: "Aint I made evil to get up and walk God's world? A walking pollution in God's own face I made it. Out of the mouths of little children He never concealed it. You have heard them. I never told them to say it, to call him in his rightful nature, by the name of his damnation. I never told them. They knowed. They was told, but it wasn't by me. I just waited, on His own good time, when He would see fitten to reveal it to His living world. And it's come now. This is the sign, wrote again in womansinning and bitchery" (pp. 119–20). Two important points emerge out of his tirade. First, his battlecry of "Abomination and bitchery" is the cry of an Old Testament prophet preaching the wrath of God upon all those who whore after other gods. His words are more than reminiscent of Jeremiah's thundering declamation against Israel's lapse into Canaanite worship, or Hosea's likening of his own wife Gomer's infidelities unto the broken faith of a nation. For the sons of Isaac, when they eschewed the tabernacle, were reverting to the worship of the Great Mother, revered throughout the Near East in her various forms as Astarte, Ishtar, Cybele. In psychic terms, then, the distress of Jehovah concerns a fear that the "fathered" impulse of consciousness might return wholly into its origins in the creative unconscious, or that the masculine mind would acknowledge its dependence on the feminine. Eupheus Hines's conviction that evil is female has a common psychic origin; the Judaeo-Christian religion becomes their common expression.

Secondly, the old man's identification of Negro blood and damnation with womansinning and bitchery confirms the underlying identity in the novel between the feminine principle and the Negro race. To Hines, Joe is damned both because his father was thought to be black, and because his mother conceived him illegitimately. At one stroke, his patriarchal identity has been forfeit, and he has been made a double party to womansinning. Yet in spite of his perdition, Hines will not let Joe be claimed by a Negro orphanage, for the same reason that he will not let the boy be mothered (it was he that let the mother, his own daughter, die, and he that spirited the boy away to the white man's orphanage, itself the abstract of a home devoid of mothering). It seems finally symptomatic of the puritan mind that man should not escape into his damnation, that is, lose consciousness of it. Accordingly, Doc Hines establishes himself as the child's tutor; the results of that education are already known.

One thing remains to be said of the antivital fanaticism of the old puritan. Although Hines is able to wreak revenge on the dark-skinned circus man who has fecundated his daughter, and though he can ensure the death of the woman herself (who, quite significantly, went off to her lover in "Lem Bush's wagon"—recalling Grove in a wagon), he is unable to share in the destruction of their vital union. Long after, when, in terms of the old man's theology, his grandson has reached the age of accountability, Hines fails to raise a lynchmob, fails to complete the work he believes the Lord God has set him: "and God said, 'It's that bastard. Your work is not done yet. He's a pollution and a abomination on My earth' " (p. 365). The point is a simple one. God is not in control of Joe Christmas's world; the Great Goddess is. Just before Joe resigns himself, after almost a week of desperate flight, to the end that is appointed him, he trades shoes with a Negro woman. His despairing hope is to put the bloodhounds off the scent. He manages that. But he cannot break outside that which he perceives as a circle (p. 321). For the road which has run through thirty years is the circle, a Great Round (like Addie and the road in *As I Lay Dying*) which surrounds him, has, in fact, always contained him. As he rides a farm wagon (this time like Lena) toward the place of his surrender, he sits "on the seat, with planted on the dashboard before him the shoes, the black shoes smelling of negro: that mark on his ankles the gauge definite and ineradicable of the black tide creeping up his legs, moving from his feet upward as death moves" (p. 321). These shoes, given to him by a woman, once again identify the Negro with the forces of the feminine, and the black tide creeping up his legs measures more than his ultimate acceptance of a racial identity (Negro murderer): it marks at last his final bondage to the goddess of death and to the matriarchate.

On the day of Christmas's death he is pursued by a young man whose dedication to duty and commitment to principle qualify him for membership among the puritans of the Puritans, though he is utterly without theology. Yet even this epiphenomenal consciousness is shaped by unseen forces—the Fates, as already noted, named the Player—into the instrument of the goddess. The symbols which so effectively convey Grimm's appearance identify his seeming spiritual agency: "Above the blunt, cold rake of the automatic his face had that serene, unearthly luminousness of angels in church windows" (p. 437); " 'Jesus Christ!' Grimm cried, his young voice clear and outraged like that of a young priest" (p. 439). The marked religious connotations, however, of both images are anathema to the convictions of Calvinism; if they are associated with any formal religion, it would be with Catholicism, the last institutional remnant of a matriarchal consciousness in the modern world.[11] If one probes more deeply, too, into the nature of Grimm's final act (the castration of Christmas which horrifies even the men from a Protestant culture), one finds that it signifies more than Grimm's conscious motive of racio-sexual protectionism. It is, at root, an archetypal act, the work of the terrible mother who appears as castrator throughout the primordial world.[12] Thus, the final course of Christmas's career is charted in the direction of his setting out. As he lies dying on the kitchen floor in Hightower's house, something terrible and profound comes into his face: "For a long moment he looked up at them with peaceful and unfathomable and unbearable eyes. Then his face, body, all, seemed to collapse, to fall in upon itself, and from out the slashed garments about his hips and loins the pent black blood seemed to rush like a released breath" (pp. 439–40). Joe Christmas is released at last from his twin demons, from the burden of being sexed and from the encumbrance of consciousness.

Gail Hightower, in whose home the resigned man dies, stands between the narrative of Lena Grove and Byron Bunch and the story of Christmas. His place in the novel, however, is more than the stitch between tales, his life more than an interaction between permanent polarities. The narrative course of his life is an integral facet in the evocation of the all-controlling archetype.

From childhood, when his imagination was spooked with tales of his gallant cavalry grandfather, Gail Hightower has dwelt willingly among phantoms. Even in the decaying odour of his adult life, "his religion and his grandfather being shot from the galloping horse [are] all mixed up, as though the seed which his grandfather had transmitted to him had been on the horse too that night and had been killed too and time had stopped there and then for the seed and nothing had happened in time since, not even him" (p. 59). It is significant that Hightower should appear to be unborn of woman, as though his very un-life were the unspilled seed of his dead grandfather. For time—the constituency of the *magna mater*—has no part of him. He lives persistently in a single past instant in which a gun crashed, impaled on that event by which he lost the only life he ever had. Perhaps it is important that a woman (presumably) pulled the trigger, blew his grandfather out of time. But his adaptation to that event is more notable, the means of reconciliation by which he thinks "that my only salvation must be to return to the place to die where my life had already ceased before it began" (p. 452). For, contrary to Lena and her positiveness, he then proceeds to live out his remaining life in one place, foulsmelling, deathcoloured, inert. The only motion, in fact, that he knows is the mind's artifice, the dream of galloping hooves at sunset. Gail Hightower, like Quentin Compson, must finally be seen as the emblem of the male intellect's desire for stasis, for the permanence of eternity, not the temporal process of change.

More than once Hightower is represented by the image of an eastern idol (p. 83), the epitome of Buddhist anti-feminism and escape of soul from the wheel of life into the unfleshed bliss of nirvana. The image arises, characteristically, as a visitor's impression of Hightower in his study. The only regular visitor to that study is another man, Byron Bunch, also a spiritual *isolato* until the advent of Lena Grove. And when Byron moves to enter the matrix-loom of fate, his spiritual advisor attempts several times to block him: "Go away, Byron. Go away. Now. At once. Leave this place forever, this terrible place, this terrible, terrible place" (p. 298). The minister's view of woman (like Joe's) is that of an evil inflicted, doom by association: "There have been good women who were martyrs to brutes, in their cups and such. But what woman, good or bad, has ever suffered from any brute as men have suffered from good women? Tell me that, Byron" (p. 299). If, then, we should compare the roles of the two most antifeminine men in the novel, we might say that Joe Christmas embodies most of all the repugnance of the male consciousness for the elementary character of the goddess (menstruation, childbearing, nourishment—Joe rejects woman-given food), while Gail Hightower typifies spirit's refusal of the feminine transformative character (her governance over time, motion, and change).

The fate of these two men, however, is not quite the same. Perhaps it is because the intensities of their reactions are not the same, because Hightower does accept, at least for awhile, involvement in the maternal fabric of existence. Though he has been finally responsible for the death of his wife (a weak and very human social creature), and though he has lived cut off from the human and natural world for most of his life, he is brought by Byron (Lena) into a redemption of sorts. The fullest expression of his new-found feeling occurs in reaction to Lena's giving birth and his part in it: " 'I must do this more often,' he thinks, feeling the intermittent sun, the heat, smelling the savage and fecund odor of the earth, the woods, the loud silence. 'I should never have lost this habit, too. But perhaps they will both come back to me, if this itself be not the same as prayer' " (pp. 384–85). He senses for the first time man's sacral connection to the feminine; he begins to take root in man's creative sources, in life's genetic principle. Or perhaps it is more accurate to say that a door has been opened for him into the primordial world, a door that had stood open once before in his youth, recalled now by Byron's woman-engendered love:

> He hears now only the myriad and interminable insects, leaning in the window, breathing the hot still rich maculate smell of the earth, thinking of how when he was young, a youth, he had loved darkness, of walking or sitting alone among trees at night. Then the ground, the bark of trees, became actual, savage, filled with, evocative of, strange and baleful half delights and half terrors. He was afraid of it. He feared; he loved in being afraid. Then one day while at the seminary he realized that he was no longer afraid. It was as though a door had shut somewhere. He was no longer afraid of darkness. He just hated it; he would flee from it, to walls, to artificial light. (pp. 300–1)

The profound antithesis between dark and light, natural and artificial, which we observed in Christmas's life is reinvoked in the youthful experience of Hightower. What becomes noteworthy is the latter's differing response, at least initially, to the attributes of the mother archetype. Where sap-flowing trees make Joe vomit,

Gail worships, fearfully and lovingly, in the darkness of the trees; where one flees the engulfment of sense in the darkness, the other feels that the dark element alone confers an actuality upon sense perception. So it is most notable that Hightower's savage adoration should be usurped in the seminary, in the conscious world of the light god which, in terms of *Light in August*, is neither seminal nor "primogenitive" (p. 107). There, at last, the lucid principle pre-dominates in him as it always had in Joe Christmas. This, then, is his failing, both in marriage and in life: that he could not give up the spirit, "Not even to her, to woman. *The* woman. Woman (not the seminary, as he had once believed): the Passive and Anonymous whom God had created [still his Christian bias] to be not alone the recipient of the seed of his body but of his spirit too, which is truth or as near truth as he dare approach" (p. 442). Since he can ap-proach so near, he is not incorrigible, presumably because for a time he has been the devotee of the goddess. Thus, if *Light in August* is the story of the great mother's terrible retribution visited upon Joe Christmas, it is also an account of her will to reclaim Gail Hightower.

That reclamation, nevertheless, is not entirely successful, al-though one observer claims that "inwardly considered, redemption is the movement beyond despair and bondage to the past to joy and openness to the future. And this is the complex movement Faulkner has created in the story of Gail Hightower."[13] Hightower has not absolutely surrendered the past, the static moment, to re-enter the stream of time. In the fading, "final copper light of afternoon" (p. 441), Hightower retreats to the romantic vision, the timeless instant of the thundering hooves and not-shapes riding through the air. And although he acknowledges responsibility, finally, for his wife's death, though he recognizes in himself a charlatan deluded by the image of "a swaggering and unchastened bravo killed with a shotgun in a peaceful henhouse" (p. 462), his final, persistent vision is of the cavalry rush through the town, of "the wild bugles and the clashing sabres and the dying thunder of hooves" (p. 467). Insofar as the man looks to the future at all, he is not as open to it as some have liked to think. The minister's wheel of thinking, rushing spasmodically toward the time to come, becomes a halo in the August night, a circle of faces arrested out of contact with the earth. More than a recognition of the compositeness, the essential identity of mankind, it is a vision of the karmic wheel of life—the rack of pain and suffering so insufferable to the spirit seeking nirvana.[14] Hightower responds to it in the following way: " 'With all air, all heaven, filled with the lost and unheeded crying of all the living who ever lived, wailing still like lost children among the cold and terrible stars. . . . I wanted so little. I asked so little. It would seem. . . .' The wheel turns on. It spins now, fading, without progress, as though turned by that final flood which had rushed out of him, leaving his body empty and lighter than a forgotten leaf and even more trivial than flotsam lying spent and still upon the window ledge which has no solidity beneath hands that have no weight; so that it can be now Now" (p. 466). Although he does not die (the text is ambiguous; Faulkner said he did not—*University*, p. 75), the wheel of life seems to rush on, leaving him suspended, arrested in that final, glorious, timeless instant of doomed courage. In his own way, Hightower is doomed as well; he cannot save himself as he could not save Joe Christmas.

Finally, only Byron Bunch is left to us, out on the road at book's end with Lena Grove, redeemed from his isolation and drawn into the female element of motion which, Faulkner once said, is life. From the instant Lena comes to him in Jefferson, he moves in orbit about her, successively giving up his room, his country choir, his job, his friend, his peace of mind, only to be balked at last by Lena from the sharing of her bed. Yet by every social (if not legal) standard, that bed should be his right. His devotion, his love, his attentiveness, have made him effectually her husband, much more so than Lucas Burch, her other running mate (running in the sense that Joe Christmas runs, away from the female, for whom the masculine is, in any event, anonymous). Perhaps it is not presuming too far if one imagines, somewhere out beyond the book's final page, Byron's yearned-for consummation. Faulkner, however, has wisely chosen to bring his curtain down before that moment, partially, it seems, for the reason Brooks suggests: "He preferred to end his novel on the dominant theme of man's inability to fulfill himself, though the theme is treated here not tragically but with humor and amused irony—even as social comedy" (*Yoknapatawpha Country*, p. 74). Since the male world of *Light in August* is totally incapable of self-sufficiency, it is deeply appropriate that Byron should be left dependent upon, in a sense at the mercy of, Lena, and yet be willingly subordinate to the unreasoning design of a greater presence. Social comedy, then, is the prevailing tone of the conclusion of the story if, by "social," is meant the effective resolution—the means—by which man is enabled to live in a world of time.

Two things remain to be said in conclusion about the mythos of *Light in August*. In the first place, while Lena and Joanna together personify the dominant impulse of their world, it seems as if the artist is now personally disposed toward the positive, rather than the negative, manifestation of the goddess. Put another way, he has a story to tell about different kinds of male response to life and its archetype (the feminine); the predispositions and rational choices of a Christmas evoke the terrible face of that archetype, yet the author (like Byron Bunch) is willingly committed to the benevolent face. Faulkner's private response to the independent and ongoing life of Lena Grove is in this regard profoundly engaging; as he expressed it to Jean Stein, "One of the calmest, sanest speeches I ever heard was when she said to Byron Bunch at the very instant of repulsing his final, desperate and despairing attempt at rape, 'Ain't you ashamed? You might have woke the baby' " (*Lion*, p. 253). The reason, one presumes, why Joe Christmas never comes face to face with Lena in this story, but why he confronts Joanna as his nemesis instead, is that Faulkner is now logically (because willfully) inclined toward separating their two functions—he wants to exorcise the terrible from the good—although symbolically, he confirms their identity. This particular structuring of unlimited power in human form can be called, in the fullest sense, the signature of mythos.

Second, Faulkner's remark about the mother and the baby suggests that Lena, in her static elementary character of the loving mother, has brought an additional kind of life to light: the work of art. In other words, the dynamic transformative character of the young woman has had great effect on the experience of the artist, just as she has been responsible for the spiritual transformation of Byron and, to some extent, Hightower. By committing himself to Lena, Faulkner has come to terms with his anima. Thus the very creation, as well as the content, of the novel stand as testimony to the presence of an inner feminine muse; its mythos is absolute, both in action and in manifestation. And *Light in August* is, in the completest sense, the book of the Great Mother.

𝒸 *Epilogue* 𝒸

Light in August is the last real incarnation of the feminine in William Faulkner's work. It is as though he had by now exorcised the "demon" archetype, or given it such quiescent fulfilment—finding in Lena Grove the ultimate expression of the value of existence—that he could turn from the heart's old driving desire to new concerns. From this moment on, the tendency in his portrayal of woman is toward socializing, toward even patriarchal usurpation. It shall be apparent soon enough how this affects *The Hamlet.*

Before leaving this section, however, we might notice how *Light in August* is the summation in the Faulkner corpus of the primordial though endlessly repeated story of the Great Goddess. For a kind of re-orchestration occurs in the novel, a coda of symbols recalled from the three previous works. The identity of trees with the primordial mother, formerly realized in *The Sound and the Fury* through Benjy's haunting memory of his sister, is evoked once again through Christmas's loathing for woman-flowing trees and through Hightower's loving fear of savage bark in the darkness. *As I Lay Dying*'s prevailing symbol of motion, so integral to the dead character of Addie, is just as vitally related to Lena's living figure. (Also one might say of Darl and Joe that they are equally "doomed with motion.") Similarly, the distrust of words exemplified in Addie receives new emphasis in Mrs. Beard's assertion that "it's menfolks that take talking serious" (p. 397) or Byron's startled recognition in Lena's place of birth that *"it was like me, and her, and all the other folks that I had to get mixed up in it, were just a lot of words that never even stood for anything, were not even us while all the time what was us was going on and going on without even missing the lack of words"* (p. 380, Faulkner's italics). Finally, *Sanctuary's* symbolic preoccupation with sex, with a corn cob and rape and sexual nausea, is reinvoked in Christmas's menstrual revulsion and in Hightower's hatred of the dark earth, but it is finally revalued in Byron's acceptance of Lena's unvirginity and the child he did not father.

In every case, the configuration of symbols evokes the all-controlling presence of the archetypal feminine; taken together these symbols answer, in James Baird's sense, our basic human need for sacrament. To put it another way, a link is touched in our archaic nature by Faulkner's primitivism, which sets off sensations of the sacred reaching back to the world of archetypal realities. In every case, the reader is expected to become ritually involved in the male element of choice—whether to accept or reject the life-giving factors. Perhaps, in a modern world, it is through art alone that one is enabled to break the bounds of one's isolation (ego consciousness), and to re-enter the sacramental world, the primitive experience of corporateness with one's "fellows in communion with the deity" (Baird, p. 56). Archetypal art, whatever its valence, then becomes the last cultural remnant of the primal stuff of revelation.

In conclusion, it is worth mentioning Leslie Fiedler's apt phrase covering Faulkner's novels of this period; he terms them "myths of masculine protest" (*Love and Death*, p. 321). Quentin, Benjy, Jason, Anse, Darl, Jewel, Horace, Goodwin, Popeye, Christmas, Hightower, and Byron all find themselves constrained, shaped, created, destroyed, and transformed by their various experiences of the daemonic feminine. To some extent, one might claim their terrors and delights as Faulkner's own. Fiedler forgets the novels *per se*, however, when he says, "Pubescent or nubile women, for Faulkner, fall into two classes, roughly corresponding to those of Hemingway, though for the former both are terrifying: great, sluggish, mindless daughters of peasants, whose fertility and allure are scarcely distinguishable from those of a beast in heat; and the febrile, almost fleshless but sexually insatiable daughters of the aristocracy" (p. 321). Nowhere is the sexual misunderstanding of Faulkner by critics better represented, and nowhere are the novels' resolutions more completely forgotten. For all of the four works considered move toward an acceptance, whether gravely or gladsomely, of the awesome forces glimpsed in special women. And in naked lyrical reverence alone, *Light in August* is the greatest of these.

PART THREE

INDIVIDUATION

Individuation, the realization of
selfhood, is not just a mental problem,
but the problem of life itself.
C. G. Jung, *The Integration of the
Personality*.

Individuation represents a
development whose [upshot] is
precisely the liberation of the
individual from the primordial
mythical world, the freeing
of the psyche.
Erich Neumann, *Amor and Psyche*.

Prolegomena to a Study of Olympian Art

One of the earliest portraits of the goddess of love in Western literature is sketched in *The Odyssey* of Homer. Together with a companion piece in *The Iliad*, it is the profoundest sort of comment on the development of Western consciousness in relation to the archetypal feminine. The gist as well as the jest of the story in question is the adulterous love of Aphrodite for Ares. Their liaison is ribaldly disclosed in a song (referred to in Homeric criticism as the "Lay of Demodokos") performed before Odysseus in the Phaiakian court. The tale has a special pertinence for Odysseus as a part of a continuing *leitmotif* focused upon wifely infidelity, but its cultural and psychic implications extend well beyond the work of art. For the story centres on the outrage of the cuckolded husband (the crippled though cunning Hephaistos), on his ruse of the artful bed bonds, and on the delighted response of his divine colleagues. After Hephaistos has sprung his net on the labouring couple, he cries out,

'Father Zeus and all you blessed immortal
gods, come here, to see a ridiculous sight, no seemly

matter . . . . I am sickened when I look at them, and yet
I think they will not go on lying thus even for a little,
much though they are in love, I think they will have no
    wish
for sleeping, but then my fastenings and my snare will
    contain them
until her father pays back in full all my gifts of courtship
I paid out into his hand for the sake of his bitch-eyed
    daughter.
The girl is beautiful indeed, but she is intemperate.'
  So he spoke, and the Gods gathered to the house with
    the brazen
floor. Poseidon came, the shaker of the earth, and the
    kindly
Hermes came, and the lord who works from afar, Apollo,
but the female gods remained each at her home, for
    modesty.
The gods, the givers of good things, stood there in the
    forecourt,
and among the blessed immortals uncontrollable laughter
went up as they saw the handiwork of subtle Hephaistos.[1]

Aphrodite seems to have become Hephaistos's
principal victim here, not because his rival is War
himself, but because she is the ambivalent object of
every god's interest. Her husband is not the only one
to announce in a single breath his longing and loathing. Argeïphontes grinningly admits, in this of all
moments, that he is eager to trade places with Ares
beneath the net (V, 339–43). The blindness of desire
is thus lightened as it is made a laughingstock.
Although Aphrodite recovers her dignity and even
some of her divinity by returning to her sacred shrine
at Paphos, where

the Graces bathed her and anointed her with ambrosial
oil, such as abounds for the gods who are everlasting,
and put delightful clothing about her, a wonder to look on
                                    (VIII, 364–66),

she has still been made the amusing subject of a dirty
joke. A jealous, because personalized, husband exposes
her to ridicule and shame (each a very human idiosyn-
crasy); a group of male gods stands mirthfully (if
somewhat leeringly) about, their female counterparts

demurring out of a sense of social nicety (no ceremonial display, this, no sacral exposure of the life-bearing powers); and the wench herself is identified with property and its patriarchal disposition. This Olympian version of inspired adultery may be free from the human tragedy of Helen's and Clytemnestra's faithlessness, but it still bespeaks the need expressed by an emergent patriarchate[2] to laugh away powers it could not otherwise control. One rightly feels that the numinous character of the goddess of fertility is now comically reduced in this irreverent story of sexual attraction.

In the fifth book of *The Iliad*, further circumscriptions are hedged about the powers of the love goddess. Attempting to protect her son Aineias, Aphrodite is pursued by the war-possessed Greek, Diomedes, who runs confidently,

knowing her for a god without warcraft, not of those who, goddesses, range in order the ranks of men in fighting, not Athene and not Enyo, sacker of cities.[3]

The Greek warrior-hero is subsequently empowered to wound the frightened goddess, to whom Zeus, father of the immortals, offers the following paternal comfort:

'No, my child, not for you are the works of warfare. Rather concern yourself only with the lovely secrets of marriage, while all this shall be left to Athene and sudden Ares.
(V, 428–30).

The female divinity who presides over creation and nurturing seems to have lost her authority over destruction; the terrible has been split from the good; Athene has taken a personality distinct from Aphrodite. All of the foregoing indicates, in terms of the mythological apperception of Hellenic culture, a sundering of the primordial unity of the mother archetype. More than that, the reduction of both her powers of awefulness and fascination suggests a tendency inherent in the personalizing (or individuation) of the feminine: inevitable usurpation by the patriarchate.

From historical evidence, it is apparent that cults of

the Olympian patriarchal deities were preceded on Peloponnese and in Minoan civilization by worship of the mother goddess.[4] When, toward the middle of the second millennium, the warrior culture of the Mycenaeans began to gain political ascendancy, the world of Homeric epic was taking shape in the form which would finally be familiar to us. The literary evidence, however, reveals many of the anomalies of historical syncretism. Vestigial elements of the mother goddess persist in the daughters and wives of Zeus, in Hera, Athene, Aphrodite.[5] Zeus himself, as his name reveals, is an Indo-European interloper (Thomson, p. 286), a clear usurper of the powers of the Minoan mother goddess. In this context, the rampant sexual violations which he conducts so vigorously tell something of the story of the conquest. The rape of Europa—herself one of the "emanations of the Minoan mother-goddess" (p. 124) whose ravishment conceives and produces Minos—connects Zeus all too easily in legend with Minoan civilization. For the purpose of political control, it is often suggested, the emerging Mycenaean patriarchate supplants the matriarchal myths with its freshly minted legends. In the broader panorama of archetypal space, however, one sees the familiar spectacle of the "male" intellect, of reason and ego consciousness, struggling to extricate itself from the "feminine" unconscious which has enveloped and contained it.

Especially in Homeric epic, this quest for consciousness's liberation from the numinous is not entirely successful; *The Odyssey*, for example, is suffused with "the overshadowing power of woman."[6] Helen, Clytemnestra, and Penelope on the human side, Circe, Calypso, and the Sirens on the immortal plane, preserve for the "male" world a dual fascination and dread of the overpowering anima. Correspondingly, the terrible beauty of Helen in *The Iliad* bears an unmistakable relation to the primordial Aphrodite. Notwithstanding these cultural vestiges of the feminine archetype, the Ionian singer(s) contradicts his inherited material. He even digresses, where necessary, to limit the authority of the matriarchate. It is not surprising that the accession of a patriarchate should mean the inevitable subordination of its archetypal basis to consciousness; reason strains to be free of its unconscious matrix. The easiest way to control the goddess is to make her an individual. As one remarks in Aphrodite, "individuation" is the certain means of circumscription; it is a part of rationality's containment of unconscious contents. Ultimately, the "patriarchate" personates.

Jung has described the human course of individuation as the process by which the ego consciousness tries to assimilate and integrate the unconscious and its chaotic, though dynamic, contents.[7] Paradoxically, this arising consciousness is at war with the element which gives it life; it often seeks an impossible autonomy; yet the degree to which it collaborates with its impersonal substance will be the measure of a full and stable human personality. Individuation, in the strictest sense, is the unending tension between protective reason and the bewilderingly devious ways of the unconscious; the totality forged from this particular stress becomes the individual.

The record of William Faulkner's agon with the anima, the tension of his conflict and collaboration with a female muse from the writing of *The Sound and the Fury* to *Light in August*, might someday obtain qualified consideration as the process of his personal individuation. It seems altogether likely that in the writing of *Light in August*, he had come to terms with it—had integrated it insofar as it is possible to integrate unconscious contents. Perhaps this accounts for a corresponding decline in artistic power when he turns once more to the female element as subject in *The Hamlet*, *The Town*, and *The Mansion*; to varying extents, the archetype is no longer the object (or factor) of literary creation.

The hypothesis that the feminine archetype had by now become impoverished, or artistically unusable, for Faulkner is an inference drawn from art to artist. The concern of the coming chapter, however, is less with artistic personality than it is with personalization in the work of art. In a strictly literary context, "individuation" here refers to a character development whose upshot is the "liberation of the individual from the primordial mythical world,"[8] and a narrative development of which the outcome is a characterless freedom.

7

Fall of the Goddess

The Rise of a Female Personality
in the Snopes Trilogy
and "An Odor of Verbena"

Eula Varner of *The Hamlet* has long been enshrined in Faulkner criticism as "the embodiment of fertility,"[1] as "earth-mother"[2] and "eternal goddess."[3] A plethora of imagistic evidence in the novel supports this notion of her mythic identity. What often goes unnoticed, however, is the Olympian *provenance* of the imagery; Eula is shaped for us by minds infected with classicism, by characters like Labove whose books include "an original Horace and a Thucydides which the classics professor, in whose home he had built the morning fires, had given him at Christmas."[4]

It is the narrator who first links Eula's appearance with "some symbology out of the old Dionysic [*sic*] times—honey in sunlight and bursting grapes, the writhen bleeding of the crushed fecundated vine beneath the hard rapacious trampling goat-hoof" (p. 95); in his own voice, he again remarks "her long Olympian legs revealed halfway to the thigh astride the wooden horses of merry-go-rounds" (p. 130). Narrative speakers likewise enjoy a common sympathy of perception: to Labove, Eula "postulated that ungirdled quality of the very goddesses in his Homer and Thucydides: of being at once corrupt and immaculate, at once virgins and the mothers of warriors and of grown men" (p. 114); her entrance into his classroom brought to "the bleak, ill-lighted, poorly-heated room dedicated to the harsh functioning of Protestant primary education a moist blast of spring's liquorish corruption, a pagan triumphal prostration before the supreme primal uterus" (p. 114); in the act of "walking down the aisle between them she would transform the very wooden desks and benches themselves into a grove of Venus" (p. 115). Even after Labove's fumbling attempt at rape is repulsed by one of the most contemptuously indifferent speeches in all of literature—" 'Stop pawing me,' she said. 'You old headless horseman Ichabod Crane' " (p. 122)—he continues to be madly fascinated, already "seeing her entering the room again tomorrow morning, tranquil, untroubled, not even remembering, carrying the cold potato which at recess she would sit on the sunny steps and eat like one of the unchaste and perhaps even anonymously pregnant immortals eating bread of Paradise on a sunwise slope of Olympus" (pp. 123–24). In Ratliff's mind and in the peripheral consciousness of Frenchman's Bend—"a little lost village, nameless, without grace, forsaken, yet which wombed once by chance and accident one blind seed of the spendthrift Olympian ejaculation and did not know it" (p. 149)—she is "the word, the dream and wish of all male under sun capable of harm" (p. 149).

The earliest doubt one ought to have about the wholehearted acceptance of Eula's mythic stature lurks somewhere in the nature of these images associated with her. They are not completely natural and spontaneous; they refer her mythic quality to a tertiary source—presumably to the same "afflatus" which inspired Homer and Thucydides, but approaching that creative source through intermediaries, not directly. The images describing Eula's awesome fertility are not dependent upon the thing-in-itself; as such, they are not fully autonomous symbols. Nevertheless, Eula is possessed of an autonomous influence; the men and boys of Frenchman's Bend flock to her in droves, compelled by the force that underlies all function of intellect. Even so reasonable a critic as Cleanth Brooks has felt the infection of the " 'mythic' atmosphere of *The Hamlet*" (*Yoknapatawpha*, p. 170), to the point of saying that "Eula becomes a kind of rustic Aphrodite" (pp. 170–71) within the story; to the "young fanatic Labove" and in a sense to "the whole community," she "becomes the archetypal feminine" (p. 172). Her effect on the menfolks notwithstanding, the statement represents a crucial misunderstanding of the myth of woman in Faulkner. No matter how "rustic" (meaning "quaintly primitive" in the parlance of a classicist) is her presentation, the Olympian Aphrodite is something quite distinct from the archetypal feminine. Eula Varner and the powers invested in her are not the controlling presence in the world of *The Hamlet*. Although she is early on the honey-pot round which the flies swirl, and though later on she is the subject of every man's elegiac longing, she herself is bartered in exchange for family honour, carried away thrall to Flem Snopes and the new economic powers. Her potential mythos becomes the record of the myth's defeat.

This narrative outcome of *The Hamlet* has suggested possibilities of interpretation ranging from tragedy to high comedy: from a view of Eula (and Ike Snopes with his cow) as life-redeeming forces refused by an impotent world,[5] to a prospect of a "convincing goddess" fashioned in a forge of humour, that we might see "the image of ourselves" reflected in both "irony and wonder."[6] The real predicament of this goddess, however, has gone largely unconsidered. For example, in concurrence with the portrait of this "girl of whom, even at nine and ten and eleven, there was too much—too much of leg, too much of breast, too much of buttock; too much of mammalian female meat" (p. 100), there are images of a counter direction. They are of rape, of sexual violation rather than of sexual fulfilment: "The three of them would be seen passing along the road—Mrs. Varner in her Sunday dress and shawl, followed by the Negro man staggering slightly beneath her long, dangling, already indisputably female burden like a bizarre chaperoned Sabine rape" (p. 96). The Dionysiac reference cited almost paradoxically in an Olympian context carries an image of "the writhen bleeding of the crushed fecundated vine beneath the hard rapacious trampling goat-hoof." These symbolic intimations culminate in Eula's seduction and marriage, the greatest rape of all; Ratliff's tensely comic vision of Flem's conquest of Hell is read by many commentators as the story of Persephone's abduction by Hades.[7]

This dual concern with sexuality, with its potential richness and its probable ravishment, is further qualified by an element of blatant whorishness. Even before she is bartered off to Flem, Eula daily passes the Varner boarder in the hall, "looking, in the rich deshabille of her loose hair and the sloven and not always clean garments she had groped into between bed and breakfast table, as if she had just been surprised from a couch of illicit love by a police raid" (p. 148). The image prefigures the fast approaching climax of Book Two—a kind of male economic violation of woman—which Ratliff again envisions as a universal feature of Snopesism, the next Snopes in line doing business with any and all women in the county as he shuts the door of the store "and puts the bar up and she has done already went around behind the counter and laid down on the floor because maybe she thinks by now that's what you have to do, not to pay for the lard because that's done already been wrote down in the book, but to get out of that door again" (p. 165). Snopeses and "whores" bespeak a new cosmic order in *The Hamlet*, a male principle of economy which is fully and finally dominant.

Although the lyrical and compassionate story of Ike Snopes's sodomy has been widely regarded as the only instance of true love in the novel (however grotesque in situation, however burlesque in romantic style), it tends imagistically to recapitulate the movement of the earlier "love" story. Eula's power of sexual attraction is reduced to perhaps its most elemental level in the "rich, slow, warm barn-reek milk-reek" of the cow, "the flowing immemorial female" (p. 168)—confirming (though not necessarily caricaturing) the natural animality of the feminine pictured earlier in the pack of suitors pursuing the woman in "a leashed turmoil of lust like so many lowering dogs after a scarce-fledged and apparently unawares bitch" (p. 131). When Houston drives the idiot off his farm in baffled, though considerate, outrage, he tries to buy off Ike's love once and for all with a fifty-cent piece. From out of the poetic splendour in which the idiot moves and breathes with the earth's suspiring, the coin is given motion, dropped, lost (whether spurned or not can only be conjectured). But Ike returns that same afternoon to bridle the indifferent cow and lead her captive to a world of lyric idyll. There he attempts to crown his abducted love with a floral diadem, but "his awkward and disobedient hand, instead of breaking the stem, merely shuts about the escaping stalk and strips the flower-head into a scatter of ravished petals" (p. 186). These intimations of rape are likewise joined once more with implications of harlotry: "Git on home, you damn whore!" (p. 178) shouts Houston at the cow standing in the creek with Ike behind her. Houston later comes to some understanding of the idiot's love for the cow and he offers the beast in trust to Mrs. Littlejohn. Nonetheless, even the sympathetic landlady is bound by rigid economic principle; she insists that Houston take payment for the animal, in a sense then buying Ike his love. It must not be forgotten, at this or any level, that *The Hamlet* posits a world in which even a man's love must be the object of his ownership. Ike's poetic mindlessness, like Eula's unconscious "divinity," is thus coerced by powers which go beyond him.

The most telling link, however, between Eula and the cow is fastened in their mutual Olympian identity: Eula is associated with Venus, the cow with Juno (p. 184). The goddess of love and the wife of Zeus might seem, on first glance, to be at cross-purposes in the philanderings of the Homeric gods. Juno (Hera), especially, is quite determined to keep her love-driven husband close to home. Nevertheless, both females have a similar effect on the Homeric vision of a promiscuous pantheon: they make divine sexuality an irreverently funny matter. Although the sexual indiscretion of the goddess-possessed Helen in *The Iliad* may awaken some of the old sense of Aphrodite's terrible fascination, more often the essential light-heartedness of masculine conquest is up-played to the hilt. Zeus seduces and laughingly do gods go cuckolding. The primary reason for this mythic reversal is fairly simple: with the development of a psychic patriarchate, the Great Goddess is transformed into the goddess of love, and the full numinous power of the feminine diminishes into mere sexuality. As a consequence, it is true of Olympian heaven (and earth) that conquest, whether in bed or in battle, is a male occupation. Patriarchal deities have "reason" to joke when alien powers come under their control, and a patriarchal world might understandably laugh with irreverence born of relief. The dark powers have been stripped from the feminine: her nakedness now no threat but threatened.

That Faulkner should turn to the Olympian world in the comic telling of his Snopes legend is significant for two reasons. First, the symbolism of *The Hamlet* reflects the ascendancy of consciousness—the male spiritual impulse—on Mt. Olympus; it is allusion which, although it retains some of the primitiveness and autonomous life of its sources, does not so much evoke a sense of the unknowable as it does the known literary figure.[8] Second, while the mode of creation in the novel is no longer matriarchal—an inexplicable imaging out of the creative unconscious—the art of conscious allusion is perfectly adapted to its themes and movement; the Olympian imagery predicts an outcome which will be similar in kind, though in degree more damaging, for the place and power of the goddess.

When Labove forsees Eula's husband (yet to be disclosed by time) as "the crippled Vulcan to that Venus" (p. 119), he signals both the humour and the threat, the comedy and the tragedy, inherent in her story. Those critics who have not wanted to laugh at Eula's humorous characterization (what one calls an "antic paganism," and another calls "a comically exaggerated 'myth' of the earth"[9]) in *The Hamlet* seem not to have accepted the full implications of the narrative. Likewise something laughable pervades the lyric brilliance of the idylls of the Cow, and no matter how sympathetic the treatment of an idiot knight held in thrall by *"la belle vache sans merci"* (Hoffman, p. 91) might be, the bare attempt to elevate the lovers to a redemptive symbol within the novel must be charged with a lack of perspective. For *The Hamlet* represents a changed cosmic order in the saga of Yoknapatawpha. The feminine has been subdued; the masculine stands in full control. Yet one cultural mutation has now obtained; conquest is achieved in barter, not in battle, and a bartered subjugation extends, with Snopes or Varner, into the bedrooms (and pastures, even plank floors) of the county.

The caricature stories of the Eula-cow goddess also contain, however, a dark and tortured intensity. They bespeak a new kind of tragedy in Faulkner, waste and destruction of a social rather than archetypal dimension (for, unlike Temple Drake, Eula has no power to mete out "justice" for the act of "rape"). The foundations of the new social order are exposed in the mind of Faulkner's new humanist hero, V. K. Ratliff, who, seeking an end to public sodomy, thinks "how this was probably the first time anywhere where breath inhaled and suspired and men established the foundations of their existences on the currency of coin, that anyone had ever wished Flem Snopes were here instead of anywhere else, for any reason, at any price" (p. 202). "The currency of coin" (and Flem Snopes with it) is the obvious power in the environs of Frenchman's Bend; the "goddesses" have both become enslaved by it, merchandise to be haggled over. They are, like Danae, ravished by the shower of gold in which Zeus descends. What is not quite so obvious in *The Hamlet*, however, is the process by which money has upset a cosmic order.

As Flem Snopes begins his rising trajectory toward Jefferson, he assumes the efficient control of the Varner business. It matters little whether he is selling plow-lines and candy or settling the annual crop accounts of tenant farmers; he is pictured in the store with the open ledgers before him (p. 61). Not even Flem's employer is safe from that ledger (much less the till). When Will Varner commands his first plug of tobacco from the new clerk, payment is quietly but inexorably demanded of him. The clerk's presence in the store, in fact, inaugurates a new kind of dealing, devoid of Jody's chiselling, yet with a new impersonality about it, conducted by a man "who apparently never looked directly or long enough at any face to remember the name which went with it, yet who never made mistakes in any matter pertaining to money" (p. 57). There is the same rigidity about Flem's contracts, a kind of binding legalism that cannot be changed for the very reason that it is law. The community of Frenchman's Bend is powerless to stop him; he becomes a monstrous embodiment of law, of utterly inflexible principle.

One finds on second glance, nevertheless, that Flem is not unique in kind in *The Hamlet*; he is merely greater in degree. The farmer whose chop bin is rifled by Ike Snopes becomes momentarily homicidal, for he sees "in this second flagrant abrogation of the ancient biblical edict (on which he had established existence, integrity, all) that man must sweat or have not" (p. 193) a violation of a principle worth more than human life. The lives of his own children have meant less to him than his stern insistence on the letter of biblical law; unsurprisingly, all of his five children left home at the moment of their majority. The same rigidity of principle (whatever its manifestation) is stamped into Labove's character, onto "a forensic face, the face of invincible conviction in the power of words as a principle worth dying for if necessary" (p. 106). Economically, too, Labove has his scruples; he will not take football cleats to shoe his barefoot family except on those Saturday afternoons when his team has been victorious. He views the shoes as the price of his heroics. Mrs. Littlejohn also has her principles; when Houston would give the cow to its beloved, she insists on the legality of payment. Likewise Ratliff, who is the silent partner in a Jefferson diner, pays "for his coffee, scrupulously" (p. 72) before leaving. So Frenchman's Bend is more than temperamentally susceptible to Snopes; in certain respects they have created him.

Ratliff, more than anyone else, perhaps, provides a measure for the mercantile ethic of Flem Snopes because he subscribes to the legality while opposing the inhuman code of pure economics. Ratliff is a shrewd dealer, but a compassionate and witty man. Before the advent of Snopes, he barters for the pleasure and the honour of a spirited contest "which far transcended mere gross profit" (p. 68). When Flem comes to threaten the community and the wellbeing of some of its individuals, Ratliff strives to champion their weakness, using Flem's incorrigible adherence to the letter of the law in a hearty attempt to turn that law to compassionate ends. But the most he ever accomplishes is a draw, and there comes a point in his thinking too—where Snopes has grown so monstrous a figure of undeviating principle—that he sees Flem triumph over Satan himself, beating him by his own law. Axiomatically, then, the law becomes a more than devilish principle. Nowhere does *The Hamlet* make this more wryly evident than in the failure of the court to compensate the terrible Mrs. Tull and the enfeebled Mrs. Armstid for the damage done them by the spotted horses. Both the judge (who is entirely sympathetic) and the court Law are revealed as being steadfastly impotent to serve the ends of anything but legal exactitude.

One of the most important aspects of this world of economic principle—or unyielding legalism—is its bond (like that of Jason Compson) with bachelorhood and a sexless masculinity. Ratliff is said to possess "that same air of perpetual bachelorhood which Jody Varner had, although there was no other resemblance between them and not much here, since in Varner it was a quality of shabby and fustian gallantry where in Ratliff it was that hearty celibacy as of a lay brother in a twelfth-century monastery—a gardener, a pruner of vines, say" (p. 43). Jody Varner's festering outrage at the nearness of Eula's ungirdled body behind him on the horse is integrally linked to his character as a "jealous seething eunuch priest" (p. 115). His holy orders, however, do not derive from the fecund goddess. His sexless antipathy has more in common with Labove who does not want Eula "as a wife, he just wanted her one time as a man with a gangrened hand or foot thirsts after the axe stroke which will leave him comparatively whole again" (p. 119).

Of Labove's face too it is remarked, "A thousand years ago it would have been a monk's, a militant fanatic who would have turned his uncompromising back upon the world with actual joy and gone to a desert and passed the rest of his days and nights calmly and without an instant's self-doubt battling, not to save humanity about which he would have cared nothing, for whose sufferings he would have had nothing but contempt, but with his own fierce and unappeasable natural appetites" (p. 106).

This antivital fanaticism so characteristic of the masculine nature is successfully directed, for once in Faulkner, against the power of woman. *The Hamlet* establishes an autonomous world of the spirit. It is not only in Labove's wrestling contest with his appetites, nor in Jody's hatred of the sexual element that the "male" intellect achieves its freedom from the generative and destructive matrix of all life. The very store, literal and metaphoric centre of the novel, maintains "an actual smell, masculine, almost monastic" (p. 125). It is closely allied with Flem Snopes, whose impotence denies the genetic basis of being. For money, the economic ethic, and the "legal" principle, have some time ago become the new cosmic order to the men who squat day after day on the gallery of the store. This same principle of spirit, once so completely and awesomely subordinate to the feminine, is now destined to ride in fullest ascendancy with the "calm beautiful mask" of woman beside it toward Jefferson. Even Ratliff, who would raise once more the old problem, the remorseless opposition of Joe Christmas to the Great Goddess, speaks less in enmity this time than in grieving masculine relief: "But that was all right, it was just meat, just galmeat he thought, and God knows there was a plenty of that, yesterday and tomorrow too. Of course there was the waste, not wasted on Snopes but on all of them, himself included—Except was it waste? he thought suddenly. . . . He looked at the face again. It had not been tragic, and now it was not even damned, since from behind it there looked out only another mortal natural enemy of the masculine race. And beautiful: but then, so did the highwayman's daggers and pistols make a pretty shine on him" (pp. 150-51). Ratliff notwithstanding, the real power over life and death lies no longer with the archetypal (she has ceased to be that) feminine. It is invested in the bridegroom who carries the pregnant mother off, holding "the straw suitcase on his knees like the coffin of a baby's funeral" (p. 146).

The love affairs of Jack Houston and Mink Snopes likewise bespeak the new independence of the patriarchate, the violent will of consciousness to assert its self-begetting and the world's determination. When the schoolgirl Lucy Pate relentlessly does Houston's homework for him, hands it in against his will, and decides even to fail with him to stay near him, he flees her, eluding the old transformative face of woman "that steadfast and undismayable will to alter and improve and remake" (p. 210). He stays away, self-exiled in Texas, for twelve years. The woman he eventually takes up with is a whore, and when he leads her out of the Galveston brothel into cohabitation, there is "a scene by gaslight between him and the curl-papered landlady as violent as if he were ravishing from the house an only daughter with an entailed estate" (p. 215). Once again, the imagistic repetition underscores the new male headspring of economy, of violation and ownership. And though the woman remains loyal to him, even loving, he pays her off; he refuses to marry her, forbidden not only by his fanatic Protestant conditioning against the whore of Babylon, but drawn ultimately by the inescapable Lucy Pate who had precipitated "a feud, a gage, wordless, uncapitulating, between that unflagging will not for love or passion but for the married state, and that furious and as unbending one for solitariness and freedom" (p. 211). Before the marriage, Houston gives Lucy a stallion, "as if for a wedding present to her, though he never said so. Or if that blood and bone and muscles represented that polygamous and bitless masculinity which he had relinquished, he never said that" (p. 218). Within six months, she is killed by the horse. It is as if, metaphorically, she is destroyed by the bitless masculinity which had never really been surrendered. Houston grieves, furiously and implacably, but he is described, like the other bachelors, as lying "on the monklike cot" (p. 192). Unquestionably he loves Lucy and her loss is insupportable, but remorse in him, as in Ratliff, seems buttressed by a hidden relief; the rational principle has, almost in spite of itself, maintained its self-sufficiency.

The love of Mink Snopes appears, on first sight, to present a different case. Mink is summoned to the bed of his employer's daughter, as is every other man before him in the timber-cutting camp. The daughter keeps her hair "cut almost man-short with razors" and when he first lays eyes on her, he sees "the habit of success—that perfect marriage of will and ability with a single un-diffused object—which set her not as a feminine garment but as one as masculine as the overalls and her height and size and the short hair; he saw not a nympholet but the confident lord of a harem" (p. 241). The mannish character of her will, however, has a striking resemblance to Lucy Pate's indefatigable will "not for love or passion but for the married state." They are two faces on the same coin, one with a male's dominance of possession, the other with an absolute commitment to law. Mink marries the lumberjack woman and sleeps uneasily with her body beside him, clothed in the ghosts of her former lovers. For he has been reared in the ethic of male conquest, "bred by generations to believe invincibly that to every man, whatever his past actions, whatever depths he might have reached, there was reserved one virgin, at least for him to marry; one maidenhead, if only for him to deflower and destroy" (p. 242). Though he misses his opportunity for ravishment, the woman becomes in time subordinate to him, shackled by her children "more irrevocably than he himself was shackled, since on her fate she had even put the seal of a formal acquiescence by letting her hair grow out again and dyeing it" (p. 243). When he becomes embroiled with Houston in a smouldering quarrel, she rescinds that acquiescence; she warns him that she will leave if he stoops to murder. Yet upon the event, she does not go very far. She even prostitutes herself to help him escape. In principled rage, Mink throws the money away, thus refusing the single assistance which might save him from jail. He thereby reveals a moral code (something alien to the rest of the Snopeses), but in a curiously moral way, he achieves his final freedom from the woman by going to prison. He defeats her figuratively, even as Houston metaphorically defeated his wife, not because he does not love her, but because the law and morality of the male spirit is ultimately inimical to passion.

In Mink, finally, one discovers forces of tragic destruction to be operative behind the comic mask of *The Hamlet* which are not singly directed from the masculine toward the feminine. Jack Houston, whose cow is beloved by Ike Snopes, and whose pasture is encroached upon by Mink Snopes's heifer, is destroyed by a mutual masculine commitment to principle, to legality, to the rational will. The long and compelling story, especially, of Mink's inflexible will is testimony to an almost admirable "male" obsession with freedom, with the justification of integrity. At the moment when the "red roar" of Mink's gun blows Houston out of the saddle, one is not convinced of the "blackness" of his crime, being yet captivated by his indomitable spirit, by the intractability of a small man who refuses to be beaten. Only consciousness's terrible alienation in the empty farmhouse, in the swamp, finally in the jail, serves as the measure of its terrible sterility. Nor can this autonomy of the will expect relief from its own kind: Flem does not go to Jefferson; he must not interfere with the machinery of justice. The male principle of spirit, having nothing left to conquer, is finally embattled against itself.

This civil war of the soul does not lack a deeply comic side. The exploitation story of the spotted horses is one of the funniest episodes in Faulkner, rivalling both the whorehouse predicament of the Snopes boys and the underworld funeral in *Sanctuary*. Implications of tragedy nevertheless linger in the face of Mrs. Armstid, pleading with her despaired husband not to purchase one of the splotched pinwheels of motion, urging him not to waste her chaps' shoe-money, quailing finally before the lash of his coiled rope. The implications spill over then into actuality, not only in the injury done Henry by the wickedly untameable herd, but in his desperate, ultimately maddened desire to find gold on the old Frenchman place. For Flem's most complete triumph in the novel involves not only the conquest of his major antagonist, Ratliff, but Bookwright and Armstid with him. The shrewdness of Snopes brings the three men to abandon reason, to exchange conscious restraint for the pure principle of possession. And though Ratliff returns to his monkishly hearty sanity, Armstid does not. Flem pauses in conclusion to watch Henry digging, spits over the wheel of the wagon, then drives on toward the town, rendered personally impervious and invincible by his freedom from feeling and the visceral world of the feminine.

One commentator objects to this masculine society of *The Hamlet*, more particularly to "the viciousness of a system that equates masculinity with the possession and dominance of a woman."[10] The real basis for remonstrance is that "Codes of conquest do nothing more than dehumanize the victor, devitalize the victim" (p. 182), striking a common note with a different sort of protest—that Faulkner's "women are seldom individualized human beings but shadowy, enigmatic creatures, incarnations of the 'Eternal Feminine' " (Brien, pp. 132–33). The one critic bemoans a tyranny over woman; the other the tyranny of feminine archetypes. What they both ask for are personalized creatures, real human women. What neither admits is that Faulkner is in the process of granting such a wish.

The reduction of Eula Varner from the Great Goddess to the goddess of love is one step in the humanizing process, in the "liberation of the individual from the primordial mythic world." The desire of Lucy Pate for the social legalities of the married state is another. The genuine love of the Texas whore for Houston, of the lumberjack's daughter for Mink Snopes, is still a further development. Perhaps the fullest "socializing," however, of any woman in *The Hamlet* occurs in the characterization of Mrs. Littlejohn. If the principle of individuation implies a coming to consciousness, to male rationality, she is the novel's prime woman-example. One critic goes so far as to say that "Mrs. Littlejohn seems . . . to stand at the apex of the pyramid of the Faulkner hierarchy of minds in this novel. She represents not shrewdness, nor cleverness, certainly not intellectualism, for she is unlearned, but above all these she stands as a figure of wisdom . . . she becomes a symbolic mind."[11]

She is at least on a par with Ratliff. It is he who, on righteous principle, takes Ike's cow away from him; he is implicitly opposed by "the man-tall, man-grim woman in the faded wrapper who stared as steadily back at him" (p. 201). In spite of her masculine character, Mrs. Littlejohn never once loses her abiding sympathy for the weak and the helpless. Nor does she lose her literal feminine difference from the male world; throughout the "spotted horses" episode, she is again and again mentioned as moving in the background, lighting the fire beneath the wash kettle, ringing the dinner bell, hanging out the laundry, frying ham in the kitchen. Each time, she pauses to look into the lot where the men are gathered and the Texan is saying "Boys," then she returns to her business of running the daily world upon which her boarders are dependent. At last, when Henry Armstid's unconscious body is carried into one of her bedrooms, the judgement which has been gathering all day is finally passed without denial on the masculine world: " 'I'll declare,' she said. 'You men.' They had drawn back a little, clumped, shifting from one foot to another, not looking at her nor at his wife either, who stood at the foot of the bed, motionless, her hands folded into her dress. 'You all get out of here, V. K.,' she said to Ratliff. 'Go outside. See if you cant find something else to play with that will kill some more of you' " (p. 310).

Mrs. Littlejohn's dominance in this scene is not the numinous ascendancy of daemonic factors. She judges the male world, but she is also detached from it (they are not dependent upon her in life and death); she ministers to its needs, but she is not hallowed by it. Like Jenny Du Pre, she possesses a practical wisdom and a sharp tongue that make her mistress of a world apart from, but not above (below), the world of men. Her judgement and her influence are merely individual and civilized. She is one of Faulkner's more successful social characterizations, the only compensation in a world where men are now victorious over what were once the supra-human powers of woman.

"An Odor of Verbena," the concluding story in *The Unvanquished*,[12] anticipates this conquest by a male code of the symbolic feminine order in a way that sheds light on what is happening to mythic women in the Snopes trilogy. Drusilla Hawk is in this one story as potentially mythic as Eula Varner of *The Hamlet*, despite how nihilistic she has been in "Raid" after having lost her fiancé (pp. 114–15), or how fully mannish she has grown riding with Colonel John Sartoris's troop of cavalry, or how "beaten" (p. 231) she has been, in "Skirmish at Sartoris," by her mother who makes her put on a dress and marry her cavalry commander. After Bayard Sartoris has learned of his father's assassination, he envisions Drusilla "in the formal brilliant room arranged formally for obsequy, not tall, not slender as a woman is but as a youth, a boy, is, motionless, in yellow, the face calm, almost bemused, the head simple and severe, the balancing sprig of verbena above each ear, the two arms bent at the elbows, the two hands shoulder high, the two identical duelling pistols lying upon, not clutched in, one to each: the Greek amphora priestess of a succinct and formal violence" (p. 252). Iconographically, she is the urn itself, not this time a Lena Grove who progresses serenely through a succession of "avatars, like something moving forever and without progress across an urn," but a vessel of vengeance, somewhat like Temple Drake, who holds in store for men both violence and the "gesture of all promise" (p. 263).

Drusilla appears, however, to be offering to Bayard in the sprig of verbena which she pins on his lapel nothing more than an obligation to uphold his father's code of honour and courage. She would have "no more bothered with flowers than Father himself would have," except that "she said verbena was the only scent you could smell above the smell of horses and courage and so it was the only one that was worth the wearing" (pp. 253–54). She does not now want Bayard to speak against his father's violent inclinations because, as she says, he has a dream, and "if it's a good dream, it's worth it" (p. 257), no matter what the cost in human life. She seems, in other words, to have become an idealist, one who can say of her own husband, "Sometimes I think the finest thing that can happen to a man is to love something, a woman preferably, well, hard hard hard, then to die young because he believed what he could not help but believe and was what he could not (could not? would not) help but be" (p. 261). Her assumption of her husband's idealistic qualities leads, paradoxically, to her own personalizing, or, as Bayard calls it, to "the incorrigibly individual woman" (p. 263). Drusilla seems at once then to configure both the mythic Eula Varner of *The Hamlet* (although appearing as *Dike*-Athene, the goddess of justice, not as Venus, the goddess of love) and the personalized Eula of *The Town*, or rather, as her masculinized daughter, Linda, of *The Mansion*.

Yet when Drusilla asks Bayard to kiss her, requesting his pledge to be worthy of "the only scent you could smell above the smell of horses and courage," he says, "I thought then of the woman of thirty, the symbol of the ancient and eternal Snake and of the men who have written of her, and I realised then the immitigable chasm between all life and all print—that those who can, do, those who cannot and suffer enough because they can't, write about it" (p. 262). Like Anse Bundren (although, initially, with much more pain), he equates woman and doing with the snake, with a medium which to man is evil and yet overwhelmingly fascinating. Later, when, in favour of him, she has "abjure[d] verbena forever more," Drusilla offers him the pistols, saying, "How beautiful: young, to be permitted to kill, to be permitted vengeance, to take into your bare hands the fire of heaven that cast down Lucifer. No; I. I gave it to you; I put it into your hands; Oh you will thank me, you will remember me when I am dead and you are an old man saying to himself, 'I have tasted all things' " (p. 274). The divine power she now arrogates to herself fulfils the symbol of "the Greek amphora priestess"; in having "abjured" verbena and having confirmed Bayard in it, she confirms as well its literal meaning—leafy branch, sacred branch—for she is the Sibyl empowering Aeneas to enter the land of the dead in search of his "father."

Astonishingly, Bayard refuses her symbolic power. He has had, like his father, enough of killing, and he too will go to town unarmed, though to establish his own code of honour, not to commit suicide. As he walks through the street toward Redmond's office, the odour of verbena which ironically encloses him becomes more than ever an emblem of a male code of honour: "It was almost noon now and I could smell nothing except the verbena in my coat, as if it had gathered all the sun, all the suspended fierce heat in which the equinox could not seem to occur and were distilling it so that I moved in a cloud of verbena as I might have moved in a cloud of smoke from a cigar" (p. 283). The overdue equinox, however, has been earlier described as "a laboring delayed woman" (p. 246); it is as if this heat itself is the labour to give birth. Drusilla, in other words, appears to be the mother of a hoped-for act of violence; much like Temple Drake, she appears as a feminine justice presiding over unexamined social codes. (This might account for the progression in associations of verbena from the smell of horses and courage for Drusilla—recalling Addie Bundren as the mare mother—to burning sun and cigar smoke for Bayard and the townsmen.) Bayard, however, is enclosed ironically in the odour because he does not accept the symbolic meaning of its giver.

Bayard's denial of the mythic powers is underscored as well in another image series: when he sets out from Oxford for home and his approaching trial of manhood, he sees "a thin sickle of moon like the heel print of a boot in wet sand" (p. 250). The image seems to prefigure the appearance of the goddess by whose power he will be required to act. Later, on the way into Redmond's office, he recalls a fragment of something he has heard his Aunt Jenny say: "No bloody moon" (p. 285). There is, this once, no moon-driven destruction because Bayard believes, like his aunt, in a reasonable order. He walks unarmed into the law office where his father's honour-bound slayer must surrender to Bayard's unconventional courage, firing two shots just to miss him, then leaving to catch at once the southbound train out of Jefferson. Bayard thus wins the respect and even admiration of the townsmen by his unorthodox display of honour, but Drusilla cannot stay to countenance a code which defies her symbolic function. She leaves behind her a token recognition of Bayard's victory—a sprig of verbena—but ironically, she leaves that which, under different circumstances, was already abjured. Woman is thus defeated and her order overturned, this time by a male principle of intellect devoted to finding a code of existence apart from the feminine element of blood.

Likewise, the only compensation in "An Odor of Verbena" for the loss of woman's supra-human powers is the development of a female personality. Miss Jenny Du Pre, like Mrs. Littlejohn of *The Hamlet*, remains as the mistress of a world apart from male stupidity and splendour. She is, like Drusilla, composed by her suffering into "the incorrigibly individual woman;" yet she refuses, unlike Drusilla, to believe in the need for honour or a feminine authority in the winning of it, saying to Bayard, "Don't let it be Drusilla, a poor hysterical young woman" (p. 276). Finally, she expresses both her pride and her concern upon Bayard's return; she passes judgement upon him and yet gives him her loving human approval: "Then she put her hands on my shoulders. I watched them come up as though she were trying to stop them; I felt them on my shoulders as if they had a separate life of their own and were trying to do something which for my sake she was trying to restrain, prevent. Then she gave up or she was not strong enough because they came up and took my face between them, hard, and suddenly the tears sprang and streamed down her face like Drusilla's laughing had. 'Oh, damn you Sartorises!' she said. 'Damn you! Damn you!' " (p. 292). The wheel has now come full circle to the Miss Jenny of *Sartoris* who, while showing a reproving love for the younger Bayard, her great grand-nephew, must finally acknowledge, in her quiet wisdom, woman's separation from the vainglory of men. Conversely, the partial individuation of Drusilla, especially in her male idealism, anticipates the later development of Eula Varner from a thwarted goddess of love to a woman who becomes honour's martyr. The question which remains to be answered, then, is what is gained and lost in that Faulknerian art which turns exclusively to individual human women?

There is a great deal of talk in *The Town* of Eula Varner as a goddess, as the avatar of every man's desire. Gavin Stevens speaks interminably of "that damned incredible woman, that Frenchman's Bend Helen, Semiramis—no: not Helen nor Semiramis: Lilith: the one before Eve herself whom earth's Creator had perforce in desperate and amazed alarm in person to efface, remove, obliterate, that Adam might create a progeny to populate it."[13] It is apparent even from this speech what fate symbols have come to in *The Town*; Gavin's bombast and his massing of allusions bespeak a desperate attempt to believe in the myth of woman where possibly little cause is left. Perhaps, in that sense, he indicates a tendency in Faulkner himself to recapture some lost or impoverished factor; but there is also evidence to suggest that Gavin is parodied, or treated with quite bitter irony.[14]

Gavin's images are threadbare and tedious; they remind one of the refrain from a song heard once too often. The trouble with all of them is that they reflect his conscious processes instead of any narrative process; they are capsule definitions of Gavin's view of Eula rather than self-contained experience. The woman is perceived, as one observer notes, almost entirely through the intellect of Stevens, "surely the greatest wind-bag in American literature, and Charles Mallison, who shows promise of being the runner-up."[15] He is a wind-bag precisely because he talks where there is nothing to talk about, elaborates where there is nothing to configure. The portrait of Eula which emerges from *The Town* is one of the most conscious and rational drawings of a "goddess" ever devised by man; and Gavin emerges as her public relations man.

Ironically, the real development of Eula's character is in the reverse direction. This new line of maturation does not even begin with the shock of seeing "Venus" strike a match on her slipper sole to light a cigarette, nor does it end with the eighteen-year fact of her faithful adultery. It starts really with the character of a woman for whom Gavin does public and bloody battle with her seducer because, "What he was doing was simply defending forever with his blood the principle that chastity and virtue in women shall be defended whether they exist or not" (p. 76). The actual woman has already been limited and contained by a code of chivalry; she will be forced to define herself henceforth in terms of a male-imposed social role (unless she possesses the power to resist the dominance of ideals, and it appears that she and her sex do not).

Charles Mallison, Sr. measures the limitations of female strength in a chivalric world: "You want two red-combed roosters strutting at one another, provided one of you hens is the reason for it. And if there's anything else you can think of to shove them in to where one of them will have to draw blood in self-defense, you'll do that too because every drop of that blood or every black eye or every public-torn collar or split or muddy britches is another item of revenge on that race of menfolks that holds you ladies thralled all day long day after day with nothing to do between meals but swap gossip over the telephone" (p. 57). Woman's revenge for being thralled is not the same thing as the feminine's response to opposition; split lips, gossip, and muddy pants are a far cry from the gasoline fire which consumed Lee Goodwin, from the juggernaut of fate that castrated Joe Christmas, from the madness which obliterated Darl Bundren. On the obverse side of the Janus-face, the creative-transformative power of woman has become non-existent now, since man is no longer changed (or resistant to change)—he merely fights, victorious or not, for his ideals.

Not too long after Stevens's fistfight with Manfred de Spain, Eula offers herself unexpectedly to Gavin. Her exact motive for doing so is not made clear in that moment; it is implied that she both answers his need and she tries to end his public campaign against her lover. The lawyer, of course, could never exchange his principles for the living woman, but he also spends so much time talking about her motives that he misses her real reason. He finally thinks she is trying to save the honour of her Snopes-husband; as circumstance will discover, she ventures one last unhurried gambit to save the name and honour of her daughter. In Stevens's refusal of her offer, one is faced once again with Joe Christmas's nonacceptance of the feminine. Only this time, no terrible vengeance is exacted from the man. The hero of reason and principle (Gavin Stevens, even) now has more power than the woman. Eula's unsuccessful gambit becomes more than the incipient admission of her power-lessness, her inability to defend her own life (without having to relinquish it) from the forces of social opinion. Eula is constricted, even constructed, in a very human mould.

She meets Gavin a total of three times in the novel; it is from this triple exposure (reminiscent of another adulteress, Hester Prynne) that *The Town* derives its structure—such as it is amongst Gavin's interminable effort to understand the little that does go on about him. But the character of Eula is not so disposed to the wild rebellion of Hester; she is less the personified tension between communal values and an amoral wilderness than she is a woman with a practical belief in the mores of her society. She seeks no less than the respectable marriage of her daughter. Two years before Stevens's clouded vision can make out any shape in the lines of Flem's grand design, Eula makes a second proposal to the Harvard and Heidelburg-educated attorney. She offers Linda as a legal bride: " 'You dont know very much about women, do you?' she said. 'Women aren't interested in poets' dreams. They are interested in facts. . . . The marriage is the only fact. The rest of it is still the poet's romantic dream. Marry her. She'll have you. Right now, in the middle of all this, she wont know how to say No. Marry her' " (pp. 226–27). Gavin, of course, once again says No. Like the bachelors of *The Hamlet*, he maintains whatever security, whatever mastery, he enjoys by keeping himself free from feminine existence. He need not be so concerned. Here, the world of woman is far more threatened than threatening. For Eula is made the victim of her own belief in those values attached by society to "bastard" and to "patronym." She is willing, for Linda's sake, to go to any length to satisfy the canons of respectable succession; she offers first herself as sex object, then her daughter as marriage object. Although her solicitude is the height of maternal concern, she is nevertheless no Great Mother who confirms so painfully the existence of a pat-riarchy. Eula Varner is not even Venus any more; she has become a fully human mother driven by social concerns alone.

The third and final time Eula faces Gavin is on the eve of her death. She tells him of her husband's shrewdest manipulation ever, how he has won the respect and affection of the daughter he did not father, and is even now converting that human feeling into the means by which he might vault over an adulterer's bed into the presidency of his cuckolder's bank. It is quite apparent to both speaker and listener that Flem's design has no more need for either marriage or its parody. Having secured the daughter, he can expose the wife, drive her off with the banker, and use his role of wronged husband to further his own social respectability. With sincerity, perhaps, Eula leads Gavin to believe that she will elope with de Spain. Probably she will, if at this moment she is able to secure Linda's future. Once more, now, she implores the champion of civic morality to husband her daughter. Gavin refuses, then at best hedges. He is as much responsible for what happens to the woman as is Flem himself. Yet outward constraint does not singly determine Eula's fate. Ultimately, it is her compulsive belief in Jefferson morality that leads to her tragic destruction. Her commitment to a social prescription for Linda's happiness is a tacit admission of her unhappy moral turpitude; she denies the legitimacy of her own life.

If Eula has been, as one scholar suggests, a rebel from the social order—an instinctual force at war with civilized suppression[16]—she now buys back that individual assertion with her acquiescence to the powers of conformity. She commits suicide to guarantee Linda's respectability; significantly, she puts a bullet through her brain without mussing that afternoon's beauty shop coiffure, the first hairdo she has had in her life. She thus repeats the socially defined role of tragic victim twice thrust upon her in the past. Will Varner had sacrificed her once before, in the interest of family honour, on the altar of marriage, and Flem Snopes surrendered her almost instantly again in a bed of adultery to acquire not only the vice-presidency of a bank but social acceptance with it. In one sense, Charles Mallison is then justified in regarding her death as a sort of vindication of public morality, as "the eternal and deathless public triumph of virtue itself proved once more supreme and invincible" (p. 337), but he forgets one thing. This final time Eula's sacrifice is purely self-willed. In this respect, the triumph in her death is less public than private. Fronting a community who later "could even forgive themselves for condoning adultery by forgiving it, by reminding themselves (one another too I reckon) that if she had not been an abomination before God for eighteen years, she wouldn't have reached the point where she would have to choose death in order to leave her child a mere suicide for a mother instead of a whore" (p. 340), she averts the maximum conquest available to a patriarchate (the name of "whore"), privately and without assistance. It costs her only her life—and the impulsive freedom her life has symbolized.

The assertion of the individual is not entirely negated, however, in Eula's acquiescence. To those who regard her as a tragic figure, she is in some sense doomed, yet the responsibility for her fate is truly her own. She undergoes some type of significant moral struggle and she accepts her end with dignity. The very notion, then of her tragic cast gives her the greatest potential in Western culture for human characterization, what William Riley Parker in his examination of the spirit of Greek tragedy has called "suffering individualism."[17]

Two questions arise. If that circumstantial potential for individualizing exists in Eula's situation, how well is it executed? And if Faulkner has now turned to ethical preoccupations in his art (the relation of an individual to her civilization), how sophisticated is the consciousness which probes the moral economy of that culture?

Eula is obscured too greatly by the swimming vision of those who perceive her ever to emerge clearly focused as a felt, known human being. Her inner feelings are not encountered directly; her outward thoughts are not even made immediate. She remains an indirect object of the mental processes of the three narrators, Gavin Stevens, Chick Mallison, and V. K. Ratliff, only one of whom is even quasi-actively concerned with her story. It might now seem that Faulkner is trying to recover the assets of a technique used so brilliantly in *The Sound and the Fury* and *As I Lay Dying*, but with this new liability: where Caddy and Mrs. Bundren exist as immediate, dramatic projections of their male "devotees," Eula is reflected upon, mulled over, and analysed by her detached *coterie* in *The Town*. She is viewed entirely from afar, from a distance both of intellect and of time—in the past tense. Though the tense of Caddy's being might also be called the completed past of Quentin's life, she continues to live in a fluid suspension of past and present in her brother's mind; as man's archetypal experience of the anima, she is a genuine expression of, and not a mere male projection upon, woman. Thus despite her "nonpresence," she has an affective life of her own. But Eula, though "present," is not immediate; she is deduced, not induced. And the deducers are not largely to be trusted.

Stevens, especially, is time and again ironically undercut. In verbal style, he comes near to being Faulkner's self-parody; in romantic character, he is continually patronized by Ratliff who knows that Stevens will never see the truth, lost as he is in his cerebral dreams of chivalry. Ratliff says at one point, "No, no, no, no, no no. He was wrong. He's a lawyer, and to a lawyer, if it aint complicated it dont matter whether it works or not because if it aint complicated up enough it aint right and so even if it works, you dont believe it" (p. 296). His tone of benevolent condescension comes near, however, to scorn in the aftermath of Eula's funeral when he says that Flem "had already milked out of Lawyer Stevens all he needed from him, which was to get his wife buried all right and proper and decorous and respectable, without no uproarious elements making a unseemly spectacle in the business" (p. 348). Ratliff's moral sense is outraged by Gavin's scruples over propriety, not so much on the principle that a morality of appearance is wrong, but because Flem is able to turn that hypocrisy to his own end. Ratliff, even more than Stevens, believes in an ethic of pragmatism.

With the creation of these several critical (non-participant, assessing) narrators, Faulkner appears to have radically restructured the leanings of his art. The Jeffersonian conflict with Snopesism here predisposes him toward moral questions. Seemingly, *The Town* seeks to probe the moral consciousness and sensibility of a culture, to picture man in the subtle terms of his social interaction. Within this ethical tradition (for which F. R. Leavis has arrogated the term "great") the demands for first-rate art are fairly specific, if (paradoxically) abstract. Leavis says of Jane Austen, "Without her intense moral preoccupation she wouldn't have been a great novelist."[18] Obviously then, one touchstone of this great artist is "a kind of reverent openness before life, and a marked moral intensity" (p. 9). But human life cannot be recorded in the absence of a milieu; civilization itself becomes the great ingredient of great art, "the 'civilization' in question being a matter of personal relations between members of a mature and sophisticated Society" (p. 11). Henry James satisfies this canon of taste as an "intellectual poet-novelist of 'high civilization' " (p. 12); his greatest achievement is the registration of a subtilized and "sophisticated human consciousness" (p. 16). George Eliot and Joseph Conrad are likewise marked by their moral seriousness and their profoundly serious interest in life. Eliot's greatness, more specifically, lies in her handling "with unprecedented subtlety and refinement the personal relations of sophisticated characters exhibiting the 'civilization' of the 'best society' and [using], in so doing, an original psychological notation corresponding to the fineness of her psychological and moral insight" (Leavis, p. 15).

One final question concerns the depth, the intensity, the subtlety, and the sophistication of Faulkner's moral vision in *The Town*. Undoubtedly, the novel gives evidence of the author's marked moral intensity, whether it be in his outrage at Snopesism or in his bitterness toward Gavin's idealistic folly. *The Town* contains, as well, a traditional society; but it is a civilization composed of a decadent (in Stevens's case paralysed) aristocracy, a complacently pious middle class, and a crass, *nouveau riche*, antagonist class—so whether the civilization is "high" or not may be the question. One of the major failings, also, in Faulkner's portrait of that civilization is the lack of personal relations between members of the society. Ratliff and Mallison analyse, aloof from events which concern them; Stevens prevents himself, by the formalized posturing of his code, from engaging in the intercourse (social and sexual) which is proffered him. The technique formerly adopted by Faulkner for the ritual telling of myth is quite ill-suited here for the subtle rendering of moral relations. As for the registration of a sophisticated consciousness, Gavin's obtuseness disqualifies him from any such claim, Chick is as yet an immature voice of the community, and Ratliff is far more subtle than he is sophisticated. The greater defect of consciousness in the novel, however, consists in the manner of its exposition. As Leavis says, "There is an elementary distinction to be made between the *discussion* of problems and ideas, and what we find in the great novelist" (p. 7). Faulkner's speakers, especially Stevens and Mallison, far too often discuss the moral problem at hand, make pronouncements upon it, instead of becoming the interaction between the moral substance and its apprehension.

But the ultimate flaw in *The Town* lies in the dimension of the moral issue itself. The novel breaks down over the sentimentalized need for Eula to become a tragic victim who redeems the respectability of her daughter. For the whole town has felt, known, believed for eighteen years not only in Eula's adultery, but in her daughter's illegitimate conception. The social register of Jefferson is not likely to forget its belief on the day Linda should accept a marriage proposal from one of its sons. Consequently it is inevitable that the girl should find a husband in some distant and liberal place like Greenwich Village (her mother's sacrifice notwithstanding). If it is argued that Eula really dies in the hope of preserving for Linda her familial identity, it is doubly ironic that Flem Snopes as a father should be better than no father at all, and that Linda should suspect the truth, yet accept Gavin's hopelessly romantic and sentimental lie. So Eula's suicide is only one more sham in a town built on a hypocritical morality; it is a self-deceiving act performed with dignity before a sincerely dishonest audience. The worst is that Faulkner, apparently, expects us to take her sacrifice seriously.

The lack of necessity in Eula's death is also just as ironic as the publicly pious, privately contemptuous monument which Flem erects to his wife's memory. The words carved in its enduring marble read,

A Virtuous Wife is a Crown to Her Husband
Her Children Rise and Call Her Blessed (p. 355)

The town, having condoned her adultery for so long, cannot now deny the words on the epitaph; but they know what they mean. If Flem is able to convert Eula's sacrifice into the crown of his own respectability, it is only because of a sentimental convention that certain things are better left unsaid. Thus the fall of the wife and the rise of the husband are both unnecessary, although now even Ratliff (the voice of sanity, humanity) has fully accepted his culture's belief in the unspoken. It is to Faulkner's discredit that he does not provide an ironic distance here on Ratliff, that he himself does not penetrate behind a callow and sentimental vision. Instead he offers us a useless tragedy in a somewhat strained affirmation of traditional morality enfolded to the bosom of individual nobility. Faulkner's characterization and his moral vision in *The Town* might well be indicative not only of his weakness in dealing with exclusively social concerns, but of his lack of understanding of the mortal female in contrast to his authentic expression of the anima. The feminine creator and destroyer in his work is much more moving and true than is the perishing human woman.

Although a retrospective consciousness in *The Mansion* hearkens back to Eula Varner occasionally in an attempt to reaffirm the old idea of her divinity—"since the god she represented without even trying to . . . was a stronger one than the pale and desperate Galilean who was all [the preachers] had to challenge with"[19]—she serves, even with her ineffable quality, as little more than a foil to Linda for whom that quality "was not transferable" (p. 212). The daughter's characterization, in fact, realizes the ultimate tendency of the individuation process as a growth toward consciousness: the complete masculinizing of the female personality.

The fundamental mutation in the character of Yoknapatawphan woman is noted by Ratliff just before Linda Snopes Kohl arrives back in Jefferson after years of absence: "But this is the first female girl soldier we ever had, not to mention one actually wounded by the enemy. Naturally we dont include rape for the main reason that we aint talking about rape" (p. 109). What Ratliff is talking about is the new undifferentiated woman, the female who is neither numinously superior nor socially inferior because of her sex. Troops do not rape her; she is now (most egalitarian) the troops. The abatement of Linda's sexuality makes her an interesting prototype of this liberated woman. She lacks her mother's social preoccupation with marriage; she lives commonlaw with a Greenwich Village sculptor for five years, refusing to be seduced into marriage because she has principles to believe in, ideals to fight for. Since she has learned some of her principles and ideals from Gavin Stevens, his oblique explanation of her attitude might be accepted without question: "When you are young enough and brave enough at the same time, you can hate intolerance and believe in hope and, if you are sho enough brave, act on it" (p. 161). She proves her old mentor true on both counts; she and Barton Kohl go to Spain because they hate injustice, because they believe in the ideal of freedom. She marries her artist-idealist only when they have a mutual war of hope to fight. Linda drives an ambulance in the Spanish Loyalist army and is deafened for her pains. She loses her husband to enemy gunners who shoot down his plane. But outwardly she doesn't grieve. After she has returned to Mississippi, it is almost as if the husband had never been, or at least had never been flesh and blood anyway, so there was nothing to miss save the idea. Her life continues to be symbolically fruitless, just as her marriage had been. She has no connection whatsoever with the Lena Groves and Joanna Burdens of an earlier world view; no physical fact, no symbolic glimpse links her to the generation and destruction of life. Contrarily, the single image which dominates Linda's homecoming is the white streak running through her hair, "a collapsed plume lying flat athwart her skull instead of cresting upward first then back and over" (p. 350). She is the modern world's version of a "knight-errant"; although she is defeated temporarily by the Spanish dragon, she finds some Mississippi tourneys soon enough to carry on with jousting.

Two roads lead Linda across the flat plain to the tower of wholly intellectual (or ideal) woman. She embarks on causes—campaigns against political, economic, and racial injustices—and she rejects the feminine-material principle of life. Although she offers her body in gratitude to Gavin Stevens, she shows tremendous relief when he turns her down (p. 239). The love she expresses for him is of a wholly Platonic order, conditioned in part by his own idealism: "We can always be together no matter how far apart either one of us happens to be or has to be. How did you say it? the two people in all the earth out of all the world that can love each other not only without having to but we dont even have to not say that word you dont like to hear?" (p. 252). The only seeming difference in their mutual masculinity is that Gavin is a prig; she isn't. When she goes away to Pascagoula to work as a riveter in a wartime shipyard, she enters fully into a masculine and sexless world. Although she loves Gavin, she cannot have him and remain faithful to the Idea of her dead husband.

The penultimate comment to be made about Linda as a fully masculine woman is that her story is not very interesting. The deafness which makes her do more talking than listening is reminiscent of Gavin himself; it is as though symbolically the intellect were solipsistic, as though it droned on forever in a vacuum where communication (coupling) was impossible.

The final point of interest in Linda's story is its connection with Mink Snopes. Linda hates her father and, as Gavin has to admit, she uses Mink to murder him. She obtains the man's pardon from the penitentiary at Parchman, knowing full well he will avenge himself for Flem's betrayal of kin thirty-eight years before. In this sense, Mink not only fleshes out the platitude that evil (preferably Snopesism) will destroy itself; he also marks the tendency of intellect to be self-annihilating. Neither he nor Linda are anything like agents, however, for the vengeance of the love goddess against Flem Snopes. In reality they both act on that rigid and immutable principle which was characteristic of Mink in *The Hamlet*. Ratliff even recalls the economic metaphor of the earlier work: that Linda is being paid up to date for her mother's grave (p. 373). But Eula Varner is not responsible in *The Mansion* for securing social justice; it has ever been the masculine spirit which grapples with such abstractions. Ultimately Faulkner suggests in the story of the Snopeses that this rational principle which has superseded the archetype will destroy itself. The wheel has almost come full circle; this is the last approach to a *götterdämmerung* in Yoknapatawpha County. For an old sound and fury rises near to the threshold of hearing once more in the conclusion of the cycle.

The great intensity which animates the story of Mink Snopes's revenge is derived in part from the furious, unbending drive of the man to be free of the earth and what it represents. Faulkner's voice is infused with much of the old power as he describes Mink's dilemma on the way toward Jefferson: "He was quite comfortable. But mainly he was off the ground. That was the danger, what a man had to watch against; once you laid flat on the ground, right away the earth started in to draw you back down into it. The very moment you were born out of your mother's body, the power and drag of the earth was already at work on you; if there had not been other womenfolks in the family or neighbors or even a hired one to support you, hold you up, keep the earth from touching you, you would not live an hour. And you knew it too" (p. 402). It is a force from which Mink (or any human being) cannot escape, and the novel ends with him on the lam from his crime in Jefferson, lying by night on the ground where

> it seemed to him he could feel the Mink Snopes that had had to spend so much of his life just having unnecessary bother and trouble, beginning to creep, seep, flow easy as sleeping; he could almost watch it, following all the little grass blades and

tiny roots, the little holes the worms made, down and down into the ground and the dirt that had to bother and worry and anguish with the passions and hopes and skeers, the justice and the injustice and the griefs, leaving the folks themselves easy now, all mixed and jumbled up comfortable and easy so wouldn't nobody even know or even care who was which any more, himself among them, equal to any, good as any, brave as any, being inextricable from, anonymous with all of them (p. 435).

It is clear that the wheel has come almost full circle. That ever-painful ego consciousness of man in Faulkner's art begins to give way ("symbolically," not logically) to the peaceful anonymity of the deathly goddess. The mother archetype (at least her Earth-aspect) shows signs of re-emergence. Only woman has not yet merged back into the field of the numinous. Mink sees her, not as the good face split from the archetype, but as the frail human opponent of overwhelming forces. She is man's temporary stay against the fateful powers.

If it be admitted that the archetype is at least incipient once again in Faulkner's work, one can make out a rudimentary arrangement of feminine lines of force in *The Mansion*'s conclusion. The "terrible mother" seems to be just as ruthlessly ascendant over the "good mother" here as she was in *Sanctuary*. Linda has no part in the "womenfolks' " role of holding infant humanity up from the earth; she appears, rather, to merge actively (though not figuratively) with Earth's drag. She is the agent responsible for bringing Mink and Flem together; consequently she draws them both down to destruction. The pattern of her final movement is also similar to Temple Drake's: she leaves a scene of ruin and death to go east. Her "mythos" is markedly different, however, in sub-stance and in aura. She is not identified with unconscious cosmic powers; instead she commits murder intellectually (and consciously discloses it to Gavin). Likewise she destroys, not in immediate response to sacrilege, but in the slow achievement of a square deal (she is collecting a moral debt from Flem Snopes for the death of her mother). On the one hand then, Linda suggests the archetypal feminine's potential for re-emergence; on the other she appears as the end product of feminine individuation: intelligent and principled in character, yet grotesque in her quacking speech and as remote from humanity as her poor ears are from sound. Finally, Linda Snopes Kohl elicits more pity than terror, more tedium than wonder. She is, in most respects, the *cul de sac* of Faulkner's humanizing process.

8

Reformation of the Whore

Woman and Goddess in a Memphis
Sportin' House

The real anomaly of *The Reivers* is not that Faulkner should have attempted the trite story of a prostitute's reformation; it is that he should have brought about as far as he did the re-emergence of the feminine archetype in a Memphis whorehouse. For the story of Lucius Priest's fall from innocence is to some extent the ritual recurrence of mankind's (the Horace Benbows, Joe Christmases, Byron Bunches) encounter with the goddess. Even Lucius's nonage cannot hinder him from participation in this age-old role of man. He brings a double focus to "A Reminiscence": the freshness of his boyhood emotions, and the articulate judgement of his elder years. Thus he can know both the anguished spontaneity and the quiescent necessity of his immersion in experience. The account of his initiation into motion and life has the same immediacy—and a similar importance—as the stories of Anse Bundren and Byron Bunch before him. Not even the supposedly patriarchal setting of a bawdy house can hinder the re-creation here of a matriarchal world view. The only major difference in this novel (apart from a pre-pailing tone of comedy which must be considered later) is the fuller personalizing of *The Reivers*' human females; as Cleanth Brooks states, "We see Everbe closer up: she is a warmer creature than Lena, less sure of herself, and clearly in love with the man who will eventually claim her" (*Yoknapatawpha Country*, p. 365).

For obvious reasons, Miss Everbe Corinthia is likened to Lena Grove of *Light in August*. She is pursued by Boon Hogganbeck in a manner reminiscent in degree, if not in kind, of Byron Bunch's pursuit of Lena; both men are also redeemed, in a way, out of their very different kinds of isolation. But the story which swirls and eddies about Everbe is unreservedly comic; the darker implications which arise out of the telescoped identity of Lena-Joanna in *Light in August* nearly offset the mild comedy of Lena's prepotency in the novel's conclusion. That link, on the contrary, which is largely comic seems to be the one forged between Everbe's predicament in *The Reivers* as the "lodestar victim"[1] of a scrapping moil of men and Eula Varner's situation as a bitch-hub of lust in *The Hamlet*. Paradoxically, however, it is Eula who is victimized, whose weakness enervates the power of godhead; Everbe triumphs in the slow serenity of a Lena Grove. Her effect upon Boon, but more particularly upon Lucius, marks the reappearance in Faulkner's art of a full-fledged mythos.

Her influence notwithstanding, Miss Everbe Corinthia is not a self-sustained representative of the Great Goddess. Her identity is shaped by the wilful idealism of an eleven-year-old boy. Lucius Priest, perhaps the youngest gentleman ever to frequent a whorehouse, fights bare-handed against the knife of her defamer to defend Miss Corrie's honour (although she is a prostitute). His quixotic act commits Miss Corrie to an equally quixotic reformation and re-emphasis of her given name (*Everbe*, eternal woman). This furious and bloody denial by the boy of a reality which is debasing recalls Gavin Stevens's chivalric commitment to "defending forever with his blood the principle that chastity and virtue in women shall be defended whether they exist or not." Everbe's consequent readiness to see herself through Lucius's eyes seems then to make her more the projection of male idealism than the authentic male expression of the anima. She appears, in her new-found conception of personal honour, to be more like Eula Varner of *The Town* than anyone else. Only Eula's decision to redeem with her life the respectability of her daughter is the stuff of tragic sentimentality; Everbe's decision to quit her business just when Boon has gone through hell to get to Memphis is the stuff of joyously unsentimental comedy.

Everbe, however, is not the primary manifestation of the femi-

nine in the novel; there is a serious side to *The Reivers* of which
she is but an indirect expression. This graver aspect is the initiation
of a boy into manhood; the rite, of paramount importance, is
accomplished through his entry into "Non-virtue" (a word which
approximates the moral term "evil" yet is fundamentally amoral).
One commentator suggests, "Non-virtue is not really the equivalent
of evil; it is a concept like Emerson's absence of good, something
toward which Faulkner has had an emotional leaning for some
time."[2] Astute as the observation is, it ignores the evidence of the
narrative. Lucius does not perceive Non-virtue as a deficiency, as
cold is the absence of heat. Virtue itself is more the absence of
something, of life perhaps, "cold and odorless and tasteless virtue"
(pp. 52–53). Non-virtue, on the other hand, is experienced as an
active entity. When Boon proposes the trip to Memphis, he sets
Lucius off on a string of appallingly successful lies that will bring
the boy to the end of his rope at the verge of their final obstacle to
departure. Approaching the farmyard of his cousin Zach Edmonds,
the boy says in resignation, "If Non-virtue still wanted either of us,
it was now her move. Which she did" (p. 62).

This ascription of a female identity to Non-virtue is no mere
accident of language. It is fundamental to the theme of Lucius's
initiation. For theft and fraud are only the means Non-virtue uses
to reach her end: a whorehouse in Memphis. Sex and woman, then,
are Non-virtue's essential representatives. Consequently, Miss
Corrie as Non-virtue's active prostitute is no longer like Eula
Varner as a helpless, figurative harlot. Whoredom has dropped its
associations with patriarchal usurpation: it means something much
closer to the ambivalence of life, to the dual (virtuous and non-
virtuous) face of the psychic factor. So when Lucius finds himself
resistlessly impelled by Non-virtue, he is only reconfirming the old
masculine dilemma in Faulkner's work—that man is forever
impelled by a feminine element to some action which his rational
part resists. How man accommodates himself to this daemonic
impulse determines finally whether he lives or dies. Horace Benbow,
who encounters "evil" in this same Memphis whorehouse, is
broken utterly by his logical refusal to accommodate himself to its
existence. Lucius, in his personal accommodation, succeeds admirably.

The person of Non-virtue is not a postulate of any of Faulkner's

earlier novels. Nor is it perceived (though it may be felt) as such by
the eleven-year-old Lucius. It is the subject of the accumulated
understanding of the old man who tells a story of what happened
to him fifty-six years before. Only after all these years can he say
he has "noticed in my time how quite often the advocates and even
the practitioners of virtue evidently have grave doubts of their own
regarding the impregnability of virtue as a shield, putting their
faith and trust not in virtue but rather in the god or goddess whose
charge virtue is; by-passing virtue as it were in allegiance to the
Over-goddess herself, in return for which the goddess will either
divert temptation away or anyhow intercede between them. Which
explains a lot, having likewise noticed in my time that the goddess
in charge of virtue seems to be the same one in charge of luck, if not
of folly also" (p. 51). His successive qualification makes it evident
that the man (as distinct from the child) not only is conscious of an
"Over-goddess" but that the goddess isn't in charge of virtue alone;
the other side of life is her province as well. If he sounds rueful or
even cynical at this moment about her duality, he soon acknowledges (even if he does revert to Manichaeism) her impelling force
in all human life: "Because what pity that Virtue does not—
possibly cannot—take care of its own as Non-virtue does. Probably
it cannot: who to the dedicated to Virtue, offer in reward only cold
and odorless and tasteless virtue: as compared not only to the bright
rewards of sin and pleasure but to the ever watchful unflagging
omniprescient skill—that incredible matchless capacity for inven-
tion and imagination—with which even the tottering footsteps of
infancy are steadily and firmly guided into the primrose path"
(pp. 52–53).

Even here, the elder Lucius does not offer us the Christian platitude that sin is simply more appealing than righteousness, that
Satan conceals his leprosy beneath the robes of an angel of light.
For no real leprosy exists in *The Reivers*; there is only Non-virtue.
That is why the sordid reality of whorehouses is not only softened
but never exposed in the novel. The criticism that "the prostitutes
are deprived of the legitimate reality of the evil which they represent"[3] is at best, it seems, unwarranted. Faulkner does not deserve
to be accused of sentimentality for his "unrealistic" view simply
because he acknowledges the necessity—nay, the value—of "evil"
in human living. Butch Lovemaiden, for example, the detestable

deputy who misuses his power to bed Everbe, is perhaps the closest thing to an exemplar of moral evil that *The Reivers* possesses. Yet even he does not violate the narrator's full embrace of Non-virtue. Although Lucius hates the sweaty ruthlessness of the man, his feelings in that moment determine the acceptance he comes to in old age:

> I was more than afraid. I was ashamed that such a reason for fearing for Uncle Parsham, who had to live here, existed; hating (not Uncle Parsham doing the hating, but me doing it) it all, hating all of us for being the poor frail victims of being alive, having to be alive—hating Everbe for being the vulnerable helpless lodestar victim, and Boon for being the vulnerable and helpless victimised; and Uncle Parsham and Lycurgus for being where they had to, couldn't help but watch white people behaving exactly as white people bragged that only Negroes behaved—just as I had hated Otis for telling me about Everbe in Arkansas and hated Everbe for being that helpless lodestar for human debasement which he had told me about and hated myself for listening, having to hear about it, learn about it, know about it; hating that such not only was, but must be, had to be if living was to continue and mankind be a part of it. (p. 174)

Living does continue; Lucius proves in the moment of "A Reminiscence" that he has continued in "the furious motion of being alive." Only he has moved from his momentary hatred of life, so akin to Joe Christmas's revulsion from the feminine realities of living, to the recognition that the terrible or the bad (Non-virtue, in short) cannot be removed from the blood without shedding all of it. (And Faulkner does not hold out the hope of life apart from the flesh-and-blood.) So in a significant respect, what "GRAND-FATHER SAID" (p. 3) is the completion of his experience, the fulfilment of his education. It is the process of his movement from a hatred of life to its joyous affirmation.

The compulsion, nevertheless, to conceptualize this feminine Non-virtue in *The Reivers* is a weakness in the symbolic factor of the work. The "Over-goddess," it is true, stands outside of time while being present in it, and she is represented in all her anagogic power (possessing that "ever watchful unflagging omniprescient skill");

but her dynamism is verbalized more than it is symbolized. She is talked about, mentalized, and projected beyond the power of woman to incarnate her, instead of appearing spontaneously and naturally in the world via symbols which import for her a sense of her very inexplicability. Everbe, in other words, cannot sustain the full significance of the archetype in herself. As in *Light in August* or in *As I Lay Dying*, Faulkner wished, it seems, to emphasize the joy of life without denying its anguish. But he could not forego either a tragic victim or "how terribly doing goes along the earth" without transposing most of the dreadfulness beyond the sphere of the doer. Accordingly, the "terrible" would have to be split off beyond the world of woman as well; he now had to provide, in explicit terms, an ultimate necessity for evil, a Non-virtuous mother who would rear her children in the naturalness of living. Only in such a context could he select the appropriate action to reveal the un-innocent joy of existence. Only within this frame of reference, as well, could personal women come to life as mirthfully legitimate agents of "evil."

Lucius first sets eyes on Miss Corrie in the dining room of Reba Rivers's brothel. She is to that extent implicated in the world's evil. But the moment she enters the room, Lucius knows intuitively that there is more to her: "This time it was a big girl. I dont mean fat: just big, like Boon was big, but still a girl, young too, with dark hair and blue eyes and at first I thought her face was plain. But she came into the room already looking at me, and I knew it didn't matter what her face was" (p. 102). Although Lucius is not yet aware of the implications of his feeling, he will eventually conclude "that your outside is just what you live in, sleep in, and has little connection with who you are and even less with what you do" (p. 304). We might take both his implicit and explicit statements to mean that what a person does is not the lasting part of what that person is. Corrie's outward action is, in fact, totally qualified by the inward and enduring part of her. She remains virtually unconscious of Boon's jealousy when she offers to ask a railway flagman, one of her regular customers, to misappropriate a boxcar, realign the priorities of a railroad, and conduct a stolen racehorse through the main streets of Memphis, all on the uncertain hope that Ned might win back the automobile which the three reivers stole in Boss Priest's absence: " 'I dont need to entertain him,' Miss Corrie said. 'I can use the telephone.' It was not smug nor coy: it was just serene. She was much too big a girl, there was much too much of her, for smugness or coyness. But she was exactly right for serenity" (p. 131). Evil in a moral sense cannot survive in the face of such serenity. At this point, Lucius's unrealized moral feelings are similar (though not identical) to Jim Casy's observation in *The Grapes of Wrath* that "There ain't no sin and there ain't no virtue. There's just stuff people do."

Women prove to be the prime movers behind the doings of men in *The Reivers*. Boon and Ned itch to be Memphis-bound simply to do a little "whore-hopping." It is noteworthy, however, that when men are drawn into motion after the feminine (like Byron is after Lena), they now must go away to the city; Jefferson has become a moral-social climate where the amoral archetype can no longer appear. Man is likewise destined, now, to return afterward to the moral and social world: the road is not endless as it is for Lena and Byron. So when controversy arises over the means of return and Boon is stymied by a lack of courage, Ned by imposed racial restrictions, Miss Reba takes charge of the entire male expedition. She not only asks Miss Corrie to secure railway assistance in transporting the horse to the race, but on their arrival she provides temporary refuge from a deputy whose lust could bring their scheme to ruin. Boon in turn provides eloquent, if bitter, male testimony to the driving force of Reba's entire sex when he uses Minnie's tooth as a surrogate for unloading his frustration. He is, of course, outraged both by Reba's firm control and by Corrie's irresistible attractions:

"I bet you are," Boon said. "It's that tooth. That's the hell of women: you wont let well enough alone."

"What do you mean?" Miss Reba said.

"You know damn well what I mean," Boon said. "You dont never quit. You aint never satisfied. You dont never have no mercy on a damn man. Look at her: aint satisfied until she has saved and scraped to put a gold tooth, a *gold*

tooth in the middle of her face just to drive crazy a poor
ignorant country nigger—"

"—or spending five minutes talking into a wooden box just
to drive crazy another poor ignorant country bastard that aint
done nothing in the world but steal an automobile and now a
horse. I never knew anybody that needed to get married as
bad as you do. (pp. 134–35)

Boon is right to an extent; woman has no more mercy on a "damn
man" in the story than Non-virtue has. Both excite him and drive
him "willy-nilly" (will-*he*, nill-*he*) into motion.

Woman, however, is not the well-nigh impersonal force in *The
Reivers* that she was, say, in *Light in August* or even in *The
Hamlet*. Reba Rivers is a particularized human creature, like
Mrs. Littlejohn in her powers of action, but lacking that woman's
commitment to masculine legality. (Her individualizing also runs
counter to that "masculine" idealism noted in Linda Kohl.) Miss
Reba is more tough-minded, realistic, and personal than any
archetypal projection. She is, in short, socialized; she needs Mr.
Binford as "the agent who counted down the money and took the
receipt for the taxes and utilities" (p. 113), who paid tradesmen and
policemen their due share of a thriving economy. Nevertheless, if
economic power devolves here upon the male, the currency of coin
does not give him unbounded power as it did with Flem Snopes.
Whores are not subjected in this book; Miss Reba drives Mr.
Binford away, however temporarily and reluctantly, when he bets
copulative-money at the race track. So her control of the male world
around her is fairly inclusive on a practical level. Not even Otis,
that wizened little parody of Flem Snopes and the gangster Popeye,
is allowed the minor triumph of stealing Minnie's tooth. Though
he has made money from Corrie's debasement (selling tickets to
voyeurs of her business), he is thoroughly defeated by Reba's and
Minnie's unexpected pursuit of him. He is banished at last to the
farm in Arkansas, a fate which another boy, Huck Finn, has described as less than desirable.

Women are socialized in a more important way, however, in
The Reivers. Miss Reba, it is said, needs Mr. Binford as "the
single frail power wearing the shape of respectability" (p. 113). A
similar need obtains with Miss Corrie. When Lucius fights for her,

he makes her want to be worthy of that respectability he has con-
ferred on her with his blood. Moreover, Boon's jealous love makes
the need for respectability all that more urgent, since she is being
unconsciously courted now toward the social state of marriage.
(Marriage was never the crux of man's archetypal response to the
feminine in Caddy, Temple, Addie, Joanna, even Lena). When
Corrie reforms, then, she successfully abrogates a social role which
Boon and others have imposed on her. Her sudden formlessness
brings man to the brink of chaos. As Boon speaks, he is "furious
and baffled, raging and helpless; and more: terrified": "Why the
hell has she got to pick me out to reform on? God damn it, she's a
whore, cant she understand that? She's in the paid business of
belonging to me exclusive the minute she sets her foot where I'm
at like I'm in the paid business of belonging to Boss and Mr Maury
exclusive the minute I set foot where they're at" (p. 197). Boon
cannot understand that she has just escaped from male-economic
dominion. Corrie, however, is still dependent on the masculine
world; she turns immediately to another male-imposed role:
Lucius's ideal of the virtuous woman. She is so unsure of herself,
in fact, that she cannot return to her proper given name without
Lucius's confirmation of its value. Thus the "Everbe" of "Miss
Corrie" is re-established, if not re-created, by unabashed idealism.

What Lucius fails, at eleven years of age, to see in his re-emphasis
of her name, however, is that "Everbe" still qualifies "Corinthia."
In his first epistle to the Corinthians, Paul rebukes the Greek
Christians for their indulgence in harlotry and fornication. His
outrage extends beyond the moral issue; it reaches down to the
persistent substratum of Greek culture—the feminine mysteries at
Eleusis. The mystery cults of Greece were matriarchal in psychology
and orgiastic in their ritual expression. Long before the Pauline
era, the Hebrew prophets of a patriarchal deity decried this universal whore of Babylon. So when the Christian heir of Judaism
denounces the Corinthians or the worshippers of Ephesian Diana,
he is venting the wrath of the male principle of spirit upon what
Eupheus Hines in *Light in August* terms "abomination and bitchery!" Contrary to this masculine resistance to the goddess, Lucius
(like Lucius Apuleius of Isis in *The Golden Ass*) is the priest of the
feminine mysteries in *The Reivers*, but he wants the mysteries on
his terms; he wants them to be ideal and eternal instead of material

and recurrent. Ironically, however, his accent on *Everbe* Corinthia only renews the full truth of her name: that the worldly female is with us always: that Non-virtue is universally present and dominant.

Lucius notwithstanding, Miss Corrie undergoes a transformation (both nominal and symbolical) of her own which gives her an intrinsic right to be Everbe. That name she once assumed upon her entry into the Memphis underworld has obvious affinities with Kore, the central figure of the Eleusinian mysteries. By examining these mysteries associated with Kore–Persephone, we might see how Miss Corrie rightfully becomes Everbe.

In their simplest form, the lesser mysteries at Eleusis represent the abduction and rape of Kore, leading up to the great mysteries which re-enact Kore's forced marriage.[4] The victimization of the girl on the one hand celebrates the transformative character of the feminine in her growth from girlhood to womanhood, while the forced marriage "is in the profoundest sense a self-sacrifice, a being-given-to-womanhood, to the Great Goddess as the female self" (p. 319). This self-sacrifice reunites Kore in the fullest way with Demeter, the Great Mother; by her voluntary immolation she becomes the eternal feminine. She then assumes the two greatest powers of the goddess, the miracle of physical transformation (birth) and the wonder of spiritual transformation. On the lower matriarchal level, Kore gives birth to a son and to continued fertility; on the mystery level, she bears a transfigured son, a spiritual, divine son. Now she is not only the mother of humanity, she is its culture-bearer.

In one important respect, Miss Corrie re-enacts the myth of Kore. Her surrender to the amorous intent of Butch Lovemaiden is both a "rape" and a "self-sacrifice" for she succumbs to the deputy only under duress—that she might win back the bare opportunity for that horserace on which Ned, Boon, and Lucius have staked so much. She crosses at this moment from irresponsible prostitution into wholehearted, responsible womanhood. She then is "forced" by Lucius's idealism into the legal state of marriage; only at this moment is she fully become Everbe (eternal woman) in the boy's eyes. But when she bears a son, she becomes like Kore a Corrie beyond capability of all abduction and forced marriage. She is at last the complete centre of the mystery of existence, eternal mother and son. Not surprisingly, Boon does not appear in the conclusion of *The Reivers*; Everbe stands alone now (the Madonna) with her natural and figurative sons. For by his involvement with Everbe, Lucius has been drawn more totally into Non-virtue than even he at first imagined. He has been spiritually transformed, moved from a hatred of life and Non-virtue to its completest acceptance. Most significantly, he also gives his name to its product, its natural fruits. Mrs. Everbe Corinthia Hogganbeck sends for him one Saturday, about a year after the Memphis expedition, to view her newborn son:

> She had a nurse and she should have been in bed. But she was sitting up, waiting for me, in a wrapper; she even walked across to the cradle and stood with her hand on my shoulder while we looked at it.
> "Well," she said. "What do you think?"
> I didn't think anything. It was just another baby, already as ugly as Boon even if it would have to wait twenty years to be as big. I said so. "What are you going to call it?"
> "Not it," she said. "Him. Cant you guess?"
> "What?" I said.
> "His name is Lucius Priest Hogganbeck," she said. (pp. 304–5)

Lucius's hard-headed cynicism denies all possible sentimentality (whatever has not been absorbed by the mythic necessity for a fused son-identity) in conclusion. For the socially legitimized mother has made no improvement upon humanity; she has borne a son just as "ugly" as his father, with the same potential for being delivered up to Non-virtue's power. And once again, he will carry the name of Lucius Priest with him.

The story of Miss Corrie, then, is no mere allegory of the myth of Kore; it is its fundamental re-enactment. The difference in Faulkner's version is that Corrie is forced into marriage not by the brute power of masculinity but by its rational idealism. In a sense, she is thus taken from within. Marriage is the crux of the Kore myth for woman, but only as something to be overcome. Marriage for Corrie, however, is also something social—answering the need for respectability. Her rape is one of consciousness, hence she is more individually human. Accordingly, the role of Non-virtue in the book is clarified.

Though Non-virtue has its human representatives, it is more influential and less influenced than they are. Non-virtue is an abstraction of the archetype, something new to Faulkner's art. It is as if, when Faulkner returns at last to a mythic dimension, he cannot recreate the myth without postulating a metaphysical feminine somewhat removed from the more personalized and human females he has been developing. The greater need, however, for a conceptual Non-virtue would seem to lie in the comic method, in the active jubilation of un-innocent existence. In this single fashion, male consciousness is enabled finally to participate to its fullest extent in the life of the goddess-muse.

Boon Hogganbeck's childlike obsession with driving automobiles is the initial impetus toward Non-virtue in *The Reivers*. His lust for a Memphis whore is the attendant and co-equal impulse. Yet Lucius is not merely tempted by Boon when opportunity comes to them both like a sudden gift horse. Thoughts of "crime" and freedom have been latent in his mind from the instant when he saw the ramifications of his Bay St. Louis grandfather's death: the absence for four days at least of his parents and automobile-owning grandparents. Consequently, "all Boon's clumsy machinations to seduce and corrupt me were only corroboration" (p. 45). Man's fall from innocence, Lucius goes on to suggest, is inherent in the embryo; it is something given to him at inception and it must necessarily mature: "When grown people speak of the innocence of children, they dont really know what they mean. Pressed, they will go a step further and say, Well, ignorance then. The child is neither. There is no crime which a boy of eleven had not envisaged long ago. His only innocence is, he may not yet be old enough to desire the fruits of it, which is not innocence but appetite; his ignorance is, he does not know how to commit it, which is not ignorance but size" (p. 46). So Lucius is inevitably precipitated into Non-virtue. The journey toward the flesh-pots of Memphis does not merely end in a female establishment; it is feminine in its actual processes of growth and motion. The car, like the wagon in *As I Lay Dying*, becomes an authentic symbol of this power of the goddess.

The crossing of Hell Creek Bottom is the central event on the outward-bound movement of the story. From it there is no turning back. As Lucius says later, "when we conquered Hell Creek we locked the portcullis and set the bridge on fire" (p. 93). The crossing is terrible, as it was for Addie, but it is muted now by an important tonal change. Boon strains demonically and desperately to heave the car through the mud, while the agony of his attempt is balanced by the comic sketch of the three (Ned and Lucius with him) "now unrecognizable mud-colored creatures engaged in a life-and-death struggle" (p. 87). They strain to cross Hell Creek, in fact, to gain the "life" which has lured them toward Memphis, but the mud-farmer who eventually hauls them across the Bottom is Charon ferrying them into the underworld. (So too, the opposing horse, whose true name is Acheron—a river in Hades—becomes not only a feminine symbol of motion but a symbol of the mother of death— that power they must in one sense overcome to return home, though also the means, epitomized in Everbe's purchase of immunity for the race, of their rebirth.) Even the Hell Creek "death," however, turns out to be emergence into life; once they pass over, they have the world before them, where to choose; they have the entire series of anxious (in the moment) and funny (in retrospect) events waiting for them just down the road. This, then, is the point about un-innocent joy: that the anguish of the moment is not the major part of the experience. Even Boon's last harried, hopeless attempt to save some of the six dollars the mud-farmer is extorting for his services turns into joyous laughter in the telling: " 'All right,' Boon said, 'but look at the other one! When he gets that mud washed off, he aint even white!' The man looked at distance awhile. Then he looked at Boon. 'Son,' he said, 'both these mules is color-blind' " (p. 91).

The tone of *The Reivers* as a whole is consistent with this one passage. Too much, it would seem, has been urged on the other side concerning the novel's supposed moral of "a gentleman accepts the responsibility," as Boss Priest phrases it for Lucius. It is true that his learning to live with his own anguished folly is crucial to Lucius's coming to experience, just as much as his tortured life-disgust is in the Lovemaiden episode. The sorrow of knowledge is the price of full life. Most of the story is funny, however, precisely when it is viewed through these knowledgeable eyes, when it can laugh where the boy couldn't. Even the news most painful to the boy—that Everbe brings the horse-racers to the track through her last fling at prostitution—is recounted in all the comic immediacy of Ned's language by the old man, whatever anguish the experience has cost him:

> "Mr Poleymus his-self had added one to one and smelled a mouse and turned everybody loose and before he could turn around, Boon went and whupped that gal and then come straight back without even stopping and tried to tear that Butch's head off, pistol and all, with his bare hands, and Mr Poleymus smelled a whole rat. And Mr Poleymus may be little, and he may be old; but he's a man, mon. They told me how last year his wife had one of them strokes and cant even move her hand now, and all the children are married and gone, so he has to wash her and feed her and lift her in and outen the bed day and night both, besides cooking and keeping house too unlessen some neighbor woman comes in to help. But you dont know it to look at him and watch him act. He come in there—I never seen none of it; they just told me: two or three holding Boon and another one trying to keep that Butch from whupping him with the pistol whilst they was holding him— and walked up to Butch and snatched that pistol outen his hand and reached up and ripped that badge and half his shirt off too and telefoamed to Hardwick to send a automobile to bring them all back to jail, the women too. When it's women, they calls it fragrancy."
>
> "Vagrancy," Uncle Parsham said.
>
> "That's what I said," Ned said. "You call it whatever you want. I calls it jail." (p. 257)

Laughter has become for the narrator the triumphant affirmation of his experience in both its agony and beauty.

It is as though the older Lucius has learned what Nietzsche's Zarathustra had to learn from Laughter: "Have you ever said Yes to a single joy? O my friends, then you said Yes too to *all* woe. All things are entangled, ensnared, enamored; if ever you wanted one thing twice, if ever you said, 'You please me, happiness! Abide moment!' then you wanted *all* back. All anew, all eternally, all entangled, ensnared, enamored—oh, then you *loved* the world.

Eternal ones, love it eternally and evermore; and to woe too, you say: go, but return! *For all joy wants—eternity.* (Nietzsche's italics)."[5] Lucius has been fully entangled, ensnared, enamoured, and yet he has learned how to want it all back (exactly the intention of "A Reminiscence"). In one respect, he has learned that the story is the fullest kind of re-enactment for he returns to the time which the story evokes. But the story utters the "everlasting Yea" now to woe even as it does to joy; in that sense, it is the fulfilment of the experience. So in a way the story through its telling becomes the eternal recurrence. In it, by it, of it, laughter teaches the teller how to rejoice in the duality of his experience. Even so, it is not the Olympian laugh which the narrator laughs from on high; it is the laughter of his actual reimmersion in the moment, in the recurrence of all that beauty and anguish.

Faulkner too, it seems, has by his constant and latest return to the archetype grasped its inexhaustibility and the indestructibility of its most ephemeral proponents. His finally comic stance has not seriously diminished his worship of the muse. Non-virtue, in fact, and the all-too-human Everbe Corinthia are focused in a sort of comic-exultant reverence, as Lena Grove before them was highlighted in a tragi-lyrical reverence. *Light in August*, it is true, goes much further in presenting the excruciations of an ego-consciousness resistant to life; in *The Reivers*, nevertheless, Faulkner finds a means of integrating the intellect with the life-giving factor of the feminine. If his means are now symbolically deficient (because abstract), the artist's last novel—published only weeks before his death—is still his ultimate (because reminiscent) celebration of ambivalent life's unambivalent joy. In a manner similar in degree, if not quite in kind, to *Light in August*, *The Reivers* represents a triumphant coming to terms in art with the suprapersonal power of the anima.

🙞 *Conclusion* 🙜

This study was begun with the intent of re-examining Faulkner's artistic view of human destiny. That view was said to be of greater concern than the willed optimism of the Nobel Prize Address would suggest; it was related both immanently and imminently to the artist's creation, in certain human females, of necessary life symbols. We have since observed how these few women, possessed of awesome forces, incarnate in verbal form the archetype of the feminine. The feminine archetype itself sums up the wholeness of man's relation to nature and to the creative forces of life; it symbolizes human relatedness (whose source lies in the primary being of the mother), as well as the moral relatedness of good and evil (whose source lies in the doubleness of life itself). Any artist's fascination by this archetype is, as Erich Neumann writes, "by no means only a personal phenomenon of his individual history; it represents an advance into a psychic realm that is of fateful importance not only for himself, but for his whole age, if not mankind in general."

Faulkner's lasting concern throughout the works we

have been exploring is with the fateful importance
for man of the emergent mother archetype. The
endurance or end of male life is entirely contingent
upon its attitude, implying will or volition, of consciousness toward her. Quentin Compson's hatred of
honeysuckle and the promiscuity of his sister Caddy,
Horace Benbow's nauseous response to Temple's rape,
to Little Belle's "seething sympathy with the blossoming grape," and to a world wrapped in the coil of
honeysuckle smoke, and Joe Christmas's revulsion
from saprunning trees and woman's menstruation,
elaborate the pathology of a masculine element seeking
to insulate itself completely from nature; each meets
with rational dissolution or destruction for his unnatural striving. Gail Hightower, on the other hand,
becomes a somewhat unwilling midwife to Lena
Grove, and thereby learns of the folly of having fled
"the savage and fecund odor of the earth," only to have
escaped into the enervating world of artificial light.
All of Faulkner's tortured, agonized men are resistant
one way or another to the creative forces of life; the
prying and polluting sexual consciousness which is
exposed in *Sanctuary* is perhaps the most impi-
ous, certainly the most impetuously chastised trans-
gressor against the life-giving factor; Byron Bunch,
by his experience of Lena's "wailing cry in a
tongue unknown to man" in the moment of her
giving birth, contrarily enters blindly and un-
reasoningly into life. Of those males who face the
urgency of human relatedness by their experience
of the mother archetype, the Bundren family—Anse,
Cash, and Jewel in particular—come most fully into
a sense of human (and family) oneness by their
response to Addie, the dead wife and mother; Darl
Bundren fails most miserably, Jason Compson most
viciously, to share in the identity or sympathy of
human life. Those males who meet with the moral
doubleness of life reveal a similar doubleness of
response; Lucius Priest succeeds most admirably in

coming to terms with "Non-virtue" while Quentin, Darl, and Horace are variously outraged by, and despairing over the presence of evil (or the terrible) in their world.

Finally, for one reason or another, the mother of life who provokes physical and spiritual transformation also appears in the guise of the mother of death. Whether, as for Benjy Compson, the aspect of the archetype will be configured positively in the icon of the Pietà, or whether, as for Joe Christmas, Darl Bundren, and Horace Benbow, it will be constellated negatively in the Gorgon-Styx-Hecate figure, depends entirely upon the will and capacity for response of male life. In our age of Western man, when an exaggerated respect for the patriarchal spirit has given rise to alienation instead of individuality, to deterioration instead of progress, and to the threat of annihilation instead of the promise of creation, there appears to have arisen in the unconscious a compensatory tendency toward renewed life-giving contact with the roots of being and the value of existence. The fate of mankind might well be dependent, as are Faulkner's males, upon the capacity for response to the reactivated archetype of the feminine. In this sense, Faulkner's work is anything but pessimistic; it is fully emblematic of the volitional condition of man confronting, both individually and culturally, myth.

The reactivation of the archetype of the anima is also of fateful importance, as we have seen, to art and artist. For the archetypal content of art has little to do with the quality of the art produced; the artist who is gripped by an archetype will find that its greatest effect is upon form. *Mosquitoes* is filled with discussion of archetypal contents but it fails rather miserably as art; *Soldiers' Pay* shows a tendency toward archetypal form but the cerebral nature of its symbols together with the historical impetus of its mythos reveals an unformulated potential; *Sartoris* momentarily approaches the dynamic of archetypal art, but it is not yet art which is generally informed by the archetype.

The threshold which Faulkner seems to have crossed in *The Sound and the Fury* is into a realm of authentic symbols, where the images engendered have a provenance traditionally associated with the muse. They now possess a life of their own as well as a life-giving association with the work of art. From the story of Caddy Compson through to the story of Lena Grove, the archetype of the feminine is communicated by symbols possessing all the dynamism and the spontaneity of the daemon itself. The varying element of formal response in this period is in every case the mythos. In *The Sound and the Fury*, Faulkner seems to have wished to avoid the terrible face of the feminine, first by "socializing" the negativity of Caroline Compson, then by muting Caddy's potentially destructive power (the result of her thwarted femininity) by holding her *in absentia* through the latter portions of the novel. The archetype is thus split into a double image of the sympathetic mother— Caddy with Benjy as the Madonna, the mother of life, and Dilsey with Benjy as the Pietà, the mother of death—but the story of the sister perforce becomes the story of the Negro servant. In *As I Lay Dying*, the tonal response to the goddess of death is now positive, so the mythos must be rearranged accordingly, investing in Addie the powers of both the loving and terrible mother, and giving her story a structural arrangement that will extend her power beyond the moment of death. The revisions of the galley-*Sanctuary* point to a coming to terms with the symbols already present; the resultant mythos carries retribution for sexuo-conscious violation to a mythic conclusion where the thought is punished as the deed, and the art itself has been left tonally subordinate to the all-controlling presence of the archetype. In *Light in August*, the old story of man's resistance to the feminine is told in the tragic tale of Joe Christmas, yet the artist seems to have wished to rest in the benign and triumphant figure of his muse; as a consequence, the mythos is disposed around two aspects of the archetype— configured in Joanna and Lena—yet the story in both narrative and theme confirms the symbolic unity of these two women.

Finally, when the artist has at last come successfully to terms with his demon archetype, has in effect exorcised it or freed himself from its compelling power, the archetype is then figuratively cast out as well in his art. *The Hamlet* is the literary record of the usurpation of the mother goddess by the patriarchate. In narrative terms, it means the overturning of a mythos (the defeat, mythically, of Eula Varner) and an attendant demystification of the symbols (the adoption of the art of allusion). Yet the Olympian imagery so used is eminently suited, both in provenance and process, to representing the new ascendancy of "consciousness." *The Hamlet*'s success as a work of art depends upon the tension of Eula's arrested archetypality or, in other words, upon the formal tension between the power of the feminine and its limitation by new powers. In psychic terms, the usurpation of the archetype means that the artist tends to turn away from anima-engendered art to new factors (as he had already done in *Absalom, Absalom!*) or at least to new concerns. Some of these new concerns are just as mythic in degree as the myth of woman; but when Faulkner returns to the content of the myth again in the latter part of the Snopes trilogy, he returns to very limited, human women and to formally inferior art. *The Reivers* is the single exception to this trend; in his last work, Faulkner makes a final return to the archetype from which his art had begun. In the story of Everbe Corinthia and her effect on a young boy (as well as a youngster of a man), he restores the old accustomed power to woman. This time, however, in arranging her mythos so as to deny completely the terrible aspect of the archetype, Faulkner has removed the symbol of Non-virtue to the cerebral plane; as a consequence, the full mythic force of *The Reivers* is somewhat weakened. Throughout much of Faulkner's career, then, and especially in his first and last works, the emergence of the archetypal feminine is of fateful importance to his art.

The age itself is the final constituent for whom the mother archetype—which is just beginning to loom above the horizon of consciousness—is said to be of fateful importance. If, as Matthew Arnold suggested almost a century ago, the function of criticism is to help a new age into being, then a new kind of mat-riarchal criticism is required: one which will attempt to integrate our understanding with the profound circumambience of the unconscious factors in arche-typal art, one which will try to explain without explaining away. If it seems paradoxical that liter-ary criticism should concern itself with religious psychology, we might remark that even the Christian apologist, Rudolf Otto, admitted the persistence of a numinous element in certain forms of aesthetic experience. Otto says as well at the outset of *Das Heilige* that it is not easy to discuss questions of religious psychology with one who "cannot recall any intrinsically religious feelings. We do not blame such an one, when he tries for himself to advance as far as he can with the help of such principles of expla-nation as he knows, interpreting 'aesthetics' in terms of sensuous pleasure, and 'religion' as a function of the gregarious instinct and social standards, or as some-thing more primitive still. But the artist, who for his part has an intimate personal knowledge of the dis-tinctive element in the aesthetic experience, will decline his theories with thanks, and the religious man will reject them even more uncompromisingly." Jung speaks more explicitly about our response to the archetypes, saying that "if they are mere images whose numinosity you have never experienced, it will be as if you were talking in a dream, for you will not know what you are talking about." Both caveats are introduced by way of forestalling either a too-easy dismissal or a too-facile adoption of an archetypal approach to literature.

The archetype of the feminine is not the only psychic factor in Faulkner's work. A reading of *Absalom, Absalom!* might suggest, for example, the presence of the shadow; Sam Fathers of *The Bear* is probably related to the archetype of the wise old man. But even where we limit discussion to the prevalence of the female muse, some rather large areas are left unexplored, particularly in the realm of signature, whether it be with the artist's language, his biography, or his most idiosyncratic formal qualities. Where the fate of man and the feminine archetype are concerned, nonetheless, a truly matriarchal mode of criticism is quite indispensable. Such a mode which, cognitively, entails a cosmic perspective (searching out the implications of mythos for human action and attitudes), and non-cognitively, involves a mode of sentience (exploring the dynamism of archetypal symbols) is required for our age, so that when the archetype comes fully over the horizon into our world, it will not be, contrary to the words of Yeats's "The Second Coming," a "rough beast [which] slouches towards Bethlehem to be born."

NOTES

Chapter I

1. See Alan Reynold Thompson, "The Cult of Cruelty," *The Bookman*, 74 (1932): 477–87; Frederick J. Hoffman, "An Introduction," in *William Faulkner: Three Decades of Criticism*, ed. Hoffman and Olga W. Vickery (Michigan State Univ. Press, 1960), pp. 2–3.

2. Beekman W. Cottrell, "Christian Symbols in *Light in August*," *MFS*, 2 (1957): 207–13, makes Faulkner's work into a virtual *Shepherd's Play*; Evelyn Scott, *On William Faulkner's "The Sound and the Fury"* (New York: Cape and Smith, 1929), first notices the unorthodox character of Benjy as a Christ symbol; John W. Hunt, *William Faulkner: Art in Theological Tension* (Syracuse: Syracuse Univ. Press, 1965), pp. 13 ff., offers the most complex reading of the Christ parallels and ironies.

3. Two possible exceptions which cannot be included in "The Myth and The Muse" are *Go Down, Moses* and *A Fable*. Most commentators now agree that, given the whole of *Go Down, Moses*, McCaslin's renunciatory act is not only futile but immoral, ending in his heirless repudiation of life. See, e.g., John M. Muste, "The Failure of Love in *Go Down, Moses*," *MFS*, 10 (1965): 366–78; and Richard P. Adams, *Faulkner: Myth and Motion* (Princeton: Princeton Univ. Press, 1968), pp. 137–54. Criticism has not pursued this question into implications of Faulkner's unbelief, perhaps because of the evidence of *A Fable*, a work admittedly based on the idea of a second crucifixion of Christ. (See relevant remarks of the author, *Faulkner in the University*, ed. Frederick L. Gwynn and Joseph L. Blotner [Charlottesville: Univ. of Virginia Press, 1959], p. 27). Even *A Fable* ends, however, not in the "truth" of the Resurrected Body of Christ, but in an image of

one of the Corporal's followers being beaten by a crowd whose patriotic sensibilities he has assaulted; as he lies in the gutter near the Tomb of the Unknown Soldier (also the tomb, unknown to him, of his prophet-martyr), an ex-Quartermaster General, one of the principals in the story of the General who sacrifices his son, steps from the crowd to kneel beside him and cradle him in his arms. Responding to the Runner's indomitable defiance, he says, in the novel's last words, "I am not laughing. . . . What you see here are tears." Thus the most extended and sympathetic treatment of the Christ story in Faulkner's work ends not in a symbol of the redeeming god but in a curious distortion of the Pietà. This metamorphosis of the Holy Mother into a tableau of purely human sympathy is not unexpected. If the focus of Faulkner's work is no longer an imaging of deity, the emphasis of *A Fable* entirely humanistic, then it seems logically to follow.

4. Galley 19. Cf. Adams's discussion, pp. 64–65, of the Christ story in *Sanctuary*.

5. *Ishmael: A Study of the Symbolic Mode in Primitivism* (1956; rpt. New York: Harper & Row, 1960).

6. Mircea Eliade, *Shamanism: Archaic Techniques of Ecstasy*, trans. Willard R. Trask (London: Routledge & Kegan Paul, 1964), p. 486. There are notable differences, however, between the modern artist of primitive feeling and the shaman of traditional societies. The latter strives to realize "*in concreto*, a mystical and at the same time *real* journey to heaven . . . to 'experience' on the plane of the body, what in the present condition of humanity is no longer accessible on the plane of the 'spirit' " (p. 494). His role as a spiritual leader is also the function of a widely received religion, one which is not a private creation, although shamanic experience occasionally attempts "to express itself through an ideology that is not always favorable to it" (p. 8). Finally, the inferred origin of shamanism reveals a "faith in a celestial Supreme Being" (p. 505). Although the celestial god may have become in fact a *deus otiosus*, and while shamanic ecstasy may have incorporated different religious forms, the prevailing symbolism of ascent in the ideology of shamanism reconfirms the importance of communication between Earth and Sky. Modern psychology indicates an opposite route by which the primitivistic artist enters into contact with the sacred: a way down through the eccentricities of personality to the unconscious core of man, where we are protagonists of fables we no longer believe, where we enter mutually into the presence of our gods.

7. Mircea Eliade, *Cosmos and History*, trans. Willard R. Trask (1954; rpt. New York: Harper & Row, 1959), pp. 5, 17.

8. Baird refers to Eliot as one of the secondary artists servile to art, "a poet to whom the whole art of poesis has been an act of reason" (p. 73).

9. *Faulkner's Women: Characterization and Meaning* (Deland, Fla.: Everett / Edwards, 1972).

10. See F. M. Cornford, *From Religion to Philosophy* (1912; rpt. New York: Harper & Row, 1957), pp. 14–21, for a survey of the presence of the *Moirai* in Hellenic poetry. Cornford, following in the Cambridge school of Durkheimean social theories, interprets the primacy of the Fates as originating in divisions of society.

11. "William Faulkner and the Myth of Woman," *Research Studies*, 35 (1967): 132–40.

12. *The Collected Works of C. J. Jung*, ed. G. Adler et al., trans. R.F.C. Hull, Bollingen Series, vol. 9i, *The Archetypes and the Collective Unconscious*, 2nd ed. (Princeton: Princeton University Press, 1969), p. 23.

13. Erich Neumann, *The Great Mother*, trans. Ralph Manheim, 2nd. ed. (Princeton: Princeton Univ. Press, 1963), p. 6.

14. See Erich Neumann, *The Archetypal World of Henry Moore*, trans. R. F. C. Hull (New York: Pantheon Books, 1959), p. 5.

15. *Man and his Symbols*, ed. Carl G. Jung (London: Aldus Books, 1964), p. 96.

16. *Psychological Types*, trans. H. Godwin Baynes (London: Kegan Paul, 1926), pp. 603–4.

17. *Writers at Work*, ed. Malcolm Cowley (New York: The Viking Press, 1959), p. 124.

18. See Jessie L. Weston, *From Ritual to Romance* (Cambridge: Cambridge Univ. Press, 1920).

19. *Faulkner's Olympian Laugh: Myth in the Novels* (Detroit: Wayne State Univ. Press, 1968).

20. Ernst Cassirer, *The Philosophy of Symbolic Forms*. Vol. 2, *Mythical Thought*, trans. Ralph Manheim (New Haven: Yale Univ. Press, 1955), p. 218.

21. Gotthold Ephraim Lessing, *Laocoön: An Essay upon the Limits of Painting and Poetry*, trans. Ellen Frothingham (New York: Noonday Press, 1957), p. 109.

22. Neumann, *Henry Moore*, p. 7.

23. *Anatomy of Criticism* (1957; rpt. New York: Atheneum, 1969), pp. 95–127.

24. T. S. Eliot, "Ulysses, Order and Myth," *The Dial*, 75 (1923): 480–84.

Chapter 2

1. Cleanth Brooks, "Primitivism in *The Sound and the Fury*," *EIE* 1952 (New York: Columbia Univ. Press, 1954), p. 23.

2. *Mosquitoes* (New York: Liveright Publishing Co., 1927), p. 11. Subsequent references in the text are to this edition.

3. *Soldiers' Pay* (1926; rpt. London: Chatto & Windus, 1951), p. 240. Subsequent references in the text are to this edition.

4. *Sartoris* (1929; rpt. New York: Random House, 1956), p. 83. Subsequent references in the text are to this edition.

Prologue

1. C. G. Jung, *The Integration of the Personality*, trans. Stanley M. Dell (London: Kegan Paul et al., 1940), p. 72.

2. Rudolf Otto, *The Idea of the Holy*, trans. John W. Harvey, 2nd. ed. (New York: Oxford Univ. Press, 1950); see esp. pp. 1–40.

3. Jung, *Psyche and Symbol: A Selection From the Writings of C. G.*

Jung, ed. Violet S. de Laszlo (Garden City, N.Y.: Doubleday & Co., 1958), p. 12.

4. See *The Great Mother*, chapters two and three.

5. Where the following discussion is not documented, it is drawn from the first eight chapters of *The Great Mother*. To the reader familiar with Neumann, my debt in its literary application will be obvious.

6. The pomegranate, filled with seeds, is a natural symbol of containment; basket, cradle, and coffin are related cultural symbols.

7. Robert Graves, *The White Goddess: A Historical Grammar of Poetic Myth* (1948; rpt. New York: Noonday Press, 1966), p. 391.

8. M.-L. von Franz, "The Process of Individuation," *Man and his Symbols*, p. 186.

9. Quoted in Robert B. Palmer's "Introduction" to Walter F. Otto, *Dionysus: Myth and Cult* (1933; rpt. Bloomington: Indiana Univ. Press, 1965), p. xv.

10. "Archetype and Signature," in *Art and Psychoanalysis*, ed. and introd. William Phillips (1957; rpt. Cleveland: World Publishing Co., 1963), pp. 471–72.

Chapter 3

1. Michael Millgate, *The Achievement of William Faulkner* (London: Constable, 1966), p. 34.

2. "Preface to *The Sound and the Fury*," trans. George M. Reeves, *MissQ*, 19 (1966), 109.

3. *The Sound and the Fury* (New York: Cape and Smith, 1929), p. 94. Subsequent references in the text will be to this edition.

4. The phrase is Faulkner's, referring to Eula Varner. He says, "You're quite right, she was larger than life, she was too big for this world" (*University*, p. 31). This quality, as it relates to Eula, shall be considered in chapter 7.

5. See Catherine B. Baum, " 'The Beautiful One': Caddy Compson as Heroine of *The Sound and the Fury*," *MFS*, 13 (1967): 33.

6. See Carvel Collins, "Miss Quentin's Paternity Again," *TSLL*, 2 (1960): 260.

7. *The Portable Faulkner*, ed. Malcolm Cowley (New York: Viking Press, 1946), p. 753.

8. William Faulkner, *Early Prose and Poetry*, ed. Carvel Collins (London: Jonathan Cape, 1963), p. 40.

9. *Ovid's Metamorphoses: The Arthur Golding Translation (1567)*, ed. John Frederick Nims (New York: Macmillan & Co., 1965), p. 253. The account of Daphne is taken from I, 545–700; the story of the birth of Adonis is found in X, 327–595.

10. Neumann, *The Great Mother*, p. 208.

11. "Lunatic" is derived from the Latin *luna*; the etymology suggests a man driven mad by the moon.

12. 'Interview with Cynthia Grenier," quoted in *Lion in the Garden*,

ed. James B. Meriwether and Michael Millgate (New York: Random House, 1968), p. 222.

13. Brylowski, *Faulkner's Olympian Laugh*, p. 66.

Chapter 4

1. See, e.g., Cleanth Brooks, *William Faulkner: The Yoknapatawpha Country* (New Haven: Yale Univ. Press, 1963), pp. 141–66; Olga W. Vickery, *The Novels of William Faulkner: A Critical Interpretation*, rev. ed. (Baton Rouge: Louisiana State Univ. Press, 1964), pp. 50–65.

2. Hyatt H. Waggoner, *William Faulkner: From Jefferson to the World* (n.p.: Univ. of Kentucky Press, 1959), p. 80.

3. Melvin Backman, *Faulkner: The Major Years* (Bloomington: Indiana Univ. Press, 1966), pp. 50–66, esp. p. 58.

4. *As I Lay Dying* (1930; rpt. New York: Vintage Books, 1957), pp. 34–35. This is a corrected edition, based on James B. Meriwether's collation of the first edition with Faulkner's manuscript and typescript. Subsequent references in the text are to this edition.

5. "The Pairing of *The Sound and the Fury* and *As I Lay Dying*," *PULC*, 18 (1957): 123.

6. Frederick J. Hoffman, *William Faulkner*, 2nd. ed. (New York: Twayne Publishers Inc., 1968), p. 68, takes this position.

7. *Theogony*, trans. and with introd. by Norman O. Brown (Indianapolis: Bobbs Merrill Co., 1953), p. 71.

8. Robert Graves, *The Greek Myths: Vol. 1*, rev. ed. (Harmondsworth: Penguin Books, 1960), pp. 136–37.

9. "Matriarchate" in this study signifies a dominant psychic situation, not its merely derivative social structure.

10. R. E. Witt, *Isis in the Graeco-Roman World* (Ithaca: Cornell Univ. Press, 1971), p. 139.

11. See David M. Miller, "Faulkner's Women," *MFS*, 13 (1967): 8, and Karl E. Zink, "Faulkner's Garden: Woman and the Immemorial Earth," *MFS*, 2 (1956): 143.

12. *Lion in the Garden*, p. 253.

13. Jane Ellen Harrison, *Themis: A Study of the Social Origins of Greek Religion* (1912; rpt. Cleveland: World Publishing Co., 1962), p. 120.

14. Mythically, the archaic world had long been familiar with the manifestation of the mare-headed mother and the fish-tailed goddess. In Greek myth, Demeter takes the shape of a mare to escape the unwelcome attentions of Poseidon, "but Poseidon became a stallion and covered her" (Graves, *The White Goddess*, p. 384). Again, excluding numerous similar examples, the goddess Artemis (Britomart) attempts to elude her amorous pursuers by assuming the form of a fish; sometimes she is successful, at times more dubiously so (Graves, p. 402). The common theme of pursuit points to the feminine desire for inviolability, that reluctance shared by Addie Bundren to meet with "coming unalone." The point of all this, however, is that a number of primitive peoples have expressed in cult the sacred identity and transformative power of the fish-mare-mother.

Vardaman and Jewel divulge from their depths the same archetypal feelings.

15. Olga Vickery, pp. 56–57.

16. Mircea Eliade, "Mother Earth and the Cosmic Hierogamies." In *Myths, Dreams and Mysteries*, trans. Philip Mairet (1957; rpt. New York: Harper & Row, 1960), pp. 187–89.

17. See respectively Mary Jane Dickerson, "Some Sources of Faulkner's Myth in *As I Lay Dying*," *MissQ*, 19 (1966): 132–42; Richard P. Adams, pp. 71–74; Carvel Collins, "The Pairing," esp. pp. 121–23.

18. See *The Great Mother*, pp. 305–25.

19. See, e.g., Peter Swiggart, *The Art of Faulkner's Novels* (Austin: Univ. of Texas Press, 1962), pp. 108–30.

20. William Van O'Connor, *The Tangled Fire of William Faulkner* (Minneapolis: University of Minnesota Press, 1954), p. 53.

Chapter 5

1. Introduction to the Modern Library edition of *Sanctuary*, 1932, p. v. Faulkner writes, "To me it is a cheap idea because it was deliberately conceived to make money."

2. Whatever the reasons, Faulkner exaggerates his claim to meretricious intent by saying, "I took a little time out, and speculated what a person in Mississippi would believe to be the current trends, chose what I thought was the right answer and invented the most horrorific tale I could imagine and wrote it in about three weeks" (p. vi). One might begin to estimate the shock value of the statement by noting that the holograph and the typescript are both dated January-May 1929 (cited by Millgate, p. 114).

3. Gerald Langford, *Faulkner's Revision of "Sanctuary"* (Austin: University of Texas Press, 1972), p. 7.

4. The galleys are on deposit in the Massey Collection at the Alderman Library, University of Virginia. I am grateful to the library staff for making both the galleys and the unbound typescript available to me. Another set of the unrevised galleys which I have not examined is at the University of Texas, Austin.

5. *Sanctuary* (New York: Jonathan Cape & Harrison Smith, 1931), p. 380. Succeeding references in the text are to this edition.

6. Harry Modean Campbell and Ruel E. Foster, *William Faulkner: A Critical Appraisal* (Norman, Okla.: University of Oklahoma Press, 1951), pp. 123–24.

7. Linton Massey, "Notes on the Unrevised Galleys of Faulkner's *Sanctuary*," *Studies in Bibliography*, 8 (1956): 200. The page proof is approximate because the unrevised galley proofs were never reduced. For the sake of further comparison, one-fourth of the story is completed in the galleys, one-tenth in the novel, before Temple is introduced.

8. The galleys are divided into twenty-seven chapters. Chapters 7–15, part of 18, and 19 contain the essential elements of the story of Temple Drake. Chapters 1–6, a portion of 12, and the larger part of the final chapters (17–18, 22–23, 25–26) are devoted to Horace.

9. Robert Cantwell, Introduction, *The White Rose of Memphis* (1881; rpt. New York: Coley Taylor, 1953), p. v. Colonel Falkner's book was enormously successful; by 1909, it had gone through thirty-five editions and a thirty-sixth was being prepared for what would prove to be the last audience still amenable to Waverly stereotypes before the onset of the Great War disillusionment.

10. Galley six locates Narcissa with Little Belle in this same complex of incest.

11. See, for example, Erich Neumann, *The Archetypal World of Henry Moore*, illustrations 50 and 77; "Jagged, wild, charged with sinister energy, this recumbent figure is more like the destroying goddess of late 1939 [Moore's chronology]" (p. 109).

12. Popeye's rape of Temple with a sterile implement occurs on the "Old Frenchman Place." Later in the Saga of Yoknapatawpha, the Old Frenchman is described as a settler whose baronial dream had vanished, leaving not even a trace of his name (*The Hamlet*, pp. 3–4). His symbolic presence in *Sanctuary*, however, suggests a symbolic name for him: the Marquis de Sade, epitome of a sort of sex gotten into consciousness.

13. *Studies in Classic American Literature* (1923; rpt. New York: Viking Press, 1964), pp. 84–85.

14. *Requiem for a Nun* (New York: Random House, 1951), p. 120. All subsequent references in the text, qualified in parentheses by *RN*, will be to this edition.

15. R. F. Haugh, "Faulkner's Corrupt Temple," *ESA*, 4 (1961): 12.

Chapter 6

1. Cleanth Brooks, Introduction, *Light in August* (1932; rpt. New York: Modern Library College Edition, 1968), p. xxiii. Subsequent references to the novel will be drawn from this edition since it is a photographic reproduction of the Harrison Smith & Robert Haas first edition.

2. William Van O'Connor, p. 82 n.

3. See, e.g., such defenders of unity as Adams, pp. 84–95; Brooks, *The Yoknapatawpha Country*, pp. 53–55; C. Hugh Holman, "The Unity of Faulkner's *Light in August*," *PMLA*, 73 (1958): 155–66; Millgate, pp. 126–37; Thompson, pp. 79–80. On the other side of the ledger, Richard Chase, *The American Novel and its Tradition* (Garden City, N.Y.: Doubleday & Co., 1957), p. 212, has argued for the greatness of the novel while frankly allowing that "The book makes a kind of triptych."

4. *The Faulkner-Cowley File* (New York: The Viking Press, 1966), pp. 28–29, Cowley's brackets.

5. See, e.g., Frank Baldanza, "The Structure of *Light in August*," *MFS*, 13 (1967): 67; Peter Swiggart, "The Puritan Sinner," in *The Art of Faulkner's Novels*, pp. 131–48; Cleanth Brooks, "The Community and the Pariah," in *Yoknapatawpha*, pp. 47–74.

6. Waggoner, p. 101.

7. Darl describes the gap closing between Jewel and the moving wagon in *As I Lay Dying* in illuminating terms of non-progression: "We go

on, with a motion so soporific, so dreamlike as to be uninferant of progress, as though time and not space were decreasing between us and it" (p. 101).

8. She is identical too with the mother goddess of Aztec myth who demands blood sacrifices—the dismemberment of her own substance—in order to fecundate the womb of earth (*The Great Mother*, p. 191), and with C. S. Lewis's Ungit in *Till We Have Faces*.

9. Zink, 149.

10. *The Great Mother*, p. 231.

11. See *The White Goddess*, p. 424.

12. See *The Great Mother*, p. 168.

13. John S. Williams, " 'The Final Copper Light of Afternoon': Hightower's Redemption," *TCL*, 13 (1968): 213.

14. Beach Langston, "The Meaning of Lena Grove and Gail Hightower in *Light in August*," *BUSE*, 5 (1961): 60, suggests that the wheel rushing on is Hightower's attainment of "*pari-nirvana*," and Darrell Abel, "Frozen Movement in *Light in August*," *BUSE*, 3 (1957): 32–44; rpt. *Twentieth-Century Interpretations of Light in August*, ed. David L. Minter (Englewood Cliffs, N.J.: Prentice-Hall, 1969), pp. 42–54, claims the lambent wheel as "the climactic symbol of *Light in August*," "an image of eternity" (p. 52).

Prolegomena

1. *The Odyssey of Homer*, trans. Richmond Lattimore (New York: Harper & Row, 1965), p. 129 (8: 306–8, 314–27).

2. Here, as formerly with "matriarchate," "patriarchate" signifies a dominant psychic situation, not its merely derivative social structure.

3. *The Iliad of Homer*, trans. Richmond Lattimore (Chicago: Univ. of Chicago Press, 1951), p. 137 (5: 331–33).

4. George Thomson, *Studies in Ancient Greek Society*. Vol. 1, *The Prehistoric Aegean* (London: Lawrence & Wishart, 1949), pp. 149–294.

5. Howard W. Clarke, *The Art of the Odyssey* (Englewood Cliffs, N.J.: Prentice-Hall, 1967), p. 86. See Thomson, p. 286.

6. Charles Rowan Beye, '*The Iliad*,' '*The Odyssey*,' *and the Epic Tradition* (Garden City, N.Y.: Doubleday & Co., 1966), p. 174.

7. *The Integration of the Personality*, pp. 3–29, 32–44.

8. Erich Neumann, *Amor and Psyche*, trans. Ralph Manheim (1952; rpt. Princeton: Princeton Univ. Press, 1956), p. 153.

Chapter 7

1. T. Y. Greet, "The Theme and Structure of Faulkner's *The Hamlet*," *PMLA*, 72 (1957): 775–90; rpt. *Three Decades*, p. 346.

2. Peter Swiggart, p. 197.

3. Melvin Backman, p. 147.

4. *The Hamlet* (1940; rpt. New York: Vintage Books, 1964), p. 110. Subsequent references in the text are to this edition.

5. Linda T. Prior, "Theme, Imagery, and Structure in *The Hamlet*," *MissQ*, 22 (1969): 237–56.

6. Brooks, p. 190, p. 173.

7. See, e.g., Brylowski, p. 143.

8. The patterns of allusion spoken of in connection with T. S. Eliot's mythical method are part of a patriarchal (conscious) art.

9. Brooks, p. 168; Hoffman, p. 90.

10. Panthea Reid Broughton, "Masculinity and Menfolk in *The Hamlet*," *MissQ*, 22 (1969): 183.

11. Florence Leaver, "The Structure of *The Hamlet*," *TCL*, 1 (1955): 81.

12. *The Unvanquished* (New York: Random House, 1938). Subsequent references to "An Odor of Verbena" in the text are to this edition.

13. *The Town* (New York: Random House, 1957), p. 44. Subsequent references in the text are to this edition.

14. Lawrance Thompson, pp. 148–58, provides the best survey of Faulkner's "quietly ironic, and yet quite bitter . . . treatment of that romantically idealistic, poetic, and quixotic upholder of the Southern Tradition, poor Gavin Stevens" (p. 158).

15. Irving Howe, *William Faulkner: A Critical Study* (New York: Random House, 1952), p. 286.

16. Olga Vickery, p. 181.

17. *Milton's Debt to Greek Tragedy in 'Samson Agonistes,'* (Baltimore: Johns Hopkins Univ. Press, 1937), p. 43.

18. *The Great Tradition* (1947; rpt. New York: New York Univ. Press, 1969), p. 7.

19. *The Mansion* (New York: Random House, 1959), p. 212. Subsequent references in the text are to this edition.

Chapter 8

1. *The Reivers* (New York: Random House, 1962), p. 174. Subsequent references in the text are to this edition.

2. Brylowski, p. 219.

3. Swiggart, p. 211.

4. *The Great Mother*, pp. 317–19.

5. *Thus Spoke Zarathustra*, in *The Portable Neitzsche*, ed. and trans. Walter Kaufmann (New York: The Viking Press, 1954), p. 435. The context of the passage makes it clear that "eternity" for Zarathustra is not the "otherworld" of the spirit, but this self-same life in its eternal recurrence.

INDEX

INDEX 263

141, 243; relation to Temple, 140; to Eula, 139
Negro mother (*Sart*), 45, 46, 66
Pate, Lucy, 206, 209
Peabody, Doctor, 99, 101–2, 107, 121, 125–26
Powers, Margaret, 36–37, 38, 43
Priest, Lucius, 227, 228–31, 234–37, 238–40, 243–44; relation to Benbow, 227, 229; to Byron, 227; to Christmas, 227, 231; to Doc Hines, 235
Quartermaster General, the, 250
Ratliff, V. K., 204–5, 206, 208, 210, 218–19, 221, 222; relation to Christmas, 205
Red (*Sanc*), 146–47
Rittenmeyer, Charlotte, 13
Rivers, Miss Reba, 134, 144, 233–34
Robyn, Patricia, 34–35, 36
Runner, the, 250
Samson, 101, 124
Sartoris, Bayard, Jr., 43, 44–46
Sartoris, Bayard Sr., 41; in "Verbena," 211–13
Saunders, Cecily, 39–40, 74; relation to Temple, 37
Snopes, Flem, 140, 199–200, 203–4, 205, 208, 216–17, 219, 223–24; relation to Otis, 234
Snopes, Ike, 14, 199–203
Snopes, Mink, 206–8, 209, 223–25
Snopes, Mrs. Mink, 207
Stevens, Gavin, 34, 214–17, 220–23 *passim*, 257; relation to Christmas, 215; to Lucius, 228
Strothers, Caspey, 41
Strothers, Simon, 41
Sutpen, Clytie, xvii
Sutpen, Judith, xvii
Sutpen, Thomas, xvi
Talliaferro, Ernest, 33–34
Tommy, 6, 141–42, 146

Tull, Cora, 111–12, 204
Tull, Vernon, 112, 124–25
Varner, Eula, 13, 32, 103, 197–202, 204–5, 209, 246, 252; in *Town*, 214–21 *passim*; in *Man*, 222, 224; relation to Little Belle, 139; Temple, 202; Drusilla, 210–11; Everbe, 228
Varner, Jody, 204–5
Vitelli, Popeye, 128, 132, 134–35, 143–48 *passim*, 149–51; in *Requiem*, 154; relation to Benbow, 141–42; to Otis, 234
West, David, 36
Wiseman, Eva, 33
See also incarnation; male principle
CULT OF CRUELTY, 3–5
HUMANISM OF, 6, 250
PUBLIC STATEMENTS OF: Nobel Prize Address, 3, 5, 242; Christian elements in work, 18; artistic responsibility, 20; artistic drive, 59; on Benjy, 73; Caddy, 61–62, 63, 64; Lena Grove, 161, 162; on *SF*, 61–62, 93–94; *Sanc*, 254; *LiA*, 160–61
NARRATIVE TECHNIQUE OF, 64–65, 93–94, 218
PERSONAL INDIVIDUATION, 195
PLACE IN ETHICAL TRADITION, 219–21

Fitzgerald, F. Scott, 84
Frazer, Sir J. G., 21, 22
Freudianism, 62
Frye, Northrop, 27–28

Gnosticism, 169
Golden Ass, The, 235
Golden Bough, The, 21, 100
Grapes of Wrath, The, 233
Graves, Robert, 91, 104
Great Goddess, the: as psychic phenomenon, xiv–xv, 56–58; as Muse, 55–56; elementary char-

Keats, John, 44, 162

Langer, Suzanne, 9
Lawrence, D. H., 148–49
Lessing, G. E., 24–26
Lewis, C. S., 256
Life symbol, 9–10, 49; dynamic of, 15, 16, 19–20; syncretism of, 17–18; archetype and artist, 18–19; feeling and form, 17, 26–30 *passim*; failure of in *Mosq*, 35–36; in *SP*, 39–40. *See also* Archetypal Feminine and incarnation

Male principle
defined as ego-consciousness, 54–55
anti-symbolic nature of, 8–9
INSUFFICIENCY OF: tragic aspect, 34; comic aspect, 34; in *Sart*, 43
EXISTENTIAL NAUSEA OF: in *SF*, 4; *LiA* 4; *Sanc*, 4; in Horace, 136–42; Lucius Priest, 231
NIHILISM OF: in Darl, 5; Horace, 5, 138; Bayard, Jr., 42–43; Mr. Compson, 83; Jason, 88–89; Addie and Dewey Dell (partial), 110; Addie's father, 105; fatalism in Joe Christmas, 169–70
RATIONAL ABSOLUTISM OF: in *LiA*, 4; in *SP*, 39–40; in Benjy, 78; Quentin, 82, 85; Jason, 86–89; Darl, 101–2, 112–16; 'composite mind' of *Sanc*, 131; Hightower, 182–83; McEachern, 4, 171; Christmas, 172; Doc Hines, 177; Joanna's part in, 175; Gavin, 214
STERILE CONSCIOUSNESS OF: in *Sanc*, 141–42; in Quentin, 63; Popeye, 147–48, 255; Christmas, 176
INCEST COMPLEX OF: definition of, 85; in Quentin, 85–86; Horace, 139–41; Little Belle's part in, 139–40, 255; Temple's part in, 140, 255
RAPE COMPLEX OF: in Apollo, 76; Zeus-Danae, 89; Poseidon, 104, 253; Zeus-Europa, 194; Hades-Persephone, 199; in Jason, 89; Darl, 115; Popeye, 147–48, 255; in *The Hamlet*, 199; reversed in Horace, 141; Temple's part in, 144–46
RESISTANCE TO SEXUALITY: in Narcissa, 42–43; Horace, 136–42, 151; Quentin, 63, 81–84; Benjy, 78; Christmas, 164, 172–76; Doc Hines, 177–78; in *Mosq*, 34–35; summary, 186, 243
RESISTANCE TO EVIL: 243–44: in Horace, 137–38; Lucius, 231
RESISTANCE TO MOTION: in Anse, 106–7; Darl, 116; Joe Christmas, 169; Hightower, 180
RESISTANCE TO NATURE, 243: in Quentin, 82; Benbow, 141; Christmas, 173–74; Hightower, 182; summary, 243
RESISTANCE TO TIME: in brothers Compson, 65; Benjy, 78–79; Quentin, 79–81; Hightower, 179–83 *passim*
TRANSFORMATION OF: in Cash, 117; Jewel, 118–20; Anse, 122–25; Hightower (limited), 165–66, 182–83; Byron Bunch, 183; Lucius Priest, 237; in *Reiv*, 227, 239–41; cultural necessity of, 244
SELF-SUFFICIENCY OF: in Flem Snopes, 205; Jack Houston, 206; Mink Snopes, 207
TRIUMPH OF: in Zeus, 194, 201; Flem Snopes, 202–5; Bayard (*Unvanq*), 212–13
INTERNECINE CHARACTER OF: in *Hamlet*, 207–8; *Mansion*, 224
IMPOVERISHMENT OF, 214–17 *passim*

REPRESENTED IN IDEALISM: of Benbow's 'composite mind,' 141–42; of Hightower, 182–83, 256; Gavin Stevens, 222; Linda Kohl, 222–23; Lucius, 228, 235 IN KNIGHT ERRANT, 223 IN LEGALISM: of Flem Snopes, 203–4; Ratliff, 204; Linda Kohl, 223–24; Mink Snopes, 224; in Hamlet, 203–5 IN MARRIAGE: in Town, 216–18; Reiv, 235 IN MONEY: Jason, 89; Snopesism, 200; Hamlet's stock exchange, 200–4 passim; Boon Hogganbeck, 235 IN MYTHIC MALES: Apollo, 55; Zeus, 55, 89, 104, 191, 193, 194; Cronus, 103; Jahweh, 105, 177; Draco, 133; Tireisias, 148; Jeremiah, 177; Hosea, 177; Buddha, 180; Hephaistos, 191, 192; Ares, 191; Argeïphontes, 192; Hades, 199; Poseidon, 192, 253; Olympians (in The Hamlet), 197–202 passim IN PURITANISM, 159–60: of Doc Hines, 176–78; Simon McEachern, 171–72; Joe Christmas, 171–72, 174; Joanna Burden, 175 IN RESPECTABILITY: of Lucy Pate, 206; Eula Varner, 215–18; Flem Snopes, 221; Lucius Priest, 235; Miss Reba, 234 IN SEXLESSNESS: of Jody Varner, 204–5; Labove, 204–5; Ratliff, 204–5; Jack Houston, 206; Gavin Stevens, 215–16, 223; Linda Kohl, 222–23 IN SEXUAL CONTAMINATION: of Popeye, 149–50; Lee Goodwin, 150 IN SUBORDINATE FEMALES: Danae, 89; Aphrodite, 191, 192–95 passim, 198, 199, 201; Olympian goddesses, 201–2;

whore, 199–200, 206, 218, 235; Venus, 214, 216; Lilith, 214; Semiramis, 214; Helen, 214 IN WORDS: in Mosq, 34; in Anse, 106–7; Whitfield, 108–9; Darl, 114–15; Byron Bunch, 186; Addie's opposition to, 108; summary, 186 RELATION TO ARTISTIC CREATION: in The Hamlet, 201–2, 214, 257; WOMAN'S PART IN: Jenny Du Pre, 41, 210; Temple Drake, 145–46; Joanna Burden, 174–75; Lucy Pate, 206; Mink Snopes's wife, 207; Mrs. Littlejohn, 209–10; Drusilla Hawk, 210–12; Linda Snopes Kohl, 211, 222–26 passim; Eula Varner (Town), 214–18; Miss Reba, 233–35)

Malraux, André, 133
Manichaeism, 169, 230
Marris, Sir William, 100
matriarchate: definition of, 106, 253; relation to Greek culture, 193–95, 236
Melville, Herman, 7
Metamorphoses, The, 76–77
Milton, John, xiv, 31, 56, 105
Minoan culture, 194; mother goddess of, 194–95
Mosher, Bernard, 219

Muse
INSPIRATION OF: xiii–xv; in SF, 61–63, 91; LiA, 160–62 OF THE POETS: Homer, xiv; Hesiod, xiv; Milton, xiv, 56; Du Bartas, 56; Joshua Sylvester, 56 NARRATIVE PREPOTENCY OF, xiv SYMBOLIC REPRESENTATION OF: as Great Mother, 55–56; Sibyl, 55; Sophia, 55; Delphic Oracle, 55–56; Athene (Wisdom), 55; Beatrice, 55–56; on Helicon, 55 AS ANIMA (see also Archetypal